OPEN MIND

OPEN MIND

Women's Daily Inspiration for
Becoming Mindful

DIANE MARIECHILD

HarperSanFrancisco
A Division of HarperCollins*Publishers*

OPEN MIND: *Women's Daily Inspiration for Becoming Mindful.* Copyright © 1995 by Diane Mariechild. All rights reserved. Printed in the United States of America. No part of this book may be used or reproduced in any manner whatsoever without written permission except in the case of brief quotations embodied in critical articles and reviews. For information address Harper-Collins Publishers, 10 East 53rd Street, New York, NY 10022.

Library of Congress Cataloging-in-Publication Data
Mariechild, Diane.
Open mind : women's daily inspiration for becoming mindful /
Diane Mariechild. —1st ed.
    p. cm.
ISBN 0–06–251093–2 (pbk.)
1. Women—Prayer-books and devotions—English. 2. Devotional
calendars. I. Title
BL625.7.M35   1994
291.4'3—dc20   94–26377
                                                    CIP

96 97 98 99   ❖ RRD(H) 10 9 8 7 6 5 4

For my teachers—
Ruth Denison,
Anandi Ma,
and Dhyani Ywahoo

ACKNOWLEDGMENTS

I am grateful to my parents for giving me the blessings of their love and spiritual guidance. My heartfelt thanks are extended to the many women who helped me in creating this book. Beverly White, thanks for asking; to my dear friends who listened to the quotes and shared their insights: Margy Holiday, Linda Moakes, Jo Palumbo, Arachne Stevens, Pati Stillwater, and Barbara Zoloth, I love you all; and to my mother-in-law, Shirley Zoloth, for editing the first draft of the manuscript, thank you for welcoming me into your heart and into your family. While working on this book I was well cared for by three amazing healers: my chiropractor, Margaret Holiday; my acupuncturist, Stephanie Lum; and my massage therapist, Karaina Black. I was fortunate to have an excellent team of editors: Barbara Moulton, Lisa Bach, and Luann Rouff. I am especially grateful to the generosity of all the teachers and lamas who have taught me the holy Dharma. May any mistakes or omissions be forgiven. May all beings be safe and protected from harm; may their bodies be strong and healthy, and may their hearts be happy and peaceful.

INTRODUCTION

From a very young age I had mystical dreams and visions, and for years I grappled with the idea of leading a cloistered religious life. I chose instead to have a family and spend several weeks or months a year doing intensive spiritual practice.

My life has been graced by many profound spiritual teachings of women. *Open Mind* is my way of sharing them. For years I have listened to stirring spiritual talks, and when the teachers, both female and male, read poetry or from other sources, their quotations are primarily from men. Brilliant, inspiring, and creative teachings from women do exist, and it is my hope that this collection will make them more accessible.

Open Mind invokes the lineage of feminine wisdom. I have drawn from the many teachings that have inspired and nourished me. My research was done in my own library with a little help from my friends. I chose quotes that are practical and encourage the cultivation of mindfulness. The quotations are from women of varied spiritual traditions and include artists, writers, and teachers both ancient and contemporary. I began collecting the quotes several years ago when my housemate asked me if I had a book of inspirational quotations from women that she could use for her daily meditation practice. Since I had no such book I decided to write one.

My first spiritual teacher was my mother. Rubbing my back and singing hymns to me each night as I fell asleep, I was taught that we are never alone, that there is always guidance and love from the spiritual plane as well as from one's earthly family. Gratitude, honesty, respect, and caring for others were not just ideals but were clearly demonstrated in our family. In my twenties I left the church of my childhood and continued to follow my own inner guidance—by listening to my dreams, my intuition, the sound of the wind and the waves and the nature spirits.

When I moved to Cambridge, Massachusetts, in the early seventies I began teaching Womancraft (feminist healing and psychic skills) workshops. The poet Sue Silvermarie attended one of my workshops and invited me to join her and several other women for a full moon ritual. Our moon circle group, which soon became large enough to break into two groups, continued for many years.

When my two sons were about eight and eleven years old, a friend invited me to a four-day Buddhist vipassana silent meditation retreat for women led by her teacher, Ruth Denison. I was overjoyed to have this time with nothing to do but practice the simple technique of being present with the breath. Although a silent retreat was new to me I didn't miss talking or the usual busy activities of daily life. I was content to pass those days in silence, doing both the sitting and slow walking meditations. The retreat filled a hunger in me for which I had no name.

The following year I met Dhyani Ywahoo, of the Green Mountain Band of the Cherokee nation, and founder and spiritual director of Sunray Meditation Society. I studied with Dhyani for ten years and during that time became a teacher in the Peacekeeper Mission, an education and training program based on the Ywahoo lineage teachings. Sunray is also a Tibetan Buddhist dharma center. During my years of intensive study and practice of both Tibetan Buddhist and Native American spiritual traditions I continued to go on silent vipassana meditation retreats. At first I would go to the Insight

Meditation Society (IMS) only when Ruth Denison was teaching. Gradually I began attending vipassana retreats at IMS led by other Buddhist teachers. Since moving to the West Coast in 1989, I have chosen to study primarily with Ruth Denison, who has given me her blessings to teach the dharma.

Open Mind is offered as an inspiration and companion to living the spiritual life. What is the spiritual life? It is an expression of basic kindness toward ourselves and toward all of life. A person who is truly spiritual lives in a way that is kind to herself and to all living things. This person lives from her deepest truth, and does not live by memorized dogma, nor does she bring harm to those who disagree with her beliefs.

Open Mind is an invitation to a deep exploration of our humanity. It may awaken us to possibility. While we accept that what seems scientifically impossible today may be an actuality tomorrow, we often resist accepting that human beings can learn to act without narrow self-interest, and express great depths of love, compassion, equanimity, and joy. Yet, even with the doubts and limitations we place on the spiritual life, there is something inside us, a deep intuition that whispers to us, saying that there is more to life than the search for physical and emotional satisfaction.

It is this intuition that calls us to the spiritual life, to seek the wholeness that is not possible when we limit ourselves to the physical, psychological, and psychic realms. We all have the capacity to be both kind and cruel. Spiritual training, becoming mindful, gives us the tools to deepen our kindness and diminish our cruelty.

It is the practice of meditation that makes the mind powerful and expansive. Analysis, logic, and reasoning won't work. We tend to identify thoughts and feelings with our mind, thinking they are the whole of the mind, when they are truly only the surface of the mind. Our minds are naturally clear, deep and spacious, like the sky. Our thoughts and feelings are like clouds floating through that sky. And in the space between thoughts, the radiant nature of the mind shines through. We can train ourselves to watch our thoughts without judgment. Greed, anger, and delusion are not permanently imprinted on the mind. They are energies that cycle through the mind. These limiting mind energies rise and fall so fast that we aren't able to notice either their beginning or their cessation, so they appear to be solid and permanent. We don't have to be held hostage by our thoughts and feelings. Every thought or feeling does not have to be acted upon. While negative thoughts and feelings cannot be forcefully stopped, we can stop running after them with more of the same.

Time for daily contemplation and meditation is a necessary part of the spiritual life. In this book I have discussed two basic types of meditation practices. Concentration practice works with visualizations or repetitions of spiritual sounds called *mantras*. This type of practice can give us a respite from the pain that we experience in our lives. For example, when I am experiencing intense physical or emotional pain, repeating a mantra or visualizing the Goddess bestowing grace upon me calms my mind and eases the tension that comes from the pain. Concentration practice provides a means for experiencing deep states of calm and bliss. However, this state of bliss is impermanent. When the bliss eventually dissolves, obscurations such as anger and greed can and do arise. These obscurations are our best teachers. They teach us everything we need to know about ourselves. Through the observation of these mind energies, we learn that we can't live freely in the world if we are always running away from unpleasant circumstances.

The second type of meditation practice is awareness practice. Here we practice mindfulness, focusing the attention on a particular object, such as the breath, or on bodily sensations or mind energies. Through mindfulness practice, concentration develops, and then insight into the true nature of reality can arise. When we see things as they are without attachment, the mind becomes peaceful.

Both concentration and mindfulness practices are described in the commentaries. I have focused more on the development of mindfulness because the development of mindfulness will support rather than conflict with whatever ritual or religious tradition we practice. Mindfulness practice is universal; it does not demand acceptance of any religious or metaphysical belief. Together, the practice of mindfulness and the practice of feminism create the conditions for a living vision of women outside of patriarchal reality. Mindfulness, like feminism, says simply: pay attention, explore, and check it out for yourself.

May you have the courage to practice through times of difficulty and times of ease. May you practice with warmth, humor, and a light heart. May mindfulness shine through all your actions and bring to this earth a great peace.

Diane Mariechild
June 1994

A woman can't survive
by her own breath
alone.
She must know
the voices of mountains
She must recognize
the foreverness of blue
She must flow
with the elusive
bodies
of night wind woman
who will take her into
her own self.

Look at me
I am not a separate
woman
I am a continuance
of blue sky
I am the throat
of the Sandia Mountains
A night wind woman
who burns
with every breath
she takes.

JOY HARJO

Joy Harjo inspires us to awaken to the realization of a universal truth. It is the truth of the interconnectedness of all life. Each of us is a part of all the living: the mountains, the sky, the elements, and all other creatures. Wind wisdom is this. It does not cling, it deeply penetrates all life, it has no boundary. Our minds can open like the wind. Our minds are able to embrace a truth that moves beyond the individual self. The quotations and commentaries in this book are an invitation to such an opening. Quiet contemplation each day is training for the mind. As the mind opens, there is joy.

SPIRITUAL PATH

JANUARY 2

A sheltered life can be a daring life as well.
For all serious daring starts from within.

EUDORA WELTY

As a sheltered first daughter, I was thrilled to read this comment in Eudora Welty's autobiography. For a long time I had associated courage and daring with physical feats and totally independent living. One who set off alone to climb a huge mountain was daring. As I grew older I realized that the spiritual search, "serious daring," does start within. It takes enormous courage to stop the busy activities that we have been encouraged to perform and look inside oneself and be willing to accept and work with whatever one finds.

They say she is veiled
and a mystery. That is
one way of looking.
Another
is that she is where
she always has been, exactly in place,
and it is we,
we who are mystified,
we who are veiled
and without faces.

JUDY GRAHN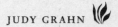

The universe appears to us as a mystery because we aren't clear enough to see the reality of creation. This is the beauty of creation. We are the ones who are veiled. Judy Grahn's poem expresses the biblical teaching "for now we see in a mirror dimly, then face to face." We need generosity, enthusiastic and strenuous effort, as well as patience, kindness, compassion, and meditative contemplation to progress along the path. It is when we lift our veils of fear, anger, pain, and doubt that through a gift of grace, the Goddess lifts her veil and we have a direct experience of the mystery. We see her face.

LIFE AS ART

When we say that life is an art, that life can only be understood if it is approached as an artistic process, we mean that, as in theater or alchemy, something is deeply interfused through its physical forms. And to understand the physical forms accurately, it is necessary to see them with a double eye.

M. C. RICHARDS

It's easy to be fooled by the outer form, especially in a culture that values slick packaging. When we take time to explore beneath the surface we find there is more to the form than its surface image. Experiencing life in this way can be threatening. We have been taught to keep cool and not rock the boat. We're afraid of feelings. We rush through our lives, searching yet not living. We think we don't have the time. Deep looking isn't about time. It is about interest. For those who have the interest to look closely, life becomes art. Deep looking is transformational. Each time we look, we look with new eyes. What is this before me? What does it have to teach me? What can I discover here in this moment? We are open. We have not come to any conclusions. We are living the question: What is this?

Stars give her strength
Sun turn her eyes
Moon guide her feet
Earth turning hold her
We pray for her
We sing for her
We drum for her
We pray

CHRYSTOS

Prayer is an opening of the heart, an alignment with the beauty of the universe. We pray to open our hearts to spiritual power, the ability to sparkle, to shine warmth and light. We open to both the power of clear sight and the power of reflection, to actions that are thoughtful and kind. The Earth in her turning holds us: no matter where we stand, we stand on the Earth. We are of the Earth, the Earth is part of us. So we must caretake the Earth and all of Earth's creatures. We are all relatives. In giving thanks for the Earth, we are giving thanks for our lives and for the precious opportunity we have to grow and to share.

Take time this evening to repeat this prayer slowly, several times, allowing the energy to pass through you. It is an awesome power and brings with it an awesome responsibility. We are blessed, and in the sharing of our blessings we are again blessed. May our hearts open. May we ever be grateful for the gift of life.

SPIRITUAL PATH

The essence of the spiritual path lies only in the beauty of the ordinariness, in the mundane, and in the freedom of separation between the spiritual and ordinary.

DR. THYNN THYNN

Leading a spiritual life is not determined by the number of retreats we attend or our ability to quote scriptures or how many rites or rituals we perform. The beauty of the spiritual life lies in its utter simplicity. One who leads a spiritual life is one who brings mindfulness to each aspect of living. In a masculinist society there is the mistaken idea that women's deep connection with the physical world serves as a distraction from rather than an enhancement of the spiritual life. Women are thought to be less capable or unable to attain the deepest spiritual insights because of the physical tasks of bearing and caring for children. In actuality, no matter how unwavering the concentration or how profound the insight, if one cannot live the truth, there is still far to go. Women's traditional work—giving birth and nurturing children, caring for the sick and the dying, gathering, planting, and feeding people—is all necessary and life-affirming activities. When done with mindfulness—that is, care, joy, and concern for all—this is the spiritual life.

Whoever you are
whatever you are
start with that,
whether salt
of the earth
or only
white sugar.

ALICE WALKER

Change is possible. The only person we can change is ourself. And the only place we can begin is where we are now, right at this moment. We must believe that we are perfect, whole, and that we are unfolding, discovering the wisdom within. When we are truly living, we are loving. They are one and the same. This love starts with us. No matter how imperfect we seem.

Here is a simple self-loving practice you may find useful. Each morning when you get up and look at yourself in the mirror, greet yourself like a long-lost friend, with all the warmth and care you can muster. Bless yourself. Wish yourself a wonderful, joy-filled day. Remind yourself that you are loved, loving, and lovable. Tell yourself whatever you long to hear about inner power, strength, and beauty. Listen with your whole being. Believe it. Live it.

HEALING/FORGIVENESS

The first step toward planetary healing is to walk toward the beauty in thee—to see the beauty in your own heart, to forgive those ideas and correct those thought forms that obscure the true wisdom fire in your mind.

DHYANI YWAHOO

In a turbulent world, where feelings of grief and fear spread like an epidemic, we can become so overwhelmed that we feel hopeless and unable to move. We *do* have the power to change ourselves. A simple first step is to see our own power, to affirm our own power, and to live as though it exists. All the ideas we have about not being good enough, or smart enough, or rich enough can be forgiven. This means they can be released. Each time we give away, or let go of, a limiting idea, there is more space for an empowering idea to come to mind. Try thinking: I have value, therefore I can do something of value because I am valuable. True wisdom burns within us. We don't have to develop it. We have to brush away whatever hides that wisdom fire.

We may think that what we think about ourselves isn't important or doesn't have an effect on the outer world. We can test this assumption by deep observation. When self-esteem is low, notice the level of energy, the feelings and thoughts, as well as the ability to work and the effect we have on other people. Is there a difference in energy, state of mind, and activities when you are feeling good about yourself?

All nature is at the disposal of humankind.
We are to work with it.

Without it we cannot survive.

HILDEGARD OF BINGEN

The first key thought here is to work with nature. So much is being destroyed on the Earth today. Many species of animals are either endangered or extinct. Since the year 1950, more than half the trees on the planet have been cut down. There are tremendous problems with water and air pollution. We now need to begin to clean up our environment and turn around the destructive trend. These changes can and ought to be legislated, yet a true change in behavior must come from a change in heart. Life is a precious gift. The Earth, all of nature, is a precious gift. We need to be thankful for these gifts and to become stewards of the planet, caring for our resources.

The second key thought is that we cannot survive without the Earth. Many people have embraced the idea that the Earth is dying. With hope, such dramatic language will cause people to wake up and create sound ecological policies and practices. What is closer to the truth is that *we* are dying. It is our greed that is killing us. If it doesn't stop and we no longer have clean air to breathe and fresh water to drink, we won't survive. The Earth will undergo transformation. She will continue, and it is the human race that will become extinct.

DEATH

Death
I name you friend.
I want to correspond
before we meet,
to speak the shape you make
inside my skin to trace
the shifting of your shape
as we draw near.
Friend I name
your coming.

SUE SILVERMARIE

The acknowledgment and acceptance of death is not a morbid preoccupation. An awareness of our own mortality brings an aliveness and a preciousness to our daily lives. We will die and we don't know when. To gently hold this thought in our minds and hearts is a way of simplifying our lives. We bring awareness to what we are doing and why we are doing it. Before you do something, ask yourself this question occasionally: If this were to be the last act I make on Earth, would I want to do it? More important than the act itself is the manner in which it is done. What is the intention or motivation beyond the action? There is usually much striving and grasping in our actions, and disappointment in not getting what we want or getting what we don't want.

I remember as a child watching the movie *A Christmas Carol* each year. There was a truth in that movie that brought us back, season after season. Scrooge was transformed after meeting his death. Are we willing to bring this knowledge close enough to allow it to work its transformation?

*All things must come to the soul
from its roots,
from where it is planted.
The tree that is beside running water
is fresher and gives more fruit.*

SAINT TERESA OF AVILA

Many of us have gotten lost in ideas and cut off from our feelings and bodily sensations. To bring forth the soul of our being, we must be in our bodies, rooted to the Earth, able to draw from the universal source of energy. If we can't, and only run our lives on "talking" energy, it's easy to become rigid and stifled. To live creatively we must be aware of this ever-present connection to the source of life. Some call this source the Goddess. When we are open to this energy, we know we are held in the embrace of the Goddess and we express a sense of well-being. Giving, sharing, and relating become natural. When we live solely in our heads, life becomes stale. When we act from our source, our lives are fresh and abundant.

Through mindfulness to the breath we awaken to the source of life. The following imagery can be useful. Once concentration is more firmly established the imagery is dissolved and the attention turned inward. Imagine yourself as a wonderful, huge, old tree. Imagine gigantic roots embedded deeply into the Earth. Feel the massiveness of your trunk. Stretch up into the branches, sway in the wind, bend but don't break. Hear the sound of the leaves as they flutter in the breeze. Feel the warmth of the sun. Imagine the rain washing over you. Drink deeply from your roots. Experience treeness.

CHANGE

With meditative concentration we can become aware of the move-
ment of the skin and under the skin. Then we have a different
outlook on ourselves and the rest of the world, because now we
know with direct knowledge that there is nothing solid or static,
least of all this body.

AYYA KHEMA

Exploring the body and mind in a slow and deliberate way
we come upon this knowing: life is change. My understanding
of change has come in part from exploring sensations of pain
in my body. At first I thought pain is pain. It hurts. Then upon
investigation the pain wasn't as solid or unmoving as I first
thought. In times of great pain, the sensations changed very
quickly but they were all painful. Yet it wasn't a solid wall of
pain. Sometimes there would be a space; however tiny, it was
apparent. Exploring the pain with deep interest and attention,
I was able to experience the painful sensations without my
story of fear of greater pain or incapacitation. The difference,
while it didn't remove the pain, was quite tangible. My mind
could be happy and peaceful while my body still hurt.

The practice of mindful movement such as yoga provides a
gateway for this understanding. Working with the body each
day we find constant change. To work with the body in a conscious way we must bring an attitude of delighted interest.
Each practice session we ask, how does the body want to
move? Working in this way we begin to notice the continual
movement. Strength and flexibility increase, but not in a linear
way. For the body to awaken we must play the edge, be willing
to come to the place of resistance and work with that.

RELATIONSHIP AS MIRROR

Aside from our formal sitting, there is no way that is superior to relationships in helping us see where we're stuck and what we're holding on to. As long as our buttons are pushed, we have a great chance to learn and grow. So a relationship is a great gift, not because it makes us happy—it often doesn't—but because any intimate relationship, if we view it as practice, is the clearest mirror we can find.

CHARLOTTE JOKO BECK

When we're young it is often easier to take risks, to fall in love, to surrender, to open to another person. We entertain the romantic notion that a certain person will make us forever happy and that we'll be able to sustain the same intensity of romantic interest, never becoming disappointed or having conflicts. As we grow in love we realize that there is more to a relationship than having the other person make us happy. In fact, our partners aren't there to make us happy. True happiness comes from within, and we can uncover this source of happiness by challenging the places where we hold onto a certain belief, expectation, or behavior. The partner with whom we are intimately involved often brings the most challenge. This is the person who knows our sore spots. Rather than resisting, withdrawing, or fighting when we are challenged, we can take the opportunity to work through the difficulties by softening and opening. The more knowledge we have around the workings of the mind, the more space there is to open to new ways of doing and being.

COMPASSION

Compassion literally means to feel with, to suffer with. Everyone is capable of compassion, and yet everyone tends to avoid it because it's uncomfortable. And the avoidance produces psychic numbing— resistance to experiencing our pain for the world and other beings.

JOANNA MACY

I was known as a sensitive child. My tears flowed easily, especially on hearing or seeing the suffering of others. I left my childhood behind but not the sensitivity. I remember once calling my parents to share with them a situation that saddened me. My father got on the phone and asked in a tender voice, "Are you still crying for the pain of the world?" Another time my mother expressed concern that I felt such great pain. I reassured her that I could also feel great joy and that I was open to both.

When we harden to the suffering of others, it limits our capacity for joy. We can't deny a part of ourselves without that denial affecting our overall capacity for feeling. This denial also makes it easier for us to harm others. Feeling another's pain is a natural response. If we are willing to experience the discomfort of others, we will be able to access our closed reservoirs of love. And love expressed does not harm.

Part of the manifestation of racism is that we don't value diversity. We've got to have a superior something or a great chain of inferiority, instead of looking at the fact that each is different and diverse and to value the whole of that.

GLORIA DEAN RANDLE SCOTT

We have been taught to fear, taught to hate, and taught to compete. We think there is only one way to be. To unlearn racism we have to change the way we have internalized power. Many of us believe that power means power *over*, whether we have power over another person or another nation. There is the mistaken belief that having power means someone must be in a superior or dominant position and someone else must be in an inferior or subordinate position. We have to unlearn blame, unlearn victim/oppressor thinking and actions. Those who are in the subordinate position are often more willing to change. Those who are in the dominant position get too many benefits and are afraid of losing them. We have never been taught to appreciate the wholeness and complexity of ourselves, let alone the diversity in races and cultures. We haven't learned that through sharing and giving, there is more.

This simple exercise is one way of transforming fear and cultivating gratitude for differences. Take a few minutes to center yourself by bringing your attention to your breath. Now visualize someone from a race or culture other than your own. Recall something that you enjoy from that culture—music, food, or art. Breathe in and receive that gift. Realize how this gift has brought enjoyment to your life. Breathe in gratitude. Allow yourself to fill with gratitude. Now breathe out thankfulness for this gift.

SPIRITUAL GARDENING

Brambles should be cut away,
Removing even the sprouts.
Within essence there naturally blooms
A beautiful lotus blossom.
One day there will suddenly appear
An image of light;
When you know that,
You yourself are it.

SUN BU-ER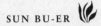

My grandfather was a gardener. He lived in a small town several miles from my childhood home. I remember each fall he would arrive by the local bus and spend the day pruning the lilac bushes that formed a hedge between our yard and the neighbor's yard. Any weeds or brambles that sprung up near the lilac bushes would be dug out. Each spring our yard would be filled with the wonderful sight and smell of purple and white lilacs.

Our work in life is similar to gardening. We need to take the same care with our minds. The unwholesome thoughts and actions coming from greed, hatred, and ignorance must be uprooted. The wholesome thoughts and actions arising from love, generosity, and wisdom must be cultivated.

RESISTANCE

Perhaps the single most important lesson from the edge (the place where forward movement meets resistance) is that simply letting go of frustration when confronted with barriers to ambition is an act of humility. And what is to be gained by humility? Nothing less than a glimpse of immortality, of what life beyond the edge really is.

CATHERINE PECK

Ambition creeps up on us so easily. I have seen this in my yoga practice. There are times when I take for granted the slow, steady progress I am making. When I have a setback due to an injury or illness I sometimes feel despairing or frustrated. Then I realize that I have gotten lost in ideas—the idea that if I keep practicing every day there is some goal I should accomplish, the idea that if I continue to grow stronger and more flexible I'll never have pain. When frustration gets the best of me, I don't want to work simply. I lose my mindfulness and become caught in the mistaken idea that growth follows an upward, linear path. It is at these moments that humor and woman-wisdom can bring me back to myself, wherever I am. I can breathe. I can relax. If today small pelvic tilts are my practice, then that is my practice. It is a full practice when I am present, and it is enough.

ANGER

But I have peeled away your anger
down to its core of love
and look mother
I am
a dark temple where your true spirit rises
beautiful and tough as a chestnut. . . .

AUDRE LORDE

In the beginning of our mindfulness practice our conditioned mind is much stronger than our mindfulness. For example, when working with anger we can bring mindfulness, bring our full attention, to the emotion of anger without judgment. As we directly experience the sensation of anger, it dies. But because our attention is not yet stabilized, the anger rises again within moments or hours. The mind has returned to its habitual or conditioned response. The conditioning, the angry reaction, is very strong. We look at our anger and we intellectualize it. We wonder what is the cause of it. We want to blame someone for the anger. We look to see who escalated the conflict. This type of exploration of anger is not a mindful exploration. It is an intellectualization.

We need to learn how to truly explore anger. This calls for a patient watching of the anger without judging, denying, or running away from it. When we can bring that kind of attention to our anger it dissolves. The more we practice in this way the stronger our mindfulness becomes and the weaker our conditioned response becomes. When the mind is no longer trapped by conditioned response, what remains is love.

The whole journey of renunciation, or starting to say yes to life, is first of all realizing that you've come up against your edge, that everything in you is saying no, and then at that point, softening. This is yet another opportunity to develop loving-kindness for yourself, which results in playfulness—learning to play like a raven in the wind.

PEMA CHÖDRÖN

To set upon the spiritual path is to be willing to meet the greatest challenges of our lives. It is meeting those places of fear that have hardened our hearts. We've been taught to toughen up, that we have to be hard to get through life. We can't show our feelings, much less our fear. We have to bluff. This technique might work in some situations but it doesn't work in the long haul. If our goal is to open to all of life then the hardness must soften. We must become vulnerable. This means we become more sensitive to how we are feeling, to how others are feeling. There is no shame in this. We need love. We need to see and appreciate the little child within. When we accept this child, we can play. Attachment is so serious. Things have to be this way or else. Stubbornness is a deterrent to the path. The spiritual path is a process of softening and opening, softening and opening. It is often in direct opposition to the ways we've been taught to be. It takes much courage to go against the grain of society. This is what we have to renounce. We must renounce anger and hatred and shame. We must renounce limitations, fears, illusions, doubts.

LOSS

Listen, listen:
longing and loss.
In the struck bell's
recurrent calling,
no moment in which to forget.

IZUMI SHIKIBU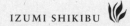

    Our lives are filled with losses. It is our attitude toward inevitable loss that determines our capacity for joy. One of my relationships ended very abruptly. One day we were together and the next day she was gone. The reason did not have to do with whether our relationship was good, bad, or indifferent. Nor did it have to do with personalities or right and wrong. The loss provided me with a precious opportunity to practice mindfulness. By bringing mindfulness to every feeling and thought that arose in my mind, I was able to work with a difficult situation. The sudden loss was like a slap in the face and I woke up. "In the struck bell's recurrent calling, no moment in which to forget. No moment in which to forget." Waking up, remembering, is joy.

I know I am made from this earth, as my mother's hands were made from this earth, as her dreams came from this earth and all that I know, I know in this earth . . . and I long to tell you, you who are earth too, and listen as we speak to each other of what we know: the light is in us.

SUSAN GRIFFIN

I had the good fortune to travel to Nepal and do a meditation retreat at Kopan Monastery. Several times during that month I took the thirty-minute walk down the hill from the monastery into the village of Bodnath. There were no paved roads, just a winding dirt path. I would see the villagers going about their daily tasks. People were busy, they walked with purpose but they did not rush. Their movements were closely connected to the Earth. Their feet truly touched the Earth; there was no gap between their bodies and the body of the Earth. With all our concrete and paved highways we can lose touch with the Earth. Our feet don't touch the Earth. They are in shoes or cars or planes. We forget that we are of the Earth.

Walking barefoot on Earth helps me to feel grounded. Here's an exercise I like to do. Press your feet into the Earth. Let them be held by the Earth. Rock back and forth from the ball to the heel and back. Then rock from side to side. Come to balance, centered on your feet. Bring your weight slightly forward and then press your heels into the ground. Now roll each foot in turn, making certain you keep pressing the edge of the foot on the Earth. Stand firmly on the Earth. Breathe deeply. Now run, dance, skip, walk, or do whatever feels comfortable. If you lose connection with the Earth, stop, reconnect, and then begin again.

PLAY

Life is playfulness. . . . We need to play so that we can rediscover the magic all around us.

FLORA COLAO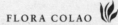

    Play is a daring, free, and delightful exploration. Play is a totally unselfconscious activity. One becomes so absorbed in the exploration that self is forgotten. Ever watch a child at play? She can be whimsical or serious, but her full concentration is called forth. The Hindus have a word for play. It is *lila* and it means divine play. It is the ever-creative, destructive, and regenerative dance of the Goddess. It is pure delight. It is free from attachment. We have become so conditioned to striving that true daring is lost. We compete, there is a goal and we are attached to winning, to being the best. We are afraid of looking silly or clumsy. There isn't freedom in our play. Playing is an attitude. We can bring this playful attitude inward and explore our minds or take it outward, exploring our environment.

I used every gift God gave me. The gift of love is the greatest. It's a difficult thing because there are people I know that I can't stand. But love doesn't mean affection. It means treating them justly even when they are terrible people. That takes a bit of doing, an awful lot of grace.

JANET COLLINS

It's easy to save our good feelings and acts of kindness and generosity for those people we love, for those people who please us. The challenge of non-attached love is the ability to demonstrate that kindness and sense of fair play to all people, regardless of their behavior or relation to us.

You can begin to practice this kind of love in simple ways. When you're driving home from work and the driver next to you cuts you off, instead of cursing take a deep breath. This person may have had some grief or pain today. Bless them. "May you arrive safely. May you be happy." At first you may be saying this with gritted teeth. What you feel is far-removed from what you are saying. With time those words will become a true expression of love and caring. It just takes practice.

TRUE NATURE

A fish cannot drown in water,
A bird does not fall in air.
In the fire of creation,
Gold doesn't vanish:
The fire brightens.
Each creature God made
Must live in its own true nature;
How could I resist my nature,
That lives for oneness with God?

MECHTILD OF MAGDEBURG

Material comforts have not given people the freedom they assumed would come from such comforts. Many of those who are materially comfortable feel lost and alienated. We have become alienated from our true nature, and the amassing of material goods can't ease the alienation. Freedom will come when our life energy is not limited by our fears and grasping. Our nature is pure. It is Goddess inspired. It is divine. Unless we open our hearts to this truth we are resisting our nature. When we look to the animal world we admire the grace with which a deer runs, the ease with which a hawk floats on the air currents. Watching a fish swim or seeing a cat stretch we see their fishness and catness. These animals are fully who they are. As we move farther away from our true natures, our movements become awkward, our voices harsh, our minds frantic. We are too busy doing. We are human *beings*. Today, remember to be.

We are reminding ourselves of the source of life. Everything we know is born of woman.

JOAN HALIFAX

Sometimes it is difficult for women to feel there's a safe place for us on the planet. This quote reminds me that not only is there a place, but there is a source and we belong to that source. We can't wait for something outside ourselves to give us this support, whether it is family, friends, or society. We have to give ourselves that respect now. When we respect the source of life, woman, we are respecting life itself. And when we are respecting women, we are respecting the source of life.

Women are the birthers of all life. Every human being shares this in common. we are all born of woman. Living with full awareness of our interrelatedness with all the living we are not able to harm. What hurts one of us hurts all of us. What harms the Earth harms each of us. We respect this great power by being trustworthy, by nurturing all life, by abstaining from harmful actions, and by living peacefully, even in simple ways, such as choosing to let go of irritation when things aren't going our way. If our attitude is to create peace, then we must always stop and think: Is what I'm doing creating peace or creating conflict?

ATTACHMENT

If you know you are not your sports car, your grades or your children's grades, your color, your degrees, your spouse's degrees, your age, your titles or your family's titles, your body, your possessions or your parents' possessions—Congratulations. You are Home again.

RUSTY BERKUS

For me, home is shelter, a place of refuge where I can be all that I am. One of the Zen koans, or riddles, asks, "What was the face you wore before you were born?" Meditation and reflection on such a question is a way of shattering our usual perceptions, our own ideas, opinions, and all the ways we have become attached. It asks us to open to the expression of our original nature. It calls us home.

Have you ever noticed how personally attached some people are to their cars? If you appreciate their car for its speed or comfort, it is like appreciating them. Likewise, not appreciating the car is not valuing them. Some people take great offense if something happens to their car. It is a personal insult rather than simply a machine that needs upkeep.

Or maybe we place an extremely high value on our scholastic endeavors. Returning to our original nature, living without attachment, doesn't demand that we give up driving cars or refuse to get a college education. It means that while we recognize that some things are necessary to move through the material world, these things won't give us the refuge that we seek. They are not our true home. "What was the face you wore before you were born?"

True love grows by sacrifice and the more thoroughly the soul rejects natural satisfaction the stronger and more detached its tenderness becomes.

SAINT THERESE OF LISIEUX

Sacrifice can be an emotionally charged word for many women who have been trained to sacrifice their own needs and wants for others. This kind of sacrifice comes from a denigration of woman power. When women are treated as unworthy and internalize this belief they often give away their power. They give to others because they don't feel worthy to receive. I doubt this is the kind of sacrifice Saint Therese is recommending. We can truly let go of personal needs for comfort and convenience when we know our Goddess nature and are inspired to grow beyond our attachment to such needs. It does not come from a place of feeling needy or undeserving. We know we are deserving. We know we are Goddess/goodness and we can increase this Goddessness/goodness through this sacrifice /gift.

An example of consciously choosing to give when it isn't most convenient is taken from my own life. I was quite busy writing and preparing to leave town when a woman called with a request. I had purchased some hand-dyed clothing from her and she wanted me to mail the article back to her so she could photograph it. It just seemed like one more thing to do, and not what I wanted. I decided to do it not because I wanted her to like me but as a conscious choice to lessen my attachment to convenience.

COMPASSION

If compassion never ceases to flow, then that is meditation. Meditation is not must sitting in the lotus positions with eyes closed. Real meditation exists in the midst of dynamic activity or life.

DAE HAENG SE NIM

Buffy Fitch and her husband lived in the Northridge Apartments that were destroyed by the Los Angeles earthquake. They were able to save the lives of twelve neighbors. In an interview Buffy said it wasn't about her becoming a hero. "It was about seeing an enormous amount of work that needed to be done. People needed to join together to do it. That's what makes a catastrophic situation less catastrophic—people joining together to help one another." Social change must start in our hearts. People who practice spiritual disciplines have the most enduring impact on life because the inward work we do makes us more effective in any situation. We are most effective when we can return goodwill for ill will and show kindness to those who would harm us; when we look for a common solution without anger or a desire for retaliation; and act on principles of care and concern without a need for reciprocation.

Some people practice throughout their entire lives just by paying attention to their breathing. Everything that is true about anything is true about breath: it's impermanent; it arises and it passes away. Yet if you didn't breathe, you would become uncomfortable; so then you would take in a big inhalation and feel comfortable again. But if you hold onto the breath, it's no longer comfortable, so you have to breathe out again.

SYLVIA BOORSTEIN

There is a rhythm, a cycle, to life. To walk in balance we must recognize and honor these seasons and cycles: day and night, waxing and waning, ebb and flow. We can't get up one morning and decide we only want to exhale. We couldn't live. We need to breathe in to open ourselves to new energy and new information, and we need to breathe out and let it go. In the letting go, the emptying, we're free to receive again. But we can't hold on to the breath or we'll suffocate. So we let go and receive a new breath. We are nourished by the breath. The oxygen feeds the blood that feeds the organ systems of the body. And we can't hold on; when it's time to let go we must let go.

Breath is a metaphor for life. Can you breathe deeply? Can you truly receive all there is to receive, allow it to nourish you and then, when it's time, let it go? Can you exhale fully without holding on to even the smallest bit of breath? Spend some quiet time today, even ten minutes, sitting alone with the breath as your only focus. Don't try to change it. Allow its natural rhythm to flow undisturbed.

UNIVERSAL LANGUAGE

One should identify oneself with the universe itself. Everything that is less than the universe is subject to suffering. . . .

SIMONE WEIL

Vipassana teacher Ruth Denison was leading a mindfulness movement session in the mineral baths. We were working in partners, one woman gently supporting the other to lie back and be held by the water. My partner burst into deep sobs. Three months before she had had her right breast removed because of a cancerous tumor, and was overwhelmed by a grief that had only briefly surfaced while she dealt with the medical treatments.

Ruth had her stand up so she wouldn't inhale any water and began gently suggesting that having only one breast was all right. Some of the woman's grief at losing a breast came from her wanting something to be different than what it was.

Ruth didn't demand that the student stop crying. She simply encouraged her to look beyond, to see through the sadness. For the time being the woman was alive and well. When we identify solely with our bodies there is much suffering. We are afraid of losing the body, and the attachment to it causes the suffering. Yes, there is pain in life. Losing a breast is a traumatic experience. Without denying the pain we can look through it to the larger picture. This seeing heals.

A fire
does not shoot its flame
downward but upward,
no matter how great a fire is enkindled.
Likewise one experiences
that this letting go
proceeds from the center of the soul
and awakens the person to
a new consciousness and a new compassion.

SAINT TERESA OF AVILA

In the Women's Sacred Mystery School* we recognized ourselves as keepers of the fire. Fire power is the power to bring light, warmth, and transformation. We honor the lineage of feminine wisdom—generations of women who have tended the hearth fires. How do we tend the fire that creates, sustains, and nourishes life? In a ritual of commitment we entrust ourselves to the training to align ourselves with, and express the energies of, love. The energy we receive from taking the vows and the community of firekeepers supports us throughout the training. We carefully tend the fire, we touch the source of life, and drawing from that power we are able to extend our sphere of influence. The influence is of an impersonal nature; it is kindness, compassion, joy, and equanimity extended to all beings. We dance, we sing, we pray. We cast into the fire the fears that inhibit love's light. In the burning away of fear, love is awakened.

* The Women's Sacred Mystery School, established in 1987, was a spiritual training program co-founded in New England.

MOTHER/FATHER GOD

Just as god is truly our Father,
So also is god truly our Mother.

JULIAN OF NORWICH

It's a joy to read the words of the fourteenth-century Christian mystic Julian of Norwich articulating the motherhood of God. The English anchoress lived during very troubled times immediately following the Black Death. In spite of the worldly distress she was able to turn inward and realize the divine light that is within. Mystics directly experience the true nature of life. Each of us is one with the power that creates and sustains the universe and this deep experience is the purpose for which we have been given life.

We have to grow into the awareness of this. To support us in this unfolding, it is helpful at times to envision this divine nature as a person. When this person is always a male, men and women may feel that females are lacking divine wisdom. God is limitless. It is fear and prejudice that have reduced God to an external and masculine authority. When people, cultures, or religions insist that we hold only one vision of God as true, they speak from fear and ignorance, not from knowledge of the Divine, who is love.

Even the softest prayer sends vibrations of prayer moving through the air, just as the guitar string stirs the piano's song.

DHYANI YWAHOO

In Western culture, prayer is often thought to be unrealistic. We envision old women in black dresses, kneeling to light candles in a darkened church. We see these old women as powerless and praying for help that will never come. We mistrust that which cannot be seen, weighed, or measured. Yet prayer opens the heart. Each time we pray we are connecting with a greater source of energy and we are amplifying that energy. Our gratitude, our thanksgiving, for even the smallest gift we have received, allows the heart to open. The more the heart opens, the larger our vision becomes. This prayer, this energy, links us with all the goodness on the planet.

TRUE SAFETY

FEBRUARY 3

When I wonder where is my refuge, my safe haven, it (the symbolic hand gesture, meaning fear not) reminds me that my real refuge is in my action, in the flow going out of the heart, in the connection.

JOANNA MACY

There are plenty of people willing to throw themselves into action.

Most people want to take sides in every encounter or conflict, distinguishing right from wrong based on partial evidence gathered by hearsay or propaganda. The world needs people who are capable of loving, not taking sides, so they can embrace the whole reality as a mother hen embraces her chicks, with two fully spread wings.

True safety comes from a peaceful heart. This heart is not barricaded from the world. The sense of peace takes us out into the world and empowers us to do whatever we can to help: struggling against sexist and racist discrimination, stopping the arms race, protecting endangered species, lessening the disparity between the rich and the poor.

If you give your life as a prayer you intensify the prayer beyond all measure. To attain inner peace you must actually give your life, not just your possessions. When you at last give your life bringing into alignment your beliefs and the way you live then and only then, can you begin to find inner peace.

PEACE PILGRIM

Peace Pilgrim was a woman who began her private mission for peace by giving up all her personal possessions, her name, and her age and setting out to walk back and forth across the country until peace came. She stopped counting the miles after 25,000 but continued walking until her death in 1981.

The path that you and I take may look very different than the path chosen by Peace Pilgrim. What is the same is this: For any of us to achieve inner peace we must go against the grain of our conditioning. It requires time and effort to go against such deeply ingrained habits as fits of emotion, compulsions, and cravings. Such patterns of thinking and behavior can be likened to a deep river and we must swim against strong currents. When I studied with Dhyani Ywahoo we practiced a meditation called Coming Home. We envisioned ourselves as salmon and we had to jump into the river and swim against the currents to come home. The water at the source was clear and calm but the journey demanded strength and commitment. We had to shake free from all fears, doubts, and learned limitations.

FREEDOM

My body lives in the city,
But my essence dwells in the mountains.
The affairs of a puppet play
Are not to be taken too seriously.
When the polar mountain fits into a mustard seed,
All the words in the universe may be erased.

WU CAILUAN

The puppet play is a poetic way of reminding us that the daily life we place so much importance on and are so busy working at is only a play. Pulled by our desires we become like puppets. We grasp at happiness but our solutions are temporary and don't provide the everlasting happiness we seek. Everlasting happiness is an inner state that doesn't depend on favorable external circumstances. Worldly success won't bring us abiding joy. Nor do we need to live alone meditating on a mountaintop to discover it. We can live in the world.

In this poem the Taoist practitioner uses the Buddhist image of a polar mountain fitting into a mustard seed, which symbolizes the attainment of mental freedom through a direct, personal experience of universal relativity. On long retreats I have been able to see thoughts, feelings, and sensations come and go so often that they no longer became personal. As I watched the constant impressions cycle through my mind, I didn't judge them. It was simply energy rising and falling. I kept watching. Mindfulness became strengthened and I felt peaceful and balanced. This was sweet joy.

My life goes on in endless song
above earth's lamentations,
I hear the real, though far-off hymn
that hails a new creation.
Through all the tumult and the strife
I hear its music ringing.
It sounds an echo in my soul.
How can I keep from singing?

TRADITIONAL HYMN

This song shares with us a secret of life. A light-hearted at-titude allows us to see beauty, no matter how much pain and suffering there is. It is an open-hearted attitude. We are singing, not out of pretense that bad things don't happen, but knowing that no matter how bad it is, the sun still rises, the stars still shine, the moon waxes and wanes, the flowers bloom. There is always something of beauty, even amidst the greatest sorrow. This doesn't take away all sorrow: it gives sorrow a place within a larger picture, one that also has joy.

SACREDNESS OF LIFE

Let us be clear that when I say Goddess I am not talking about a being somewhere outside of this world, nor am I proposing a new belief system. I am talking about choosing an attitude; choosing to take this living world, the people and creatures on it, as the ultimate meaning and purpose of life, to see the world, the Earth, and our lives as sacred.

STARHAWK

To recognize the sacred is to make holy, to make whole. To recognize the sacred is to see the connection with the divine, to know that we are divine. To recognize the sacred is to respect and revere all of life. When we bring the attitude that all life is sacred to everything that we do, our thoughts, words, and actions are transformed. Understanding life as sacred allows us to slow down and greet each person and each circumstance in a more gentle way. When we revere each person, each object, each situation, we treat them with loving care. When we rush or when we are afraid or angry, we often do harm. Belonging to the divine, the holy, the whole, we respond to everyone, including ourselves, with kindness, clarity, and compassion.

UNIVERSAL CONSCIOUSNESS

Remember that you are this universe and that this
universe is you.
Remember that all is in motion, is growing, is you.

JOY HARJO

Each time I remember I belong to the universe, I receive enormous support and comfort. I forget the petty, selfish side of myself. I know I am not alone and separate from the whole universe. I don't remain stuck in my own perceptions, thoughts, and feelings. When I remember the universe is my home I feel blessed and want to extend this blessing to others.

Playing with this phrase as a mantra or prayer is one way of extending our field of awareness. Try repeating this phrase three times when you get up in the morning, three times before each meal, and three times before you go to bed tonight. You may want to extend this practice for three days or three weeks. Notice how it feels in your body to remember that you are the universe, to remember that things are in motion, moving and changing inside you. You might play with bringing a movement to this phrase, touching your heart as you remember you are the universe and extending your arms out from your heart, bringing the palms together in a prayer position and then bringing them again to your heart.

WOMEN'S ABUNDANCE

We who bleed
we who pour libation to the earth each moon,
weave toward the sea.
These are priestesses who carry me.
Each moon, each woman
nourishes this soil that suckles us.
We the bloodrich, we the generous.

SUE SILVERMARIE

Monthly ritual circles are a wonderful way for women to celebrate their abundance and generosity. During my time of study with a Native American teacher, we performed a ritual during one of the retreats in which the bleeding women collected some of their blood, went out onto the land and dug a small hole, put some tobacco in the hole, and then poured the blood in and covered the hole. Prayers were made for the community. Women prayed that whatever energy needed release or transformation would be discharged and transformed. Relieved of their usual daily tasks, this was the sacred duty of the women during their moontime.

While this ritual might not be appropriate for all women, we can each find some gesture that reminds us of the power of the bleeding time and begin to incorporate it into our lives. Try placing a single red flower on your altar or desk during your bleeding time.

Finally the oyster knows itself
to be not different from the pearl:
soft flesh made precious in pain,
all a jewel in God's fiery sea.

LYNN PARK

One spring on a meditation retreat in the high desert, we were treated to the beauty of many wildflowers, some of which, rangers reported, had not bloomed in one hundred years. The heavy rains that preceded the blooms created dangerous flooding. After the danger subsided, the land blazed with the color of the flowers, the air was sweetly perfumed, and thousands of butterflies delicately kissed the flowers.

There is no high drama in Lynn Park's poem, no saying I'm so glad for the pain, it made me what I am. Rather, it is a simple statement of truth. Life brings both beauty and pain. Take a moment to breathe deeply and visualize a precious and beautiful pearl. While resting gently with this image reflect on the making of a pearl. An oyster caught a grain of sand within her shell. Maybe it was painful and she tried to stop the irritation by releasing liquid to cover the sand. The pearl formed. The beautiful pearl is not separate from the pain and irritation. When looking at beauty in our lives we see that it often follows a time of struggle or irritation. The irritation serves as the polishing necessary to refine oneself.

SILENCE

Moon shell. . . . You will remind me that woman must be still as the axis of a wheel in the midst of her activities; that she must be the pioneer in achieving this stillness, not only for her own salvation, but for the salvation of family life, of society, perhaps even of our civilization.

ANNE MORROW LINDBERGH

We live in a culture that has overdeveloped the masculine, or active, principle. This imbalance has engendered the pain of aggression and violence. Another pain, not so easily observable, is the inability to be still. People have not been trained to develop stillness. It isn't respected in Western culture. Even those who desire stillness don't know how to achieve it. There are methods that we can practice to still the mind, to witness the process of mind, to enable us to be observers of the movements of mind and body. The mind always creates thoughts. With training in meditation we learn to be conscious of the movement and less identified with it, so we can touch the place of stillness within. As we become less attached to this movement, we can bring the contemplative quality to all aspects of life. Even when we are in active periods of life, we can keep the stillness within and move from that space. Our activities will be infused with lightness, a quality of serenity and peace.

SMALL CHANGES

But we have been ripening
To a greater ease,
Learning to accept
That all hungers cannot be fed,
That saving the world
May be a matter
Of sowing a seed
Not overturning a tyrant,
That we do what we can.

MAY SARTON

Doing what we can is the crucial understanding in Sarton's poem. As we grow in wisdom we see that we might not be able to make all the changes that are necessary and we might not be able to make changes as fast as we'd like, but we can begin with a small step, like the planting of a seed. When I was young I was often indignant about the suffering in the world and eager to make great changes. I'd watch my mother knitting children's hats. "This won't change the world," she'd tell me, "but one little child will have a warm head." By her example I learned to slow down and move with confidence, knowing that each little bit helps.

What is one thing you can do today to ease the pain of someone else? Make it very small, very simple. Do it today.

SOCIAL CHANGE

FEBRUARY 13

The practice of meditation teaches us to be humble about our per-
ceptions and to look more deeply into things in order to be closer to
their reality. If we are too sure of our perceptions, when things turn
out to be different we will suffer, and a shock like that can cause us
to say that life is illusory.

SISTER CHAN KHONG (TRUE EMPTINESS)

Sister Chan Khong was born in a village on the Mekong
River Delta in 1938. Propelled by her passionate dedication to
social change, she began working in the slums of Saigon as a
teenager, distributing food, helping the sick, and teaching children. In 1964 she joined Zen Master Thich Nhat Hanh in
founding the School of Youth for Social Service, which grew
to an organization of over 10,000 people organizing medical,
educational, and agricultural facilities in rural Vietnam, and
rebuilding villages destroyed by the war.

Sister True Emptiness carries out her responsibilities in the
world with ethics and compassion. Meditation does not remove her from the world. It brings her into the world with
nondiscrimination, with true love. She can feel the hunger and
pain of all beings as her own. Knowing the truth of interbeing
she can function in the world in a nonattached way with great
energy and joy.

What is the greatest kind of love?
Great Love
does not flow with tears.
Rather,
it burns in the great Fire of Heaven.
In this Fire
it flows and flows swiftly
yet all the while
it remains in itself
in a very great stillness.

MECHTILD OF MAGDEBURG

Whenever I read this passage from Mechtild I am touched deeply in the place beyond words. Articulating this love is not easy. What I hear is something about the awesomeness of love. I hear that the power of love is the power of transformation. I hear that love is brilliant. Its light allows us to see with pristine clarity. I hear that the warmth of love's energy is so subtle that it can't be said to be either moving or still. These words portray a love that is not clinging or sentimental. Great love is the alchemical fire that transforms our baser instincts into gold.

I know these words contain a great truth and I hold them closely so I can absorb that truth. I repeat the words again and again, first aloud and then silently. There is no mental analysis, only the transformation that comes through their resonance in my heart.

CHILD OF GOD

I'm convinced that I'm a child of God. That's wonderful, exhilarating, liberating, full of promise. But the burden which goes along with that is, I'm convinced that everybody is a child of God. The brutes and bigots, the batterers and the bastards are also children of God.

MAYA ANGELOU

One of my friends, who is a survivor of both physical and sexual abuse, shared with me her struggles with the acceptance that Maya Angelou describes. "As I've opened my heart to myself, I have had to open my heart to recognizing that the people who abuse have also been harmed in their own ways. I'm not letting them off the hook and saying the abuse is okay. But I do need to keep my own heart clear. To keep from becoming bitter I have had to realize that they are also children of God. It isn't up to me to hate them or to enlighten them. It's up to me to step out of the way and not keep getting hurt."

*My feeling is, the better we feel about ourselves, the fewer times we
have to knock somebody down in order to stand on top of their
bodies and feel tall.*

ODETTA

Self-esteem isn't feeling good about ourselves at someone
else's expense. There will always be someone to knock down
or someone trying to knock us down. There will always be
tension and fear, even when not outwardly struggling with
others. Self-esteem comes from an inner certainty, a connectedness with life, an equanimity that is maintained regardless
of the blame or praise we receive.

"The better we feel about ourselves, and the more willing
we are to help others to stand tall, the more able we are to
have a good time. There's no sense in putting anybody down,
then you have no peers," was a friend's response to Odetta's
words. We have been raised in a very competitive culture.
When we grow up with a feeling of scarcity, whether it is articulated or not, we see other people in competition with us.
We're in a race to get the good things in life. When we are able
to respond to people as partners, part of the one family of life,
who are working *with* us, we are all co-creators of the world,
and the world is a very different place.

BEAUTY

Beauty and grace are performed whether or not we will or sense them. The least we can try to do is be there.

ANNIE DILLARD

Annie Dillard, in her daily walks to Tinker Creek, showed us how to truly see. She took the time to look whether it was at a spider, a bird, a flower, or a tadpole. She stopped and she looked. Beauty is happening all around us. Can you take a moment this very day to stop, breathe deeply, and look? Even if you live in the city, look at a tree or some flowers in a window box that you pass every day on your way to work. Take a minute to observe them. Do it every day for a week. Notice what feelings or thoughts arise as you practice deep looking. Is there a time when no thought arises? Can you see simply the color and the shape? When the mental conception quickly arises, can you notice it and come back to the color and the shape?

We can do anything we want to do if we stick to it long enough.

HELEN KELLER

    These words come from Helen Keller's personal experience. Deaf and blind because of a childhood disease, she persevered and learned to communicate despite the enormous odds against her. This isn't to say that on our journey we won't tire or feel frustrated or despairing. It is then we need to call upon our graciousness to keep going. We may have to slow down, we may have to move backward a few steps to something easier, but we continue to persevere.

    A meditation student on a retreat was having severe back pain and needed to lie down during some of the meditations. She did so in the back of the meditation hall. It was more difficult to keep attentive to the breathing in this position but the student worked with pressing her lips together to feel a bodily sensation and gather her focus. When this no longer worked, she silently repeated a mantra and worked with her energy in that way. When the teacher commented on the student's practice she said that this method demonstrated good self-esteem, in that she didn't fall into self-pity but kept practicing. It also demonstrated humility, by her willingness to fall back to an easier level of practice.

GODDESS/DEVOTION

Mother and God, to You we sing;
wide is Your womb, warm is Your wing.
In You we live, move, and are fed,
sweet, flowing milk, life-giving bread.
Mother and God, to You we bring
all broken hearts, all broken wings.

MIRIAM THERESE WINTER

This sacred song written by Miriam Therese Winter is a means of celebrating and opening the heart to the creatress of all life. Goddess or God is an aspect of our being. We often personify the qualities of the creative, abundant force of life. This force that has created and sustained us is not separate from us. It is difficult for us to comprehend the vast and beautiful qualities of this energy. We cannot know it through our intellectual mind. Playing with the analogy of the abundant, giving, spiritual mother is a way of awakening us to this source that is beyond all descriptions. It is a lovely reminder that we are never far from this embrace.

This song can be part of our morning and evening devotions. Allow its energies to penetrate deeply within your heart. Feel the solace that comes from knowing we have the support of the Earth beneath us and the Sky above us. We can feel and act from this support.

Attachment to what we call "spiritual" is the very activity that hampers a spiritual life. If we are attached to anything we cannot be free or truly loving. So long as we have any picture of how we are supposed to be or how other people are supposed to be, we are attached; and a truly spiritual life is simply the absence of that.

CHARLOTTE JOKO BECK

In the New Testament we read that Jesus healed people on the Sabbath. He was demonstrating that even attachment to religious rules inhibits our spiritual progress. For the same reason, Tibetan Buddhists serve a bit of alcohol and meat during their sacred ceremonies. The Mexican Indian sorcerer Don Juan described this truth in a similar way. He said, "I cling to nothing, therefore I have nothing to defend." And a present-day meditation teacher, when explaining the meaning of the Buddhist Heart Sutra, said, "There's nothing worth clinging to."

Here is a simple way to explore this teaching: You have been wanting to see a particular movie for some time. Your partner, however, has a very different idea of how to spend your time together. What do you do? Do you insist on having things your way? Do you attempt to get her to see why your choice is better? Do you give in because you want this as a point of negotiation the next time you have a difference? Do you repress your needs for hers? Notice what you do and why you are doing it. How do you feel about your choice? Explore without judgment, simply to gain information.

LOSS

Through the years
I've become used to sorrow:
there was not one spring
I didn't leave behind
the flowers.

IZUMI SHIKIBU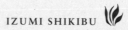

Izumi is sharing a simple truth. It isn't dramatic. It isn't embroidered with layers of images. It is this: Flowers are born and flowers die. In that dying, in that loss, there is sadness. Sadness acknowledged in this way is not held. It is seen, felt, and released. Izumi knows that life is cyclical. There are losses. There is sadness, and there is more than sadness. There is joy and beauty as well.

My teacher Ruth Denison explains that when the mind acknowledges the truth of impermanence it relaxes into itself. There is an acceptance of life and a lightness that comes from seeing through the confusion. The mind is balanced.

This is to love:
bear with a fault and not be astonished,
relieve others of their labor and
take upon yourself tasks to be done;
be cheerful when others have need of it;
be grateful for your strength when
others have need of it;
show tenderness in love and sympathize
with the weakness of others.

SAINT TERESA OF AVILA

It is a challenge to express this kind of love. More often than not when we say "I love you" we're really saying "I love me." We love what the other will do for us and how the other makes us feel. To love in the way Saint Teresa is describing means we must put aside selfish desires and angry impulses. The more we are able to do this, the more loving energy is available to us. We've been taught that loving means we care enough to point out the faults of our loved ones. This isn't love, this is criticism. To love is to see the beauty and the wisdom beyond the faults. We all make mistakes. We must look to correct our own mistakes. Love is tender. We don't take advantage of others when we see their weaknesses. We offer assistance when asked and we encourage others to see their own strengths and to help themselves. Love is a wholehearted willingness to serve. In the small town where I once lived a beloved member of the community was badly burned in a fire when a cabin heater burst into flames. Within forty-eight hours friends and neighbors gathered and rebuilt the cabin. Above all else, love is kind.

TENDERNESS

How can we touch each other, my sisters? . . .
We keep our tenderness alive and the nourishment of the earth
  green.
The heat is central as lava.
We burn in each other. We burn and burn.
  We shout in choruses of millions.
  We appear armed as mothers, grandmothers, sisters, warriors.
  We burn.

MERIDEL LE SUEUR

Basic mindfulness is a continuous practice during the women's vipassana meditation retreat. We work with the breath, awakening to the knowledge that we are breathing. We can feel the touch of the breath. We are all breathing the same air. The air that I breathe in and out is breathed in and out by the woman sitting next to me. At the end of the sitting my teacher will sometimes say, "Take a minute to recognize the support of all the dharma sisters. We are all practicing together. It is safe here."

We are learning to keep our tenderness alive. As each of us finds in her heart the ability to be tender to herself and to others, this gentle touch is felt by the Earth and by all those walking on the Earth. Our actions become less harmful. The fire is burning away the dissatisfaction, the inability to see. In that burning we awaken to our oneness, we awaken to our interconnectedness. We become mindful of the effects of cutting down a forest or burning fossil fuel or using water. Mindfulness is tenderness. It is careful and considerate. It is time for women who recognize our interconnectedness to bring this sensibility to the world.

(The flower) says: Just be, Alice. Being is sufficient. Being is All. The cheerful, sunny self you are missing will return, as it always does, but only being will bring it back.

ALICE WALKER

Self-criticism and self-condemnation play too strong a role in our lives. We think we should feel this way or we shouldn't feel that way. Only a limited range of feeling is acceptable. True happiness can only arise when we accept all of our feelings. We need to accept and experience the sadness. When we can graciously allow it into our field of being, it can be directly experienced and then released. The release is not through force. It comes naturally with the direct experience.

When a relationship ends and you are the one who is left, it can invite feelings of blame, anger, and self-pity. Yet it can also be a rich and fertile time to welcome uncomfortable feelings. It can be an opportunity to work with all the sadness and anger over what could have been or what you think should have been. Work directly with these feelings. Allow them to be seen, felt, and experienced. Don't work with the content, that is, the story of how "she done me wrong." Don't hold onto blame for yourself or your former partner. Without the story, the feelings are simply energy available for transformation. Whenever I practice in this way my equanimity soon returns and with it comes a profound sense of peace.

GENEROSITY

FEBRUARY 25

To acknowledge privilege is the first step in making it available for wider use. Each of us is blessed in some particular way, whether we recognize our blessings or not. And each one of us, somewhere in our lives, must clear a space within that blessing where she can call upon whatever resources are available to her in the name of something that must be done.

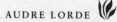

AUDRE LORDE

During meditation retreats, participants are asked to volunteer to help with the running of the center. The task serves as a mindfulness practice as well as a practical means of keeping the costs of the center down. We were challenged by the teacher to see if there was something more we could do once we finished our assigned jobs. Rather than thinking, I want to meditate, I don't want to do housework, we were asked to reflect on these things: I am privileged to spend a number of days in this beautiful desert retreat center. Here I can practice in safety, protected by the precepts (the ethical code of behavior we all chose to adopt) and in the company of my sisters. Here, I am able to receive precious teachings.

We can explore the ways in which we give. What is the motivation behind the giving? Are we giving from a place of gratitude and sharing the abundance? Or are we giving with resentment because of the cultural conditioning that says this is what a woman is supposed to do? The smallest act of generosity given with a clear heart and mind is a great gift, not only for the giver and the receiver but for the whole world. Could we make the time to take our friend's children for a Saturday afternoon or walk a disabled woman's dog?

If you don't know essence and don't know life,
You split the creative and receptive into two paths.
But the day you join them together to form the elixir,
You fall drunken into the jug yet have no need of support.

TAN GUANGZHEN

The creative and receptive are two expressions of the one energy of life, just as breathing is a process of inhalation and exhalation. The active, or creative, aspect is complementary and equal to the receptive, or integrative, aspect. Like the beating of the heart, the valves open and close to keep the blood circulating. One motion isn't more important than the other. They are not opposites. They are complementary. Together they form the whole.

One of the misconceptions that exists in many cultures concerns gender. We have forced women and men into stereotyped roles, falsely assuming that only women can express the receptive and only men can express the creative. Yet these streams are manifestations of the one river of life, and exist together in both women and men. To awaken is to bring these complementary flows into balance. To awaken to this flow is bliss.

NATURAL CURIOSITY

*A more interesting, kind, adventurous, and joyful approach to life is
to begin to develop our curiosity, not caring whether the object of
our inquisitiveness is bitter or sweet. To lead a life that goes beyond
pettiness and prejudice and always wanting to make sure that everything turns out on our own terms, to lead a more passionate, full,
and delightful life than that, we must realize that we can endure a lot
of pain and pleasure for the sake of finding out who we are and
what this world is, how we tick and how our world ticks, how the
whole thing just is.*

PEMA CHÖDRÖN

We are all born with the natural curiosity. Watch how a
baby learns. She touches, tastes, and explores. When learning
to walk she falls down and gets up, again and again. It is her
innate curiosity and her motivation to grow that moves her
along life's spiral path. She doesn't say, "Wow, I've fallen before so I better not try this again." If that were the case not one
of us would learn to walk. As adults we need to retain a childlike curiosity. This is different than being childish. People who
act childish create problems by wanting everything their own
way. They act as though the world revolves around them. We
want to transform the childish qualities and retain or renew
the childlike wonder and ability to take risks.

After great longing
the wild orchid appears
sets down its tubular feet
in the softened walls
of the heart.
Breathing in
tendrils wrap their succulent
arms around your hunger
breathing out
pink light sprays
across the interior of the chest.
A sweet mist aerates the mind
and grief gives way
to rain forest
purple orchids spinning.

JEAN BOUGHTON

Every person, every creature on this planet, wants to be happy. We don't know how to make it happen. As human beings we have the opportunity to find real happiness. Happiness comes not from denying our sadness but from opening to the sadness. We must take the risk to feel the sadness, the pain in our own lives, and the pain in the lives of all peoples. This pain will break our hearts open. When the heart is broken, the seeds of joy that have been watered by our tears will blossom.

INTERCONNECTEDNESS

The opening of your heart never ceases
It comes in on the tide
of breath
It goes out on the tide
of breath
The whisperings of a lover
a chant, a song, a prayer
to your wholeness
to the sacred awakening of the heart.

MARCELINA MARTIN

A great gift of womanhood is the ability to recognize the interconnectedness of all life. True power is the power to be connected to, the power to be in harmonious relationship with. Awakening this power will bring peace to the world. The dominant culture views power as power over another person, another group, another culture. Power is expressed as aggression and the mind that views power in this way is a greedy mind that sees and wants and grabs. This kind of power creates enormous pain and suffering.

True power is subtle. It is an alignment, a harmony with all of life. It is connected to and working for the good of all life. It is impersonal. It has no preference. It does not say I will only give to you if you give to me. True power gives and connects because that is its very nature. This power to connect is magical and at the same time absolutely ordinary. It is awakening to life. It is welcoming to life. It celebrates how precious life is. To be alive—to experience the tide of the breath. And to notice what you are experiencing. To love, and to know that you are loving. This is power.

We need rituals of memory . . . because a political movement, the public policy and tactics of our movement, does not come from our ideas, but from the bloody and joyful substance of our lives. We need to be conscious about what our lives have been, to grieve and to honor our strength, in order to break out of the past into the future.

MINNIE BRUCE PRATT

On the spiritual path we often talk about the necessity of letting go. However, there is a difference between letting go and denying or pushing away. Without remembering, without accepting and embracing what has happened, we can't let go, we can't open into the present or move into the future with clarity. We must embrace, acknowledge, honor, and accept our experiences, both good and bad, joyful and painful, by saying, "Yes. This is what happened. This is what is." In that acceptance our heart is opening and in that opening, there is a release.

We may think of letting go as a separate action. We collect a lot of baggage and then hopefully, we can let go of the experience. In the beginning we may only be able to let go after the experience is finished. As we become skillful we bring a more spacious attitude toward all our experiences. We can open to each experience without either trying to make it last or get rid of it. Then the letting go is inherent in each action.

PURIFICATION

One cannot force or grasp a spiritual experience, because it is as delicate as the whisper of the wind. But one can purify one's motivation, one's body, and train oneself to cultivate it. Because we come from a culture which teaches us that there is always something external to be obtained which will lead us to fulfillment, we lose contact with our innate wisdom.

TSULTRIM ALLIONE

A well-known meditation teacher has labeled the grasping for spiritual experiences as spiritual materialism. We live in a glittering marketplace and as westerners we have been taught to "go for it." We are educated to think that we can go for what we want, that we can acquire anything. We can achieve success in our work, in relationships, and so forth. The rules that govern the spiritual plane are different. We can't acquire spiritual experiences in the way we can acquire objects in the physical world.

We can begin to purify ourselves, to make ourselves ready for the spiritual experience. Purification means we purify our bodies by sensible living habits. We purify our minds from negative thoughts. We purify our motives, our intentions, by transforming our greed and self-striving and by our willingness to serve other beings. We purify our desires by eliminating our wishes for material possessions or self-aggrandizement. We strengthen our desire to know and do the will of the Goddess, to align ourselves with the dharma, the universal law of interconnectedness, understanding, and love.

We are here to witness the creation and to abet it. . . . We are here to bring to consciousness the beauty and power that are around us and to praise the people who are here with us.

ANNIE DILLARD

If you've ever spent any time with a child you know their love of the witness. "Mommy, watch me do this, watch me do this!" The witness is a natural aspect of our minds. It is what the mind does when it is at peace. We don't have to force our minds to be the peaceful witness. That is always present. We are often tormented by agitation, restlessness, fear, doubt, and other disturbing states of mind that cover up the witness. We can rediscover the witness by choosing to look deeply and investigate the process of mind. If we have the patience to watch long enough, we see that the disturbing states of mind come and go. We don't have to base our decisions or actions upon them. We don't have to repress or express them. If we truly see the nature of these mind states—their impersonal, constantly changing quality—our identification with them shatters. In this open state spontaneity, kindness, joy, equanimity, and gratitude abound.

SPIRIT

Holy Spirit,
giving life to all life,
moving all creatures,
root of all things,
washing them clean,
wiping out their mistakes,
healing their wounds,
you are our true life,
luminous, wonderful,
awakening the heart
from its ancient sleep.

HILDEGARD OF BINGEN

Reading the words of Hildegard of Bingen, the twelfth-century Christian mystic, is a precious opportunity to uncover women's history. Saint Hildegard was a lover of the Earth and all creation. A great renaissance woman, her talents were many: poet, painter, musician and prolific composer, dramatist, doctor, prophet, and physicist. It is an inspiration to know that there were and are women mystics who have broken the bonds of suffering to discover true freedom and bliss. Our path may not be the same but we know that freedom can be won.

Hildegard is reminding us that the source of life is spirit. Each of us intuits this truth, though our hearts may be sleeping. There is a wisdom and joy beyond the body that cannot be contained in the body. Our breath can reveal this knowledge. *Inspiration,* to breathe in, is to fill with spirit. It is through life, through the human body, that we can discover this truth.

From the moment of time's first-drawn breath,
Love resides in us,
A treasure locked into the heart's hidden vault.
Before the first seed broke open the rosebud of Being,
An inner lark soared through your meadows,
Heading towards Home.
What can I do but thank you, one hundred times?
Your face illumines the shrine of Hayati's eye,
Constantly present and lovely.

BIBI HAYATI

What an incredible, magical journey this life is! So many treasures hidden away, awaiting our discovery. Most exciting is the knowledge that the treasure of love is within us. This love is in our hearts. We are born with this love. Before any forms were created, this love existed. To know the presence of such love is the greatest joy. There are many people who are born in such distressed conditions that they never intuit this love, never having felt love from another human being. It is our duty, those of us who intuit this love, to deepen our awareness, appreciation, and expression of this love. We live in this world. Let the world touch us, let it break our hearts. Then we can uncover the love and joy that has always been present. Sharing this love will end suffering.

ALONE JOURNEY

MARCH 6

Anything we fully do is an alone journey. No matter how happy your friends may be for you, how much they support you, you can't expect anyone to match the intensity of your emotions or to completely understand what you went through.

NATALIE GOLDBERG

When I began teaching outside my home community I experienced what Natalie describes as an "alone journey." The workshops and retreats I led throughout the country were delightful experiences for me. I met hundreds of women who demonstrated enormous courage in exploring their inner landscape. It was an honor to witness their transformations as they moved through fear and pain into an expression of their creativity and wisdom. Each retreat was so complete in itself I was unable to describe, to my satisfaction, what I had experienced to my friends. At first it felt lonely—the traveling, the intensity of the experience and no one with whom I could adequately share it. Gradually I understood that this was neither possible nor desirable. I took good care to slowly reintegrate back into my daily life. While I was gone my friends had also been involved in many experiences that I could not share. As I made my peace with this knowledge I could reconnect with my friends and share when it felt right. I could hold the experience in my heart and let it work its magic there.

Always we must come around the circle to find the harmony in ourselves. It is never really lost; we have only to accept it and let ourselves resonate with the whole universe.

DHYANI YWAHOO

Today let us take the time to sit and breathe deeply. Be a witness to the life that moves within us, the breath. The breath, the life force, allowed to flow without interruption or force, is harmony. Many people don't start soul searching until there is a painful situation in life, something that pulls the rug out from under them. Old coping mechanisms no longer work. Yet as painful as such situations are, they provide a wonderful opportunity to stop habitual patterns and effect a true change or transformation.

It isn't necessary to wait for upheavals. We have the opportunity now in the breath. Try watching your breath for ten minutes. Sounds easy, but you'll often find yourself distracted by the many thoughts that constantly go through the mind. One of the things that I find helpful is to give myself a touch point, like the base of my tongue. I use this as a focus for my attention by periodically checking to see that my tongue is relaxed and resting on the floor of the mouth.

FEMINISM/SPIRITUALITY

MARCH 8

I want a women's revolution like a lover. I lust for it, I want so much this freedom, this end to struggle and fear and lies we all exhale, that I could die just with the passionate uttering of that desire.

ROBIN MORGAN

International Women's Day is an excellent time to reflect on this excerpt from Robin Morgan's poem "Monster." Robin Morgan wants an end to the fear and the lies. Sexism comes from fear, and fears create the lies that are harmful and limiting to both women and men. There is a common ground shared by feminism and spirituality. Spiritual practice is dedicated to freedom, to ending fear and lies. This freedom is only possible through self-knowledge. Fearful and dishonest individuals cause harm and create societies that are harmful. Large-scale societal change will not be possible until we look deeply within ourselves and experience a profound change in our relationship with ourselves.

We intuit the power of woman, the power of woman's blood. Our power is to birth, to nurture, to sustain, and to transform. Everything that is born is born of woman. All life springs forth from the empty void. This space, this emptiness, is part of all creation. And everything is empty of the possibility of independent existence. With this understanding, that nothing can exist alone in and of itself, we come into balanced relationship with all of creation. This understanding is love.

The day is a gift without time
Moment after moment I unwrap her
I move through her in grace,
no more ahead of myself, or behind,
than a tiger, than a seagull.
Let me remember
I can open tomorrow the same way.
A slow present
lived as free of time
as the life of a tiger, a seagull.

SUE SILVERMARIE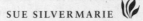

An attitude of scarcity informs our lives. With all the hustle and bustle of modern living, what is most scarce is time. One of my teachers would say, "Time is the most tangible illusion." Sue Silvermarie's poem "Calling In Sick" is the story of a day away from work. Yet, with mindfulness, even on work days, we can cultivate the awareness of a day unfolding. It can be learned by performing every activity with total attention. When sitting in front of your computer, know that you are sitting. Feel the pressure of your sitting bones as they rest on the chair. Wait calmly for your files to appear on the screen. While walking from the bus station, be mindful of each time your foot touches the pavement. Enjoy the sensations. During the bus ride keep your attention focused on your breathing. Let your mind rest. Don't plan your next task. Each act done completely creates space, an opening. Without thoughts there is a gentleness and openness in the mind. This is freedom.

EQUANIMITY

Equanimity is born from wisdom and love and, as such is not an isolated quality in itself.

DR. THYNN THYNN

Equanimity is an English word that describes what Native Americans call "walking in balance." The teachings vary from tribe to tribe yet there is a common understanding of the interconnectedness of life. To walk in balance we move from that center of connectedness to all living things. Life is sacred and we are in relationship with all beings, all creatures that walk, swim, crawl, or fly. The ability to walk gently upon the Earth, to be mindful of the delicate relationship with the environment and all living creatures comes from deep wisdom that is love. Equanimity is not indifference. We mistakenly think that a calm attitude comes when we are disconnected from or indifferent to what is happening. In modern times we have forgotten the web of the universe and our deep, lasting interconnections. Our lives have become quests for satisfying endless desires. We have lost our balance. Balance cannot be forced.

Dr. Thynn Thynn, in her dharma talk, spoke of the relationship between wisdom, compassion, and equanimity. Compassion is our ability to feel what others feel. Equanimity helps us transcend our emotional involvement so that we can see things objectively. Wisdom allows us to find solutions to our problems that will be of benefit to all. When all these qualities are present, we walk in balance.

Female genius . . . is the flowering of experience from a particular point of view of an individual who is courageous enough to experience life deeply, to experience all the pangs and joys, the awesome vision of death and infinity. Genius and madness and sainthood are all entwined in the vision of life being greater than oneself, and if one can stand the vision and speak of it, though never really capturing it in words and symbols, that is the work of the genius.

ARIEL RUTH HOEBEL

   Those whom we consider to be gifted with genius appear to be very different from ourselves. The genius seems unreachable. Yet we all have a spark of genius within us. A genius has a greater vision. There may be intense focus on one particular aspect but that aspect is held within a larger picture. We can learn to live from within this larger picture. It isn't something outside ourselves that we can never reach. The gift of genius is the gift of courage. Genius takes risks and makes mistakes in finding ways to express this vision. We may not understand the whole vision but we trust that it is there and that it is possible to live within it. The vision nourishes us.

SELF-RESPONSIBILITY

I believe the lasting revolution comes from deep changes in ourselves which influence our collective life.

ANAÏS NIN

In October of 1991 I was privileged to attend the First International Conference on Buddhist Women. One of the most impressive figures at the conference was Ven. Hea Choon Suk, a seventy-three-year-old *bhishuni* (ordained nun) from Korea. Her strength and self-assurance were an inspiration to all. She treated every person equally with humility and warm loving-kindness.

Ven. Hea Choon Suk became ordained at age thirty-three and has practiced meditation for forty years. Her meditation practice consists of five points, the last of which is "whenever difficulties are encountered, think it's my responsibility." The development of self-responsibility without blame, either for self or others, leads to a lessening of attachment to the goodness or badness of a situation. We look to each situation in a less personal way. When the attachment is lessened energy is released. We begin to see what we can change and what we cannot change and we develop the wisdom to tell the difference. This deep looking needs to be supported by a daily meditation practice and the cultivation of an attitude of respect for all of life.

Our erotic knowledge empowers us, and becomes a lens through which we scrutinize all aspects of our existence, forcing us to evaluate those aspects honestly in terms of their relative meaning within our lives. And this is a grave responsibility, projected from within each of us, not to settle for the convenient, the shoddy, the conventionally expected, nor the merely safe.

AUDRE LORDE

Eros, love, our erotic knowledge is our passionate connection to life. When we are passionately alive, connected to life, that passion informs everything that we see. When we see with the eyes of love, the world appears fresh and new. There is beauty even within deep suffering because the world is sparkling with aliveness. With passionate connection we are able to take in the whole of living, all the pains and all the joys.

This passionate connection transforms our lives. It is dangerous. We no longer have the safety of our habits and assumptions, limiting views, or self-protecting stances. We can no longer hide behind comfort and convenience. We risk all, without knowing if there will be a return for our effort. The awakened state is an honest state; there is no denial of pain, no refusal to accept pleasure.

LOVING-KINDNESS

MARCH 14

What strikes you, my sisters, strikes us all. The global earth
is resonant, communicative.
Conception is instant solidarity of the child.

MERIDEL LE SUEUR

In the Buddhist tradition there is a wonderful meditation called *metta,* which is translated as loving kindness. Here is a simple metta meditation. It is a means to recognizing our solidarity as a planetary family.

Sit comfortably and take a few deep breaths. Continue to focus on the breath and imagine your whole body filled with the energy of loving kindness. Breathe in loving kindness and allow that energy to infuse your whole being. Wish yourself well. Say mentally: May my heart be peaceful and happy. May I be safe from harm. May I be kind. When the metta phrases are flowing easily in your mind, expand the meditation in this way: As you exhale imagine the energy of loving kindness flowing from you and surrounding and infusing someone you love. Breathe in loving kindness and breathe it out to those you love. Imagine the energy surrounding friends, partner, family, children, co-workers, the people in your community. Let the energy expand to fill your country, reaching even those you aren't comfortable with and those you have not met. Let the energy of loving kindness surround the globe. Without preference, send this energy to all beings. Silently pray: May I be well, may all beings be well.

Our true nature is not some ideal that we have to live up to. It's who we are right now, and that's what we can make friends with and celebrate.

PEMA CHÖDRÖN

Expectations are destructive. However well-intentioned we may be, the expectation puts the power outside of us. Expectations create pressure and conflict. Failure is programmed into expectation. This failure leads to disappointment, despair, anger, and pain. Whether we suffer from the pressure of other people's expectations or our own, it is the expectation that hurts. Spirituality is being mindful right now. It is loving who you are and how you are in every moment. Especially those moments of despair and rage. It is softening and loving, knowing it's going to be okay. Spirituality is learning to make friends again and again with our shameful parts, our confusing parts, our wild parts, our silly parts, the whole of ourselves. Right now.

I awoke this morning with stiffness and pain in my back. I couldn't jump out of bed and get on with this writing like I planned. I had to apply a moist heat pack before I did my stretches. I realized once again, this is how it is. There is this body and it has pain. Sometimes more, sometimes less, it is usually present. That has to be okay. Cursing the pain or cursing myself for not unlocking the key to this pain won't help. Softening and loving myself does. Loving that spine. Softening and opening. Conflict stops with acceptance. There is space, there is equanimity. There is love.

DEEP SEEING

MARCH 16

Seeing is never from memory. It has no memory. It is looking now. The total organism is involved in seeing. Not thinking about what is said from memory, but listening and looking openly now.

TONI PACKER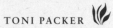

The next time you watch a sunset, notice if you are present with it. Are you able to see the colors without comparing them to yesterday's colors or the sunset you saw in another place or with another person? Whenever we see something, that sensory input is experienced as pleasurable, unpleasurable, or neutral. This reaction happens so quickly we don't notice it. We can't stop this reaction but we can notice it. If we don't notice it our minds become conditioned to our likes and dislikes. We continually compare, evaluate, and judge everything we see.

Here is one way of experimenting with deep seeing. Take a moment to shut your eyes and follow your breath. Now slowly open your eyes and look out onto the world. See a tree or a flower, a bridge or a teacup. See it as though you are seeing it for the first time. As you practice this kind of seeing you will notice how thoughts and memories are evoked. If you are looking at a yellow flower, you may see all the other yellow flowers you have ever seen or the flower will remind you of a happy or sad experience. When old thoughts, memories, or feelings are superimposed on what we see, we are not purely seeing. Each time a memory or thought or judgment comes in, stop. Close your eyes and then slowly open and begin again. In time you will have uncovered the childlike curiosity that exists buried within you. You will look and see what gives this flower its yellowness or this fruit its fruitiness.

Woman is the creator of the universe,
the universe is her form;
woman is the foundation of the world,
she is the true form of the body.
Whatever form she takes . . .
In woman is the form of all things,
of all that lives and moves in the world.
There is no jewel rarer than woman . . .
There are not, nor have been, nor will be
any riches more valuable than woman.

SAKTISANGAMA TANTRA

I love the Hindu Saktisangama Tantra. It speaks so eloquently of the power and strength of woman. I need to hear these words. I need the reminder of this great power, Sakti, the active feminine power of creation. All forms are born of this power. As woman, this sacred creative power flows through me. As woman, I accept my responsibility as a co-creator of this world.

In Women's Sacred Mystery School, the Saktisangama Tantra is chanted three times as part of our daily morning meditation. After the recitation we sit in silence and allow the power of these words to penetrate deeply into our cells. Read these words. Hear these words. Know the truth of these words. Absorbing the truth of these words imbues us with divine pride. We know we are Goddesses. We know our abundance and we live and give from this sacred space.

COMMITMENT

Commitment isn't something that just happens by chance. Commitment is a capacity. And it grows as a muscle grows: by being exercised.

CHARLOTTE JOKO BECK

Commitment is easily confused with promise. Promises are filled with the hope that we might be able to fulfill them and a fear that we won't. Promises are often lightly made, especially when we feel the heat of passion and romance. We make many promises, which we are sometimes willing to keep as long as we feel we're getting something of value in return. The power of commitment goes beyond the hope and fear of promise.

Mothering my two sons taught me the greatest lessons about commitment. Pregnancy was the first commitment. My body was no longer mine alone. It was inhabited by this other being, whom I nurtured and grew inside me. Then I gave birth to this child and my body still served him, this infant suckling at my breast. As my child grew so did my commitment. This was a child of the universe, given to me for a time to guide and care for, not for days or weeks but for decades. Of course I would grow tired, of course I would have conflicting needs, but commitment wasn't based on whether my children were pleasing me or paying attention to what I said. They needed love, support, and attention. As a young mother in my twenties I didn't sit down and think, I must be committed to my sons. Sometimes I must set aside my own needs. I simply responded to the situation, and although mistakes were made, we all grew in our ability to express love and commitment.

I need to discover how to point out injustice without rancor, how to help women meditators break free of their idealization of male teachers so that they can protect themselves and other women and children from abuse. How to do this while remaining grounded in the compassion, sympathetic joy, and equanimity that are the heart of this spiritual path.

SANDY BOUCHER

Many women have suffered sexual abuse at the hands of ministers, priests, religious leaders, and teachers. One would expect religious leaders, of all people, to have a greater sense of compassion and integrity and not to fall prey to such greed and misconduct. However, we need to understand that those on the spiritual path are human and have human failings. We need not invest them with supernatural powers. Sexual abuse is difficult to confront. It's too easy to feel that we're at fault, we've asked for it. And when the perpetrator is a religious leader the problem is compounded.

No one has the right to cross our boundaries in this way. No one has the right to misuse their power and their position to ask for, demand, or expect sexual favors. The perpetrators of this abuse have used our compassion and forgiveness as a weapon to silence us. It is true that we need compassion. It is true that we need to forgive. It is true that we need to recognize our own greed and violence. But it is also true that we must speak out about this abuse. We must say, "No, this is harmful, this is inappropriate." We need the support of our spiritual communities, teachers, and religious leaders to help us heal and to stop further abuse.

MEDITATION

The art of meditation removes . . . separation, so that we can return to our basic nature and truly know it. Meditation has nothing whatever to do with self-improvement. It is an extraordinarily deep, prayerful experience, and its purpose is to become one with the Cosmic Buddha—or, if you like, have an experience of God.

ROSHI JIYU KENNETT

Many people today are searching for a way to reconnect with their spirituality. They want to find the purpose of life. They want to have a direct, meaningful experience of life. Meditation is sometimes viewed as a practice for making one-self more relaxed or as a centering exercise. It is seen as a way of connecting us with our creative energy, or opening us to healing energy. We hope to change for the better. While these practices have some merit, they are not meditation. They are creative visualization techniques. In truth, meditation is not about making us other than who we are. One of my teachers used the image of peeling an onion as an analogy to the process of meditation. As you peel away the onion there are tears. The tears flow as layer after layer is peeled away until nothing is left. Now there is only empty space. There is nothing to separate us from our true nature. We can call this true nature Buddha or God or Goddess or Divine Wisdom.

Spiritual life is the tearing down of all the castles, of all securities.
For only then, and then only, we can reach the Ultimate Security.

IRINA TWEEDIE

Enjoying the securities of life is fine; indeed, it is necessary to have shelter and enough food. But we have made a religion of comfort and convenience, and our needs are endless. The problem is in our grasping, and we grasp not only for material things but for position and power. We also hold tightly to our beliefs, attitudes, and opinions, thinking that such things are the ultimate truth. Without them, we would be nothing. We are taught to believe that if we let go, we will be left with nothing. Yet life experience teaches us time and again that letting go is the only path to freedom. It doesn't matter whether or not there is some truth to our beliefs. As long as we cling to them we will not be free.

On this first day of spring let us plant seeds of freedom. Let us begin to train our minds through the practice of mindfulness. Take a simple act such as drinking a cup of tea and be mindful of each aspect: reaching for, touching, and lifting the cup. With this focused attention the scattered thoughts are dispelled and the mind comes home. The mind is at rest and free.

BITTER/SWEET

Although the wind
blows terribly here,
the moonlight also leaks
between the roof planks
of this ruined house.

IZUMI SHIKIBU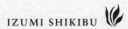

The same life that offers us painful experiences offers us beautiful experiences. In the midst of pain and unpleasant circumstances, what is the difference between a person who goes through life with a sense of joy and serenity and one who is angry, bitter, and filled with remorse? The difference is attitude. If the attitude is one of an open heart, then there is both a willingness to accept the pain and an openness to seeing the beauty. When we are openhearted, we must be open to all of life—and that includes the bitter and the sweet. In an attitude of surrender and acceptance, everything is welcomed. This is no meek, begrudging acceptance; it is with eyes wide open that we acknowledge: This is life. This is all energy. This energy can be transformed; we can learn and grow from all our experiences.

Compassion means
that if I see my friend and my enemy
in equal need,
I shall help them both equally.
Justice demands
that we seek
 and find the stranger,
the broken, the prisoner
and comfort them
 and offer them our help.

MECHTILD OF MAGDEBURG

Justice and compassion are powerful qualities that arise from an open heart. They are not qualities that a closed heart can easily offer or sustain. Working to cultivate compassion necessitates working with our resistance. What is the fear that prevents us from feeling this natural concern and warmth for others? What prejudice makes us decide that only certain people are worthy of our compassion? Exploration of such questions is a means to promoting inner growth.

Visualization can also facilitate this growth. Imagine a friend standing before you and make an offering to her. It may be a silver platter heaped with fresh fruit or the keys to your car. Notice any feelings or thoughts that arise as you make the offering. When you feel truly connected to both the person and the act of giving, make this change: Visualize someone with whom you are not strongly connected and repeat the process. Finally, imagine making the offering to someone with whom you are angry, or whom you dislike. Without judging the thoughts and feelings keep breathing and allow them to be released.

FREEDOM

What's the need to bow and pray
To beg for long life?
Clearly the original spirit
Is thoroughly pure.
Shatter space to become completely free,
And wishing jewels and relics
Are all empty names.

FAN YUNQIAO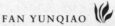

In Taoist teachings the phrase "shatter space" refers to the final step in the practice, when one merges or becomes fully aligned with the Tao, universal harmony. "Wishing jewel" is a Buddhist metaphor for granting whatever is desired, a metaphor for the liberated mind. That the jewels and relics are "empty names" indicates that the process itself is transcended. There must be no attachment to rituals and rites: these are simply the means to bring us to enlightenment.

In the Christian tradition it is "thy will be done." People can misinterpret this as giving away your power, giving someone power over you. This prayer phrase expresses the willingness to align with the great law of the universe, the law of interconnectedness, harmony, and love. Until this alignment is achieved there can be no true freedom.

HEAVEN ON EARTH

*Each one of us, I believe, is a gift the earth is giving to itself now,
a unique gift. Every anguish, betrayal, disappointment can even help
prepare us for the work of healing. You don't need to be extraordinary. If the world is to be healed through human efforts, I am
convinced it will be by ordinary people, people whose love for this
life is even greater than their fear. People who can open to the web of
life that called us into being, and who can rest in the vitality of that
larger body.*

JOANNA MACY

We can make heaven on Earth, here and now, through our
appreciation of beauty; through our acts of generosity and
sharing; through our kindness to others; through our joyful
embrace of life's preciousness. We can make heaven on Earth
through our strenuous effort, by our willingness to face with
courage those places that have tightened or hardened, by our
willingness to touch the edges and soften and open them.
When the mind is spacious, the fragrance of love permeates
the air.

MIRACLE OF BIRTH

MARCH 26

I tell you, roses want to bloom out of the wood,
the goodness in people wants to break free
of the blind ego.
Birth is a miracle in every germinating seed.

MARGE PIERCY

When my partner's brother became a father for the first
time at age forty, he said with awe in his voice, "This is the
whole thing, this is all there is." The miracle of birth is transformative. You can't witness it and not be moved. It changes
our perception. It re-orders our priorities. We need to remember this. Miracles happen everyday.

Take some time to do a short walking meditation. Imagine
that as you inhale you inhale goodness and that as you exhale
this goodness a rose blooms at your feet.

Listen the way a cat listens, a kind of listening with the back of your mind, just letting be without any hesitation or interference. Nothing is ever repeated or predictable or the same but all is unexpectedly fresh if we listen this way.

FLORA COURTOIS

My housemate's cat lies in a patch of sunlight on the floor while I work. She sleeps peacefully, but if there is a new noise she is instantly awake and alert. She remains relaxed and open in a way that allows her to respond immediately to changes in her environment. When we listen in this way, it is without reaction. We pay attention. We listen and see what is happening. We don't have to react. We can absorb, bringing the information into our inner space and then choosing if we wish to respond. Whether it's done quickly or slowly, we can make a decision as to if and how we want to respond.

SELF-CREATION/PELE

MARCH 28

Self-creation is an art of fire:
   each person
   forms
   (her) spirit's housing
   and
   celestial cistern.

M. C. RICHARDS

The Goddess Pele lives in Hawaiian hearts as supreme personification of volcanic majesty and power in a universe in which all natural forces are regarded as life forces and related to human life. On a recent visit to the Big Island I experienced both the serenity and the fury of Pele. Four of us hiked through the rainforest to the barren lava floor of one of the dormant volcanoes. Before entering the forest we silently asked Pele's permission to enter. Her response was immediate and welcoming, "Come, daughters of Pele." We walked single file in silence down to the crater's floor. We stretched out flat on the ground near places where cracks allowed hot steam to escape. Pele's warm breath soothed the ache in my bones.

The following day we heard that the lava was flowing from one of the active craters, so we returned to the park that night. The power of the lava flows, even at a distance of three-quarters of a mile, was tremendous. While not close enough to hear the volcano's roar, we heard an occasional blast as trees, touched by the flow, exploded and burst into flames. Watching the fiery fingers of lava move down the sides of a cliff as it made its way toward the ocean, we could smell the gases from the heart of the Earth, an Earth changing before our eyes. We stood in silence at the edge of the womb of creation.

And lilacs in their splendor
Like lost friends
Come back through grief to tell her
Love never ends.

MAY SARTON

When we are in deep sorrow it becomes our whole world. It is difficult to see beyond the intensity of the feeling. Yet nothing is solid and there are spaces even in grief. Even in sorrow, if we chance to see a flower—really see it—the beauty of that flower can teach us about the end of grief. A flower blooms for a short time before it dies. The next season it blooms again.

My mother used to say, "Give me my flowers when I'm alive." I knew what she meant; she wanted to enjoy beauty while she was alive. The flowers at a funeral are for the living. They remind us in our grief that life, so fragile and beautiful, will end, and in time, will return again. Love never ends.

WOMAN

MARCH 30

*I am a woman, a human being of extraordinary strength, wisdom
and grace. My woman's body was created in the body of a woman.
I am daughter, sister, mother in thousands of generations of
women. . . . I am a woman, part of and the whole of the first circle,
the circle that transcended space and time, the circle of women
joined.*

ANN VALLIANT AND KATHLEEN KLIMEK

In the 1970s many women returned to the ancient practice
of gathering in full moon circles to celebrate the Goddess. We
would often speak these powerful words together or one
woman would read them while the others were in a meditative
state. It was an important part of our spiritual journey as
women to remember and reclaim the Goddess within us. We
were not attempting to excavate the bones of a Goddess from
a distant past. Studying the matriarchal period in history was
a step in a spiral journey that led us to awakening the Goddess
within ourselves. These words powerfully affirm the sacredness of ourselves and therefore of all life.

Repeating these words enables us to see ourselves as an important link in the motherline. Try repeating them in the
morning, standing in front of a full-length mirror. Repeat
them in the evening by candlelight. Say the words for yourself,
your mother, your grandmother, your daughter, your grand-
daughter. Create a Goddess circle and with hands joined, recite these words with your women friends.

Try to treat with equal love all the people with whom you have rela-
tions. Thus the abyss between "myself" and "yourself" will be filled
in, which is the goal of all religious worship.

ANANDAMAYI MA

There was a brief period in my life during the time my children were in elementary school when we lived with two other
women. One of the women had a young son. We connected
easily and began sharing our lives like family. It was easy for
me to show kindness toward her, to be loving and enthusiastic
about spending time with her. It was more difficult with the
other woman. She didn't seem to want to be drawn into our
circle and didn't do her share of the household tasks. It was
more challenging to treat her with the kindness and love that I
freely gave the other roommate.

Yet life situations such as this are opportunities to see
where our edges are. Where do we hold back love? Where do
we give unequal treatment? If we extend ourselves just a little
bit today and every day, we will soon find ourselves kinder
than we were before. It takes perseverance. Our personal lives
make a difference. Inequality of treatment taken to its extreme
is hatred, racism, sexism, and all other "isms." Equality of
treatment is love.

LOVE

Do not shun power
nor despise it.
But use it correctly.
When is power used correctly?
Power is made for service.
I am your servant;
I am not your master.
Be a servant.
Not a master.

MECHTILD OF MAGDEBURG

A first reading of Metchild's words "be a servant" can elicit negative connotations. We recall the history of slavery throughout the world and the horrible abuses, as well as the present-day treatment of people who do domestic and un-skilled labor. The work isn't highly valued, the conditions are poor, hours are long, and pay is low. Let us put aside those im-ages for a moment and consider another meaning of servant.

A servant is one who serves, one who has a purpose. Then we must look deeper. What is it that we are to serve? And what is our purpose? To Native Americans, each of us has a particular life purpose, abilities we need to develop that are not for ourselves alone but to be given in service to the whole community and the whole circle of life.

Form is the language of the universe singing its praises. Its rejoicing is seen everywhere—in the sun through a web of hair, in the flower and its petals, in the subtle folds of a garment, in the human body.

DIANORA NICCOLINI

I housesat for friends in Inverness Ridge for three wonderful days. I watched the fog swim over the fir trees in the morning. The fog brings a lushness to the forests. It dripped from the moss clinging to the trees, it fell from the sky like a soft rain. When the sun burned through the fog its rays sparkled through the spider webs that hung on the bushes and fences. I watched the deer forage for food in the backyard. I spent hours walking along the beach, enthralled by the gray winter ocean. A few inquisitive seals swam along the shoreline, keeping pace with my movements. Flocks of gulls preened on the beach, undisturbed by the solitary woman walking quietly by.

There is beauty all around us. Can you find time this week to notice the "universe singing its praises"?

GREED

The fruits of consecration
are sweetness and patience,
sureness in the middle of panic and confusion
when baboons put on business suits.

LYNN PARK

I love the humor in this quote. The image of baboons putting on business suits is a delightful way to describe how our lives are often run by our animal nature, by our fear for survival. We are propelled by our survival instinct. We try to disguise this. We dress it up. There is another way to live. We can live without being sucked in by greed and fear. We can consecrate our lives, dedicate ourselves to the practice of mindfulness. It is mindfulness that makes life sacred. Mindfulness, or the pure attention that we bring to each idea, thought, or person, is love.

We can make friends with our greed. Each time you feel its pull imagine that you bow to it and offer to your greed whatever it wants. Play with this. Feel the wanting, the fear, the desire, the hope, the hopelessness. Make room for all the feelings. Then in your mind's eye create the wildest fantasy, feed that greed. Imagine how it feels to become totally satiated. Feel the greed, satisfy it, then let it go. Breathe and release. It is only a thought. You can choose to repress it, express it, or simply allow it to be. What is your choice?

It is here, my daughters, that love is to be found—not hidden away in corners but in the midst of occasions of sin. And believe me, although we may more often fail and commit small lapses, our gain will be incomparably the greater.

SAINT TERESA OF AVILA

When reflecting on this passage it might be useful to change the word *sin,* as it is a highly charged word. Rather than sin, read obstacle. An obstacle is whatever stands between ourselves and the realization of our true divinity. Life's obstacles can be opportunities for the realization that we are love and can embody that love. Our practice is to be mindful of our thoughts, to look deeply into the source of our actions. We have a choice. Will the choice be to deepen our attentiveness or not? We will make mistakes. It is our commitment to keep trying that is essential.

Our speech is one example. Do we choose words that hurt or heal? Do we gossip? Do we speak harshly and condemn others? Do we speak only the best about ourselves and others? Before we speak we can ask ourselves three questions: Is what I am going to say true? Am I speaking with sensitivity? Is it necessary to say this?

WOMEN'S WISDOM

APRIL 5

Shechinah, I pray that Your spirit may pervade
those whose tears will not flow; that they may
experience the release of feeling that connects
us to each other, to the tradition of our ancestors,
to our progeny and to all humanity.
For the blessing of tears,
I thank God I was born a woman.

WOMEN'S HAGGADAH

The Haggadah is the special text used for Passover that includes the story of the Exodus. This prayer is one of thanksgiving for women's ability to feel and to connect. We pray that all people may feel this connection and know the oneness of all life.

Women's wisdom is the wisdom of connection, but the tears that can easily flow from our eyes have been used against us as proof that we are overly emotional, irrational, and unrealistic. Yet it is this knowledge of connectedness that is lacking in today's world. When our tears can freely flow, when we can feel compassion for another's pain, abuse will stop. As long as we feel separate and disconnected we can deny other people's humanity, cause harm to one another and to the Earth.

The dharma, the law of interconnectedness and love, has the power to break open the heart. Women have often come to me in tears after hearing a dharma talk. I once thanked a woman for her tears. She was quite surprised, never having thought of her tears as a gift. She deeply received the thanks and in so doing her heart opened wider and she felt great joy.

*I know that we all have a hunger for spiritual things and if it gets
pushed under—then there is a hunger that always exists.*

MARIE SHERMAN

My mother's faith is a living one. She taught me from early
childhood that actions speak louder than words. I would often
accompany her when she visited people who were elderly,
sick, or in mourning. She was always there with a smile and a
pot of spaghetti sauce.

My mother felt sorrow for those who had no spiritual practice or religious beliefs. When such people have the inevitable
pain that life brings, they have no understanding and no context to work with. Such people are often bitter and angry at
what they term the unfairness of life. One friend, whose husband had died eight years ago, was still bitter about his death
and had never accepted it. "He was such a good man, he gave
so much of himself, and so many other terrible people are still
living," she would lament.

"When your father died," my mother told me, "I figured
his circle was finished. Naturally, I wanted him to be around
longer but it didn't happen that way."

LOVE

APRIL 7

Love is the foundation of the world. Where there is love, there is peace. Where there is selfishness, there is misery and suffering. Learn from Mother Nature who gives of herself even though exploited by man. Do only good deeds and look upon all as the children of God.

MATA AMRITANANDAMAYI

It takes enormous endurance to put the other person first, especially when your efforts are met with indifference. To continue to give your best you must be patient and not have expectations of others. Even when another doesn't respond, remember that you are growing. You are polishing the rough edges that make human relationships difficult. This is the purpose of the spiritual life, to love—and it is this loving that brings peace.

There are many fine people who have a deep commitment to justice and equality that emerges from their sense of decency and goodwill. Their commitment is seen as political, not spiritual. The two remain separate for them because they view spiritual practice as self-serving and not necessarily evidence of peace and justice. It is sad that many people who consider themselves religious live their lives in ignorance of interconnectedness and through their own prejudice and hatred create much harm in the world. It is important to distinguish between the spiritual practice and the human limitations of the practitioners: their pain, fear, prejudice, or even hatred. Spiritual practice is training the heart to transform doubts and fears so that we may love fully. Spiritual teachers like Mata Amritanandamayi are living embodiments of this great love.

The secret of the receptive
Must be sought in stillness;
Within stillness there remains
The potential for action.

ZHOU XUANJING

The receptive, or feminine, aspect is spacious and open, not closed and passive as some mistakenly think. To be receptive means to be open. To be open we must allow our compulsive or habitual thoughts to float through our minds without repressing them, grasping them, or allowing them to motivate our actions. So much of our thinking isn't fresh or original insights, it is habit. We spin around and around with our thoughts, digging ourselves deeper into self-created ruts.

A friend who works in the corporate world shared some of her business philosophy with me: "Don't speculate on knowable facts. Look up the answer." Here is another way of expressing the need to cut through habitual thoughts. How often do we worry or wonder about things for which we can find an answer, if only we would stop and look or listen. Stilling habitual thinking is the beginning of spiritual practice. This practice isn't passivity. It is a clearing of the mind to release positive energy from the prison of habitual thoughts.

When you find your mind spinning into a rut, stop and take a deep breath. Then, while paying attention to the breath, think: I breathe in clarity, I breathe out confusion. When the mind stabilizes, continue the focus for a few more breaths, this time saying, "I breathe in clarity, I breathe out clarity."

GODDESS WITHIN

APRIL 9

I found god in myself
and i loved her / i loved her fiercely

NTOZAKE SHANGE

    While in a circle with friends at a ritual for my fiftieth birth-
day, we passed around some cedar oil that my friend Lili had
made from trees in Inverness. Each woman blessed herself and
then made a blessing for me. I saved the oil imbued with blessings to use when I again want to create a special ritual.

    The spiritual practices of traditions throughout the world
are designed to unveil the divinity within us. There are many
prayers, rituals, and chants to awaken us to this ever-present
connection. A simple self-blessing will call forth this energy.
As you bless yourself you are blessing the divine in all beings,
in all creatures. The energy of this blessing will resonate
throughout the atmosphere. Choose a quiet time and place.
Pour some water or unscented oil into a small bowl. Gently
dip your fingers into the bowl and touch your body, whispering blessings. Touch your forehead, eyes, nose, lips, breasts,
belly, vulva, feet. Choose words that are important to you,
such as "Bless my eyes, that I may see clearly."

ACCEPTANCE

In the first five minutes of paying attention, you learn that pleasant sensations lead to the desire that these sensations will stay and unpleasant sensations lead to the hope that they will go away. Both the attraction and the aversion amount to tension in the mind. Both are uncomfortable. So, in the first five minutes you get a big lesson about suffering; wanting things to be other than what they are.

SYLVIA BOORSTEIN

Two friends of mine were temporarily living in a small, beautiful house overlooking a field surrounded by rolling hills. Each time I visited I found one friend totally delighted with the beauty of the space. She enjoyed and was inspired by the beauty. Although she knew her stay would only be a few months she fully enjoyed the time she had. The other friend was often rushed and her mind was continually jumping to unfinished tasks and future plans. There was an air of disappointment around her. She could never rest peacefully in the beauty that surrounded her.

Take time each day to be appreciative of what you have. It may be a quality of mind, it may be an object, it may be a friend, it may be the place where you are. None of these things will stay the same. Knowing this, can we appreciate it now, for what it is, whatever it is? Can we accept it, without wanting it to be better, or last longer, or be different from what it is?

LOVE

I am the Mother of the virtuous, I am the Mother of the wicked.
Whenever you are in distress, say to yourself: I have a mother.

HOLY MOTHER

These are the words of the Holy Mother, a twentieth-century Indian saint. She is a human being who has fully manifested her godliness or goddessliness. She is the embodiment of divine love. Her words indicate that her love is impersonal; it is given to all, regardless of their behavior. The Holy Mother is there reaching out to every individual, whoever and wherever they are. For all who are in need, it can be a great solace to know that there exists someone who cares. The knowledge of this caring and the knowledge that we are not alone can give us strength to go through the many trials and tribulations of earthly life. Her loving energy is always available to us, and it will not be withdrawn if our behavior is disrespectful. The more we are aware of this energy and the more we work to transform our limiting behaviors, the better able we become to receive this energy.

In spiritual maturity, the opposite of injustice is not justice, but compassion. Not me against you, not me straightening out the present ill, fighting to gain a just result for myself and others, but compassion, a life that goes against nothing and fulfills everything.

CHARLOTTE JOKO BECK

Pick up any newspaper, or listen to the news, and you will find stories of rape, homelessness, and abuse. When we hear stories of police brutality or a mother neglecting her child we feel an energy arising in us. It is easy to take sides. We react. The reaction doesn't help. We need to be able to allow the suffering to break open our hearts and realize that both victim and perpetrator suffer. This does not condone the violence of the perpetrators. Nor does it suggest that perpetrators should not be punished. It simply acknowledges their pain. All this suffering comes from people who are controlled by their pain, fear, greed, hatred, or violence. We need to train our own minds, to purify our negative thoughts of greed, hatred, and violence. At the same time we need to reach out and help those who are suffering.

Reaching this level of openheartedness is quite challenging. Begin to cultivate openheartedness by reading a news story that would ordinarily cause you to take sides. Breathing slowly and deeply, allow yourself to feel compassion for the victims. Let that suffering fill your heart. Breathe it in. Let that suffering move through your heart and out again. Now, allow that the perpetrators also have pain. Make no distinctions, simply allow the pain of all people, victims and perpetrators, to fill your heart. Now breathe out the pain. Let it go back into the Earth.

LISTENING

Listen to the past, future and present right where you are. Listen with your whole body, not only with your ears, but with your hands, your face, and the back of your neck.

Listening is receptivity. The deeper you can listen, the better you can write. You take in the way things are without judgment. . . .

NATALIE GOLDBERG

I have season tickets to the Women's Philharmonic. What a joy to see and hear a full orchestra of women, led by a woman conductor and performing works composed by women, some of which have never been performed before. One night the symphony performed a piece by Fannie Mendelson that was quite remarkable. It was only the second time in history the piece had been performed. As the sights and sounds filled me, I was drawn to the pianist. I felt as though I could see the music moving through her. She played with her whole body. When she wasn't playing, she listened to the orchestra with her whole body. She lifted her head and drank in the music through every pore of her skin. Her ability to listen with her whole body profoundly affected her ability to play.

The Holy Spirit is our harpist,
And all strings
Which are touched in Love
Must sound.

MECHTILD OF MAGDEBURG

As students in Sunray Meditation Society we were taught how to amplify the clarity in others, rather than see the faults and try to fix them. We learned to purify our own energy so that when we came into the company of others, through resonance, they too would be drawn into a clearer energy field.

Resonance is something we have all experienced. An example of this happened when some friends and I were camping in the country. The land was owned by a collective that was having some difficulties. At first we got caught up in thinking about how we could remedy the situation. We felt hopeless and saddened by it. Two of the women, however, continued to patiently build the deck they had promised to build. They hummed along to the classical music that was playing, laughing and obviously enjoying themselves and their work. Within a short time the rest of us were enfolded in that energy and our discomfort was transformed into joy as our energies were focused on the work at hand.

LOVE

Into my life you came like a storm of monsoon banging down
from the eastern sky.
And you scattered me, like the wind disperses dry grass and the
petals of flowers.
Out of myself you scattered me into Nothingness,
Beyond the Nowhere, beyond the Beyond.

IRINA TWEEDIE

Irina Tweedie is speaking of her guru, her beloved teacher, who guided her to the wisdom place, the place of love. True love is a shattering experience. Irina's powerful, poetic words describe this shattering, the dissolving of the personal self, the ego, into the universe. What is shattered are the ideas, concepts, feelings, and beliefs that we think describe who we are. We can no longer hold onto our old ways of perceiving. It is only when the little self is shattered that we are open to the universe, that we are love. One meditation teacher calls this opening to the "wound of love." In this sense love hurts. It hurts because we are clinging to our own ideas and ways of being. Unless there is surrender, and we stop clinging to our personal likes and dislikes, we will never be scattered like the flower petals in the wind.

We can take small steps to let go of attachment to a personal preference. One way to soften our personal preferences is to do a simple act with mindfulness, such as allowing a friend to choose what movie you will see or what you will have for dinner. Order something you dislike for dinner and be mindful as you eat. Playing in this way, we can lessen attachment to rigid likes and dislikes.

*The earth is at the same time
mother,
she is mother of all that is natural,
mother of all that is human.
She is the mother of all,
for contained in her
are the seeds of all.*

HILDEGARD OF BINGEN

Many of us who were raised in Christian families have become alienated from our religious tradition. The essence of the teachings seems to be lost in male-dominated, hierarchical institutions and has become twisted with guilt, punishment, and woman-hating. Lost and without roots we search for other traditions that speak more fully to our hearts. There is a danger that we will remain in a reactive rather than responsive place. While it isn't necessary to continue the traditional Christian practice, we do need to make peace with the religious tradition of our family.

What a joy it is to bring forth at this time the words of Hildegard of Bingen, the grandmother of Rhineland mystics. We need to know that there are spiritual masters in every tradition and that many of them have been, and continue to be, women. Women need to know of such foremothers for they provide us with inspiration as models with whom we can identify. Men need to know of these women to cut through the illusion that spiritual mastery is the sole provenance of men.

ENLIGHTENMENT

The alchemical path, you should know,
Goes directly upward—
The mystic jewel
Is only in our hearts.

CUI SHAOXUAN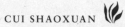

Enlightenment lies within oneself and can't be found outside. Every religious tradition has its rituals and rites to open the heart, to awaken to the inner light. When we are attached we think our path is better than another's path, or mistakenly believe there is only one prayer or one ritual that contains the truth. Regardless of the tradition or path we follow, its rites and rituals must eventually be transcended. They are only a means, and attachment to anything, even a religious ritual, inhibits the full opening of the heart. The open heart is a space that we are always within. We may not realize it, but it is always there.

Take a few deep breaths, then continue breathing and imagine that as you exhale you are exhaling through your heart. Allow it to soften and open. There is nowhere to go, nothing to do. Just breathing. Breathe freedom. Breathe peace. Breathe.

. . . Sisters we/ are the ones who got to turn it right around.
Its not our way/ to put a thing outside our body
and call it enemy/ "None of it was true about our enemies,
we/have none/ women never birth enemy faces."
It's NOT our way/ to hurt the earth or make the wars
and that's WHY we, sweet sisters
are the ones who got to turn it all around. . . .

SUE SILVERMARIE

While taking the bus home from the airport I passed a military cemetery. As my eyes went from the tombstones back to the book in my lap, I had an extraordinarily visceral experience. In that moment I felt within my body the pain of centuries of aggression and warfare. I was reading a novel about the first people on the European continent and thought, here we are thousands of years later, still filled with fear and hatred, still at war with one another. Our weapons are larger and more impersonal now. The feelings of fear, greed, hatred, and violence are the same. When will the violence stop?

Imagine yourself in your favorite place in nature. Breathe deeply and draw in the Earth's energies. Breathe out, allowing your energy, combined with Earth's energy, to return to the Earth. Feel, sense, or imagine great love for the Earth. Breathe in Earth's energy and breathe out love for the Earth. Continue receiving and sending this energy, gradually extending it to all creatures and all people living on the Earth.

GOD

God Herself becomes the dwelling place we build for ourselves. It seems I am saying that we can build up God and take God away since I say that God is the dwelling place and we ourselves can build it so as to place ourselves in it. And indeed we can!

SAINT TERESA OF AVILA

When I read this quote to my partner, Barbara, her response was enthusiastic. "I like this quote because it says that we can be the architects of our vision of God. There is no one absolute way to envision God. There is no one particular vision of God that is God. Whatever our own individual creation of God is, is what God is. God can become a personalized construct and how each of us perceives, creates, or constructs that God for ourselves is how God is."

One of my teachers would say, "God is an aspect of being." Rather than making God into an idea that we argue for or against, we can look to the wholeness that is within each of us. Each person must make their own journey to discover that wholeness.

In Buddhism, finding fault with another is wrong.
By finding fault with another, we're finding our own obscuration.

JOAN HALIFAX

    We often find fault with those behaviors that are most like our own weaknesses. The next time you start to criticize someone, stop and take a few deep breaths. Be attentive to your body and try to sense any tension there. Is there something you are afraid of? Have you been holding something back? Does this situation remind you of something from your past? Is this simply an old habit that you can watch enter and leave your mind? You do not have to let such feelings or ideas motivate your behavior. Before you speak, ask yourself several times, is it necessary for me to say this? What will happen if I do? What do I really want to say?

DARKNESS/LIGHT

APRIL 21

Help us to be the always hopeful
Gardeners of the spirit
Who know that without darkness
Nothing comes to birth
As without light
Nothing flowers.

MAY SARTON

This stanza, taken from Sarton's poem "Kali," shows us clearly why we need both the darkness and the light. We want to be happy and embrace the light, so we spend precious energy trying to push away or deny whatever we consider the dark. We forget that both are necessary and that we can't have one without the other. The winter landscape can appear cold and bleak, yet beneath it lies the seed that with sunlight will become a rose. In darkness is fertile power, the mystery, the great unknown. In light is the clarity and vision that come from having the courage to embrace the dark.

It is not so much a question of whether the lion will one day lie down with the lamb, but whether human beings will ever be able to lie down with any creature or being at all.

ALICE WALKER

In Buddhist teachings we are reminded again and again of the precious opportunity we have as human beings. We can know the Dharma, the law of interrelationship, the way of understanding and love. We have a body and a mind in which to perceive this truth. Yet this mind frequently operates out of habit, out of conditioning. We have fears and doubts. We resist, we condemn, we judge. It is this mind that creates *dukka,* or suffering. Suffering can range from the slightest dissatisfaction to the most painful unhappiness.

We are conditioned to build up the ego, or the small self, by thinking of our personal wants and desires as more important than anyone else's. We get angry or annoyed with others whom we perceive as different, or who have different wants or needs than we do. We think of ourselves as separate individuals, not as individuals within a universal context, individuals who are interrelated with all life. Peace won't come through defending our separateness. Peace will come through the transformation of conditioned behavior. When we wake up to the deep interconnections that exist between all peoples and all of life we will no longer be able to harm one another.

PRESENT

Don't live for the present; don't allow transitory things to influence you. Live in eternity, above time and space, above finite things. Then nothing can influence you.

ELISABETH HAICH

Can you imagine someone who doesn't let things influence them? Someone who lives serenely without being pushed and pulled by praise or blame? We might imagine that such a person would have to harden themselves to life. Rather, the opposite is true. Such a person is open to all of life's experiences. This is a person who *knows* that life is change. This person doesn't become too inflated when something good happens or too distressed when something bad happens. When you know who you are, that you are spirit, and that there is no separate self that exists in and of itself, there is nothing to defend. There is nothing to protect or disappoint or hurt or imprison. There is only freedom.

The feminine energy, Buffalo Woman's energy, is very strong in many of our hearts at this time. Buffalo Woman is willing to shine out through each of us who quiet ourselves and call.

BROOKE MEDICINE EAGLE

In the Native American tradition Buffalo Woman symbolizes the strong, creative, nurturing, and transformative feminine energy. This energy has always been present on the planet but it has been hidden or twisted by our denial, our misconduct, and our violence. It is time for women's wisdom to ripen, so that all creatures may taste its fruits. Most of humankind has awakened from the preconscious state—one close to body, instincts, and nature. Unfortunately, many have denied the body, instincts, and nature while in the state of conscious ego development. As humankind continues to develop we need to integrate the preconscious state into the present ego state; however, this is not the final state of evolution. We must go beyond ego to a more subtle state of consciousness, one of realization or communion with the circle of life. This is a spiritual journey to uncover the Goddess within. We must put aside doubt, fear, hatred, and violence. Connected with, in communion with, in union with another, we cannot harm. Buffalo Woman is the embodiment of this energetic, creative, caring connection with all life.

UNITY

I cannot say
which is which:
the glowing
plum blossom is
the spring night's moon.

IZUMI SHIKIBU

I had a wonderful vacation in Hawaii. Six of us stayed on Hookena Beach on the Kona coast, which is the dry side of the Big Island. We lived for a week in thatched huts without windows. A generator provided enough electricity for lamps, and we showered outside with a teepee of vines above our heads.

The beach, less than a hundred yards from the huts, was created by huge black lava rocks in quite wonderful shapes. Formed when Pele spewed forth her fire, the lava had slowly rolled to the sea, where it hardened into folds that looked like the back of a huge turtle or the roughened hide of a rhinoceros. The first day there I carefully walked across the rocks and laid down on them, close to the water's edge. Now and then waves would wash over me. The day was warm and humid. It had rained the night before, and the changing shapes of great clouds danced across the sky. Eventually the sun burned through. There was no sound except the sound of the water hitting the rocks. The waves kept washing over me and the rocks until all sense of separation was lost. Any ideas or thoughts that floated into my mind were taken out with the tide. I simply became another form, another shape, like the rocks on which I laid. I lost all sense of time, all sense of a separate self.

When we recognize that "body" and "spirit" may be seen as the warp and woof of life's fabric, we can resist being crushed. Spirit escapes all nets. It remains unconfined by walls. It is not obedient to authority. It cannot be taught to march "in step."

ELSA GIDLOW

It is said that we are spirits attempting to live in bodies. The body can be imprisoned, the spirit cannot. Spirit can be neither contained nor controlled. The spirit does not adhere to the rules of the phenomenal world. It is part of the world and it transcends the world. Our spirit may be buried. We may not recognize its existence but it is always present. We have been given the precious gift of life, the gift of a body, that we may learn how to manifest spirit in all that we are, in all that we do. There is both pain and joy in the world. The body will become sick, age, and die. Everything in the world changes so rapidly we mistakenly think that there is something solid and permanent to which we can cling. Although we may have many pleasurable experiences in life, we will not find lasting happiness or freedom through the body and the senses. We can learn, through careful and deep observation of the body, the senses, and the formations of the mind that there isn't anything worth hanging on to. When we realize this, we recognize the formless, what some name the spirit. When we remain open to and live by this spirit, the energy that is the foundation of the world, we are free.

PURIFICATION

APRIL 27

Our people call this time we now live in the Time of Purification . . .
it is also a Time of Returning. It is the returning of that which has
never been lost; the regathering of ever-widening Circles of Women
for the growth and healing of Earth Mother, generating outward
from these nurturers and bearers of the nations to enfold and include
all that lives, all of which is part of her.

JOAN HENRY

Let us invoke the lineage of feminine wisdom through this
blessing. Dip your fingers in warm, fragrant oil and beginning
with the head touch them to your body, whispering, "Bless
this mind that it may be clear, open, and peaceful. Bless these
eyes that they may perceive truth and beauty. Bless these ears
that they may always hear the song of the Goddess, the Spirit
of Life. Bless this nose that it may smell the sweet fragrance of
wisdom. Bless this mouth that it may speak when necessary,
that it may speak truth, that it may speak with sensitivity.
Bless these hands that they may freely give. Bless this heart
that it may be open, warm and loving. Bless these breasts that
the power of nurturance be known. Bless this belly that there
may be creative connection to all life. Bless this vulva that the
power of sexuality may be honored and enjoyed. Bless these
feet that they may walk in balance and beauty."

I believe that what woman resents is not so much giving herself in pieces as giving herself purposelessly. What we fear is not so much that our energy may be leaking away through small outlets as that it may be going "down the drain." If it is woman's function to give, she must be replenished too.

ANNE MORROW LINDBERGH

We have been given the gift of life; therefore, we have something to give. Our giving empties us and enables us to continue receiving. It keeps the energy flowing. When we awaken to the knowledge of this cycle we can give fearlessly, knowing that our giving comes back to us. That is the nature of energy. One of the key words in this quote is "purposelessly." Each of us has a life purpose. We generate much fear and confusion because we don't know that we have a purpose, or what that purpose is. This lack results in the creative life energy being withheld or dissipated.

Even if we may not know our life purpose, or doubt that we have one, we can still begin to explore the motivations behind our actions. Giving in an unconscious or unclear way may mean we give because we're afraid or we want to be noticed or liked, or we may give in order to gain something. Unclear giving drains our energy. In fact, we probably have a mixture of motivations, some selfless and some very much a part of our own agenda. Just beginning to notice the motivations behind the giving helps to clear the energy. When the motivation is clear, the energy flows in an unobstructed way, that is, in a circle. We don't have to be attached to the outcome of our giving. We can give because it is our nature to give. And we are replenished because that is the nature of energy.

NOURISH SPIRIT

APRIL 29

Nurture the spirit, be sparing with energy,
As though holding a full bowl.

SUN BU-ER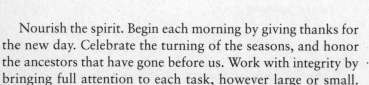

Nourish the spirit. Begin each morning by giving thanks for the new day. Celebrate the turning of the seasons, and honor the ancestors that have gone before us. Work with integrity by bringing full attention to each task, however large or small. Practice generosity. Know that you have been given the gift of life and you have much to give. Be willing to take risks, to fall down and get up and begin again. Make beauty wherever you go.

An imbalance can be created by withholding energy or overusing energy. Too often we overdo through overwork or emotional excesses. Watch a master dancer. She is sparing with energy, using just as much effort as needed for each movement, no more and no less. At times a gifted dancer seems to fly. This ability comes through long and devoted practice. The native elders would say, "If you don't move it, you'll lose it." We can put this wisdom into practice by making our bodies strong, flexible, and balanced through a movement practice such as yoga or tai chi.

Here is your eternal testament—
  This cup, this chalice, this primordial cauldron
  of real menstrual blood
  the color of clay warm with promise,
  rhythmic, cyclical, fit for lining the uterus
  and shed for many,
    for the remission of living.

ROBIN MORGAN

In ancient times, when God was a woman, the blood offering on altars was menstrual blood. It was given as a reminder of the sacred connection of all life. It was a reminder of the power of woman and the power of transformation. Menstruating women have been honored throughout the world, yet in modern times the power of the blood has been denied or denigrated. We need to create space in our lives to welcome the time of bleeding as a time of turning inward. We all need a time for contemplation, a time to reflect, to see what within us is seeking release. How fortunate woman is to have a special reminder of these needs. In Native American culture, as in tantra, menstruation is respected as the time of woman's greatest power. The dreams of a menstruating woman have been consulted as important oracles. The bleeding woman would stop her usual activities and spend the days of her "red time" or "moon time" in prayer and meditation. She prayed for her whole community, that they might release the old and give birth to the new.

DHARMA

For Dhamma* is greater than its messengers. One sees with amazement over time that a life lived in Dhamma, even imperfectly, is the greatest effort one can make for a better tomorrow. Dhamma, the great transformer, has everything to do with transformational politics—and nothing at all.

CHARLENE SPRETNAK

"The world today is so complicated and the problems are so huge that it's easy to get weighed down by that awareness. Just the issue of global pollution is enough to put me over the edge," my friend and dharma sister, Jo, declared in a recent conversation. I asked Jo if her spiritual practice was any help when she felt this way.

"There is an image I carry that helps me when I feel that my little political action isn't going to make any change. I remember I'm just a little stone thrown in the pond, so even the small effort I make for change makes ripples and widens to fill the whole pond."

The spiritual life, learning to be present to each moment, opens us to the fear, the terror, the joy, and the ecstasy of the world. This presence is the courage to open to the pain and work toward its healing while knowing that we cannot heal all of it. When supported by equanimity, this knowledge doesn't weigh us down: it allows us to do what needs to be done with a light heart.

* In the Pali language, *Dhamma* is the equivalent of the Sanskrit word *Dharma*, meaning Ultimate Truth or Universal Law.

How sad now never to see men holding hands while everywhere one looks they are holding guns.

ALICE WALKER

Why do we expect men to be holding guns? Why do we glorify it? Why do we think it is masculine to be aggressive and warlike? Why is it acceptable to us to see men holding guns? Why is it unacceptable to see men holding hands? Why are we more terrified of caring and love between men than we are of violence between men? Which action, that of holding guns or holding hands, truly harms us? Which action brings peace?

If peace is what we want we need to make it our primary concern. We need to stop fearing those who are different and stop glorifying violence. Take some quiet time and ask yourself these questions as part of an ongoing dialogue with yourself. Really listen to your answers. Feel the bodily responses that you have. Don't settle for your first response. Go deeper. Ask again and again and again.

KINDNESS

The deepest secret in our heart of hearts is that we are writing because we love the world, and why not finally carry that secret out with our bodies into the living rooms and porches, backyards and grocery stores? Let the whole thing flower: the poem and the person writing the poem. And let us always be kind in this world.

NATALIE GOLDBERG

My friend Linda told me a story about a delivery man she saw on the street in San Francisco. As Linda walked by the delivery truck she saw the driver walk up to two homeless men who were sleeping in a doorway. The driver said, "Excuse me, I'm sorry to disturb you but I need to bring things through this door." He was so gentle and loving it brought tears to her eyes.

Kindness is simple. All that is needed is to treat others in the same way we wish to be treated. None of us like to be ignored, talked down to, or interrupted. We become agitated by being pressured or rushed. We don't like to be the butt of a joke or talked about behind our backs. "Let us always be kind in this world."

I have a love for life that is bringing with it sensitivity and care, real care. . . . If you strike back you injure life. . . . When you have that certain sense you cannot be vindictive or unforgiving, no matter how much wrong was done to you.

RUTH DENISON

There are many bay trees surrounding my house. Some days I watch the squirrels racing up and down the trees. Other days I am drawn to the pattern the light makes as it filters through the leaves. When I am open and completely focused on seeing the tree I can feel the wind moving the leaves as though it is also stirring in my heart. There is no separation. The sensation is quite tangible. When that kind of sensitivity is felt toward all living things, the heart is open. I could not injure the tree because I would be injuring myself.

Sensitivity to life and the ability to let go are skills we can develop. This nature ritual will help to cultivate these abilities. If you have been injured or harmed by another person, it may be possible for you to find a place in nature where you feel safe. If so, find a tree that you appreciate. Visit this tree as often as possible. Hug the tree, climb into the tree, sit or stand by it. Stay with the tree long enough for you to feel its presence. Allow your connection with the tree to heal you. Let the tree take your pain. Even if you can't feel the tree, keep practicing the exercise and pretend it is working. Eventually it will. As you develop sensitivity to the tree you will gradually be able to extend that sensitivity toward yourself and other people and creatures. Be gentle with yourself. You have all the time you need.

EQUALITY

MAY 5

I taught nearly forty years and I taught my students that every person is a human being. Every human personality is sacred, potentially divine. Nobody is any more than that and nobody can be any less.

MARGARET WALKER ALEXANDER

In my years of training with Dhyani Ywahoo of Sunray Meditation Society, Dhyani would emphasize that the teachings are not designed to make us Native Americans. The teachings are to assist us in becoming the best human being we can become. In other words, we are to open to our divinity, the "divine potential" that Margaret Walker Alexander speaks of.

The last line is a key for me. Ms. Alexander is asking us to cut through the arrogance that gives us the mistaken notion that we are better than someone else because of our race, color, or nationality, or because we have more money or a different sexual orientation. When we treat others disrespectfully we are not guided by the truth. We are acting out our hatred and prejudice. The line also invites us to settle for nothing less than the full expression of our inherent divinity. When we open into that divinity our compassion and warmth is extended toward all life. With an open heart, all people are treated as equal. Every woman is an expression of the Goddess and every man an expression of God.

The following affirmation reminds us of our divinity: I am an expression of the Goddess. May all my thoughts, words, and deeds express this divinity.

To take refuge is 'to retreat into a shelter that is safe from danger,' and, because of a continuous practice, I did have access to the Triple Treasure.* I surprised myself. I did act according to the belief that every experience is a powerful teacher, and I did transform, combust, move the energies of this negative experience.

JUDITH RAGIR

There is a body of "new age" thinking that says we choose each of our life experiences because there is something we need to learn. This statement, while containing a partial truth, also contains much confusion. The harmful effects of this thinking lead women to feel guilty for "choosing rape" or "choosing childhood incest." This kind of thinking lacks compassion and is harmful. A clearer and more skillful understanding is that all our life experiences can be powerful teachers, whether the experiences are beautiful or horribly painful. If we are willing, we can embrace each experience and take the energy of it and allow it to transform us. Then there is healing. This is the power of woman, the power to transform.

So clear thinking is not: I have been raped because it was an experience I needed to grow. The clear thinking is: I have been raped and I am able to take the energy of this horrible and painful experience and transform it. Then I will heal and this healing will be of benefit for us all because of our deep and often unseen connections.

* In Buddhism the three refuge vows—the Buddha, the Dharma, and the Sangha—are referred to as the three jewels, or the triple treasure.

NO-SELF

When have you ever seen that an "I" was born? Have you ever seen an "I"? The "I" has never been and never will be born, only the body. The true, divine self is perfection itself, so a development in it is not possible.

ELISABETH HAICH

On long meditation retreats we have the opportunity to let energy and concentration build so that a deep exploration of the body is possible. When we stop thinking about the body and look to the simple experience of the body we notice many changing sensations. These sensations include heat, cold, itching, tingling, buzzing, vibrating, twisting, stabbing, numbing, throbbing, aching, hardness, or softness. With every sensory experience we have there is an immediate reaction of pleasure, displeasure, or neutrality. This level of experience and reaction usually goes unnoticed; we are not conscious of trying to grasp the pleasant sensations and experiences and push away the unpleasant. This constant grasping and pushing away creates a persona that we mistakenly perceive as solid; thus, we identify ourselves as a person who likes this and doesn't like that. While we cannot stop our immediate reactions to the sensory experiences we can become aware of them. The more we notice that we experience a warm, pulsing sensation as pleasant or a stabbing sensation as unpleasant, the less we will build a story of fear or grasping around the sensations. The actual reality, the direct experience of the body, is simply changing sensations. The deeper we look, the clearer it becomes that nothing is solid and unchanging. The less stories we create, the more space and energy we have to act in appropriate ways.

I stand in awe of the millions who live the life of earth, doing its work, suffering its conflicts, manifesting its human destiny, imagining. The whole world is our religion. Blessed with an inner child, we may see it new.

M. C. RICHARDS

It is easy to separate ourselves from people who are from a different race or class if we focus only on our differences and come from a place of reaction and distrust. While there are many races of people and a wide variety of lifestyles, when we get down to the basics, all people want to be happy and free from pain. No matter how different we appear on the outside, on the inside we have these roots in common. Also within each of us exist the roots of greed, hatred, and delusion. And the three opposites exist within also: generosity, loving-kindness and wisdom.

Take an honest look within yourself. Are you able to experience these roots? All our actions come from them. This is true for everyone. There is no person who is totally pure or totally evil. Seeing these roots in a balanced way we can begin the work of uprooting the greed and cultivating the generosity. Seeing ourselves in a balanced way we don't need to get caught in disappointment or blame. Looking deeply within we see that when we act in a greedy way, there is discomfort; and when we act in a generous way, there is joy. This knowledge from our own direct experience gives us the energy necessary to uproot the greed and cultivate the generosity.

LIFE/ESSENCE

The fields, the mountains, the flowers and my body too are the voice of the bird—what is left that can be said to hear?

ASAN

Usually we identify ourselves by some or all of the following: the work we do, our age, where we live, our sexual identification, our socio-economic class, and our cherished beliefs and opinions. The labels we attach to ourselves can be useful in moving through the world. Trouble begins when we become attached to these definitions and believe in the absolute existence of this separate self. When we deeply examine all the different aspects of the self we must come to the conclusion that there is nothing that can and does exist alone, in and of itself.

In nature, have you ever had the experience of being so present and so alive that all sense of separation is dissolved? I have had such experiences when I am deeply attentive to the life around me, whether I am watching the seals peeking out at me as I walk along the seashore, listening to the sound of the waves crashing against the rocky shore, or observing deer grazing on the hillside or elk sleeping in the afternoon sun. I become totally unselfconscious, not in a way of denying anything, but in a way that the usual sense of self drops away and what is left is the essence—the life force that infuses all forms on the Earth. It is in these moments that we are in touch with the truth of ourselves.

Teachings can only bring us back to who we truly are. . . . Our lives and deaths can be of the Beauty Way. But we must start now; we must become refined. The grinding away process to become truly who we are.

JOAN HALIFAX

Spiritual teachings can't give us anything that we don't already have. What teachings do give us is a means for uncovering the truth that is already inside us. A teacher can't do it for us. We must do the work ourselves. The material of our own lives is all we need to awaken. We can learn from every experience, if we so choose. Memories, thoughts, and images won't serve us here. They form a barrier that isolates us from our inner knowing. Wisdom is different from knowledge. Knowledge is a process of gaining information. We can learn how to program a computer, how to drive a car, how to plant a garden. These are technical skills and our memory serves us here. Wisdom is beyond emotion and intellect. It can't be acquired.

Wisdom is a deep understanding of life. Another word for wisdom is love.

PURPOSE

To this day I believe we are here on earth to live, grow and do what we can to make this world a better place for all people to enjoy freedom.

ROSA PARKS

Most of us know Rosa Parks, the founder and president of the Rosa and Raymond Parks Institute for Self-Development, as the woman who became the catalyst for the Alabama bus boycott that was the beginning of the civil rights movement. Ms. Parks' words are refreshingly clear and simple. Blessed with the gift of life we have both the opportunity and the responsibility to honor life by growing into our fullness. For authentic growth the choices we make must not be selfish ones, without regard for the people and environment around us. The words *responsible choice* come to mind and remind me of an old seventies poster for the women's movement with a picture of a strong woman and the caption: NO ONE IS FREE UNTIL WE ARE ALL FREE. For freedom to grow we need to open to the world—by transforming the selfish fears that cause us to grab and clutch for ourselves alone. Freedom is abundance.

We women should concentrate more on spiritual evolution and truly act as mothers for society. There is tremendous energy within women that needs to be recognized and used for the welfare of the world. If women truly see themselves as mothers, then they can give pure, unconditional love to anyone. This is what the world definitely requires today.

ASHA MA

Genevieve Vaughan is one of many women today who is acting as a mother for society. Ms. Vaughan created the Foundation for a Compassionate Society and Change of Heart, Inc., to give women a chance to practice women's values while still living in the patriarchy. Vaughan defines women's values as freely giving, which has as its basis the love and care a mother gives a tiny child. She describes current patriarchal values as an exchange, giving in order to receive. Whether the giving is done in relationships or between nations we can see that it isn't clean. There are always strings attached and this perpetuates conflicted relationships. As long as the ego is involved, Vaughan suggests, "it needs to be continually recreated and confirmed . . . this can also be done by violence against the other."

It is natural to give freely. We have been conditioned to think and feel the opposite. We can practice this natural way of giving. For the next three days begin acting on every little impulse you have to give. Remember that our conditioning is strong and we may have feelings of fear, scarcity, or embarrassment over this giving. Be the gentle witness to this conditioning.

EARTH WISDOM

MAY 13

. . . Sisters/ our planet's goo—ood / oh / she's sweet.
Don't we know it! / Praise the planet!
This green earth / she's a generous woman,
sure a rich sweet mama.
Don't we feel it? / Don't we feel her as she rocks us?
Oh, let's close our eyes and feel her
she rocks our hearts to beating
Listen to her loving us / listen to her lullaby. . . .

SUE SILVERMARIE

My partner and I received as a gift a marvelous book of photographs of Earth taken from the moon. The text, written in English and Russian, is the personal impressions of Earth given by a group of astronauts and cosmonauts who have formed the Association of Space Explorers. What the explorers share in common, regardless of their race or nationality, is an appreciation of the great beauty of space, the night sky, the planet. Able to witness Earth from so far away, it became clear to each explorer that our geographic borders are artificial, and that humankind is "a single community living on spaceship earth." They recognized that the planet is quite fragile, and that we must do whatever we can to protect it. The explorers were awed by the magical energy of life and understood that there is a common human experience that transcends our differences. The intention of *The Home Planet* is nothing less than awakening people to a "cosmic perception of the world" and a desire to unite all peoples of the Earth in the task of safeguarding the planet, our home. Very few of us will have the opportunity to travel into space, but we all have the potential to awaken to the wonder of our planet.

Learning to love differently is hard,
love with the hands wide open, love
with the doors banging on their hinges . . .
. . . .
It hurts to thwart the reflexes
of grab, of clutch; to love and let
go again and again.

MARGE PIERCY

We believe we truly care about our partners and lovers. We think we want to make them happy, to please them. In actuality, our caring for them is often mixed with enormous self-interest. If we try to please the partner it is because we want them to like us or do something for us. We want emotional security or sexual or sensual gratification from them. As soon as we feel we are not getting the kind of gratification we want, we leave the relationship and go to another.

We need to look at our relationships and ask the question—what is the purpose of the relationship in our lives? A relationship can act as a mirror for us by reflecting back to us those places that are in balance and those that are out of balance. Relationships become mirrors by our willingness to see our reflection. If we don't allow relationships to be mirrors they become just another way to satisfy our grasping. They become a means of escape.

KINDNESS

MAY 15

There is hunger for ordinary bread, and there is hunger for love, for kindness, for thoughtfulness; and this is the great poverty that makes people suffer so much.

MOTHER TERESA OF CALCUTTA

One of the problems in our society today is denial. Denial makes us unable to accept that all people are the same in that we all have a hunger for kindness and for love, as well as for food. We are often trained to be competitive, rather than co-operative. Competition is fueled by fears; fears of not getting enough, fears of losing what we have. These fears can cause mistrust of others, rather than concern for others. We are not often trained to be kind, loving, and thoughtful. Kindness is simple but not always easy. This is the primary work of those on the spiritual path—to get beyond the fears and conditioned thinking so that natural kindness can be expressed. A seeker once asked of the Dalai Lama, "What is the purpose of the Tibetan meditations, rituals, and chants?" The Dalai Lama replied, "To become a kind human being." It is kindness that is so needed in the world today.

WOMAN POWER

We are the trees of the earth
our roots stretching deep and strong,
the stone of the firmament,
sister to the stars
that gave birth to the soil.

ALMA VILLANUEVA

It is easy to get lost in the business of our daily lives and forget the essence, the source of all life. All women share a universal perception that comes from being female, regardless of our race or culture. The ability we have to create and nourish life connects us to all of life. There is a vulnerability here that is our power. We know directly how fragile and precious life is. This knowledge makes it harder to take things for granted. It makes it harder to deny the humanity of a person because they come from a culture or race other than our own. The next time we feel threatened by difference let us remember our power. The next time someone tries to degrade or harm us, let us remember our roots, our strength, and our source.

Remember imitating trees and animals as a child? Stand tall, feeling the stretch from the bottom of your feet to the top of your head. Feel the power of the abdominal muscles as they support the back. Let the head rest gently on the neck. Feel the weight in the hands, let the shoulders relax back and down. Now begin to imitate the trees. Bend and sway as you keep mindful of your groundedness. Reach and let the stretch move your arms—first up over your head and then extending out to the sides. Now move without losing the sense of connectedness to the Earth. When you are ready come back to standing, bend and sway and then return to stillness.

DISCIPLINE

MAY 17

Art serves me. I don't serve it. But I have to be a servant before it serves me. In other words, I have to be disciplined. There is no such thing as freedom without discipline. The one who is free is disciplined.

JANET COLLINS

One of the hardest lessons for students in the Women's Sacred Mystery School to learn concerns discipline. The school provides a structure that nourishes rigorous training. We rise early in the day to meditate before breakfast and continue working late into the night. There are periods of silent meditation and walking, creative and interactive exercises, yoga, dance, women's council, chanting, and ritual. The schedule is strenuous and can be a place of resistance. At one time or another all the students experience it. "I work hard all week and this weekend should be about relaxing and socializing. I want to talk to these interesting women, not sit in silence."

In the beginning the discipline can feel like deprivation. We come up against old habits, and it is through the discipline we create a space where we can carefully observe the old habits without reacting or repressing them. Each time an old habit is broken there is more freedom.

MOTHER OF US ALL

We all come from the Mother
And to Her we shall return
Like a drop of rain
Flowing to the ocean

ZSUZSANNA E. BUDAPEST

What a delight it has been for me in my travels to be able to sing Z. Budapest's wonderful chant with hundreds of circles of women. I love this joyful reminder that we all come from one source, this great ocean. The greatness of the ocean is contained in each drop of rain. Each of us, sisters of the sea, flow from and return to our source. We are never parted from this source. This energy is continually available to us.

Chants such as this are wonderful reminders in this modern world, where many of us are constantly on the move and separated from our families and friends. It can be quite challenging to find and stay connected with our roots. Knowing that we all come from the "Mother" tells us that we are all relatives. We are never alone. It is to this "family" we need to establish clear connection.

CONFRONT DARKNESS

The way I must enter
leads through darkness to darkness—
O moon above the mountains' rim,
please shine a little further
on my path.

IZUMI SHIKIBU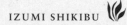

The wonderful qualities of joy, loving-kindness, and equanimity that are the fruits of the spiritual path are natural qualities that are always present. To access these natural states of mind, we have to confront, to meet face-to-face, those mind states that have hidden the natural qualities. Izumi describes what is necessary to effect a meeting with the natural, spacious qualities of mind. We must go through the shadows, enter the darkness, hopelessness, despair, disappointment, anger, fear, and hatred that have overshadowed our true nature. We must be willing to meet the darkness head-on. It is a great risk, going from darkness into darkness. We don't know what we will discover. We must make the journey alone. But it is not without support. There is light there. Those who have gone before us are like the moon shedding light on the path.

Holy persons draw to themselves
all that is earthly.

HILDEGARD OF BINGEN

A whole person is a holy person. She is vitally alive, without clinging to life or trying to force a particular outcome. She is present and able to respond to whatever situation this earthly life offers. The holy person is a lover of the Earth. Sometimes we mistakenly think of a holy person as one who wants to leave the suffering of the Earth. We sometimes picture holy people with their heads in the clouds, unconcerned with earthly matters. The whole person, the one with an open heart, is here with feet firmly on the Earth. She may lead a simple life or she may be involved more actively in worldly affairs.

What holy people share is a quality of sensitivity toward life, a compassionate care and loving-kindness, a clear and insightful mind. The earthly experience isn't pushed away. The greater our willingness to let go of personal preferences, the greater our openness to all of life. In this way we are healed, we are whole, we are holy. It is the experience of earthly life that gives us a precious opportunity to express our holiness.

One ought to struggle for its own sake. One ought to be against racism and sexism because they are wrong, not because one is black or one is female.

ELEANOR HOLMES NORTON

Fear of difference is a strong fear and it manifests itself in the "isms" of which sexism, racism, and heterosexism are a few. It is this fear that translates into hatred and aggression. Safety in the world doesn't come from making everyone the same. It doesn't come from denying rights to people who are different. True safety comes when our hearts are open and we are able to celebrate diversity. We can more easily open to difference when we honor the ways that we are also similar, the ways in which we are all connected.

One day I was in the supermarket with a friend who was wearing a brilliantly colored tie-dyed shirt. As she went through the checkout, the checker commented on the beauty of the shirt, asking where my friend had purchased it. My friend paused and then said, "I got it at the Gay Day parade." She then continued to talk about tie-dyed shirts with the checker. This allowed the checker to take in the information she had received—that my friend was a lesbian, and that lesbians buy food in supermarkets like she does, enjoy fun clothes, and even know how much salt added to the water will prevent tie-dyes from running.

The process of the practice is to see through, not to eliminate, anything to which we are attached. . . . Our mind doesn't matter. What matters is nonattachment to the activities of the mind. And our emotions are harmless, unless they dominate us (that is, if we are attached to them)—then they create disharmony for everyone.

CHARLOTTE JOKO BECK

What does the phrase, "our mind doesn't matter" mean? Just this, the mind is going to have desires, thoughts, expectations, doubts, fears. This is the process of the mind. We aren't bad because of this. It is a function of being in the body. To practice is to see through this process of mind movement. Seeing through means cutting the attachment. If we are attached, for example, to our comfort, then the need for comfort controls us. Our behavior is directed in continually seeking to fulfill the desires. There is no peace. Our ability to live happily in the world is limited if personal comfort is our first priority. It isn't the comfort that is problematic, it is the attachment to the comfort. If, for example, we are given a choice between sleeping on a bed that is more comfortable and one that is less comfortable, it isn't wrong to choose the more comfortable bed. But if attachment is strong, then when the time comes that we don't have such a choice we will have disappointment, anger, or distress. If we are strongly attached, then not only will we attach to comfort, we will attach to the emotions that arise when we aren't comfortable. What is important is to be aware of our preferences and our feelings about them and not be strongly attached to either. In this way we can have preferences, make choices, and stay balanced even when we don't get our first choice or when we are in uncomfortable situations.

PURPOSE

MAY 23

Don't forget your purpose.
This is all a holiness—
but don't tell anyone.

LYNN PARK

In the Buddha's teaching, clear comprehension is one aspect of complete mindfulness. In clear comprehension, one must know the regulating force, the purpose, behind all thoughts, words, and actions. Clear comprehension includes both knowing the purpose of life as well as one's own particular purpose. Many people today have forgotten that there is a purpose for living, something beyond one's need for survival and pleasure. Many people aren't consciously aware of their special purpose or gift in life. Not knowing creates sadness and feelings of being lost.

The drive for material success and the competition fostered in Western culture stems from a lack of awareness of one's purpose. When the purpose is known, human beings are connected to the whole circle of life. Each being has a place, a purpose. Energies that might have been competitive are expressed in caring for and working in harmony with all living beings.

My teacher, Ruth Denison, says that knowing our purpose simplifies our lives. We're not held back by superficial excuses. She suggests that before we react we stop, breathe deeply, and allow ourselves to contact this sense of purpose. Knowing our purpose, Ruth says, lets us begin the practice that allows our wisdom to ripen.

IMPERMANENCE

When I am alone the flowers are really seen. . . . They are felt as presences. They live and die in a few days; they keep me closely in touch with process, with growth, and also with dying.

MAY SARTON

Springtime in northern California is a special time for me. Two of my favorite places where wildflowers grow are Abbott's Lagoon and Chimney Rock. Here the purples and blues of the iris and the lupine glow next to the bright yellow and orange poppies, the tiny blue forget-me-nots, and the brilliant red of the paintbrush. Each walk becomes a feast of sight and smell with new flowers blooming daily. Primrose, beach daisies, larkspur, manzanita, and fiddleneck. I am filled with joy at such incredible beauty. They are Earth's gift to us all; if we pick them they die instantly. In the fields and meadows their blooms only last for a short time. Perhaps it is the fragile, short-lived beauty of a wildflower that makes it so precious. The ghost of death blows through each bloom.

NO-SELF

This whole everything, which is no separate thing, never remains the same from one instant to the next, and yet each moment is totally sufficient, whole, and without conflict. We are not separate from all this! There is no separate movement of "me" and "mine" except in thought-feeling and memory. Deeply realizing the beauty of this is love and joy and the ending of insecurity.

TONI PACKER

On my fiftieth birthday my son presented me with a copy of one of his favorite childhood books, *The Giving Tree*. It is a tender story of the gift of giving and the serene acceptance of another's capacity to love in return. He inscribed it with these words: "To have the sensation of being dissolved is actually positive. I am happy to know there is more than just me or you. It is scary to give up what you know, because what you gain or trade is unknown and must be experienced firsthand in order to truly know. For some reason, unknown to me, I have never been afraid of this. I have always known that to love and to lose your separate identity is good. I owe this to my mother. I am lucky."

The mind becomes spacious and light when it can give up anger, seeing it as a destructive force, out to do harm. The faculty of anger has a disturbing force which robs us of harmony and peace and kindness for ourselves and life around us.

RUTH DENISON

Feminism and psychotherapy have taught us to reclaim our anger as a means of empowerment. We are taught that it is disempowering to repress anger. In the process of learning not to repress anger we have sometimes fallen into the opposite extreme, inappropriate expression of anger. True empowerment comes from neither repression nor inappropriate expression of feeling.

Empowerment comes from opening to the anger and accepting the anger without judging it as bad and to be denied or good and to be expressed whenever we feel it. Anger is to be felt and allowed. When we have a direct experience of anger, we feel all the sensations of anger in the body—the heat, the tension, the shortness of breath. We see, we feel, we accept. In that opening anger is transformed; it is neither repressed nor expressed. The transformation makes available more life energy, which we can use to create balanced actions that are beneficial for all life.

Anger can be a warning bell that signals something out-of-balance. We may need to speak about the anger. Yet we speak with peace and clarity, rather than fear or irritation. This doesn't guarantee that our words or actions will be well-received. What it does guarantee is that we are planting seeds for peaceful resolution by not continuing a conditioned pattern of behavior that will only stimulate more anger.

REFUGE

Taking refuge in the Buddha means that you are willing to spend your life acknowledging or reconnecting with your awakeness, learning that every time you meet the dragon you take off more armor, particularly the armor that covers your heart.

PEMA CHÖDRÖN

Patriarchal consciousness, which has existed for thousands of years, has engendered so much denial, hatred, and degradation of women that we might be mistrustful of taking refuge in a man. We feel that to take refuge in the Buddha is the same old story, a woman putting all her faith and trust outside herself and into a man.

Let us look deeper into the meaning of refuge. Buddha means awake. Taking refuge is a courageous step. We are taking refuge, not in a man, but in our own potential to awaken. Taking refuge in the Buddha means that we are willing to do whatever it takes to reconnect with the awakeness that is already within us. Rather than running from our fears we are willing to face them, to strip them away until nothing is left but the exposed heart. To awaken is to live with courage and balance from that soft, vulnerable space.

I have been with you
from the beginning,
utterly simple.
I will be with you when you die,
say what you will.
We shall never be finished.
This is possible,
a small gift, hush.

ROBIN MORGAN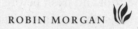

We are always within the embrace of the Goddess. This is a magnificent secret. This interrelationship exists whether or not we awaken to it. This connection is timeless and unchanging. Our death is a physical change, a shedding of the body, just as we would discard an outgrown or worn-out coat. It is possible to awaken to the reality of eternal life.

We live in a material world and we become attached to material possessions, including our bodies. Eternal life does not mean we stay in this same physical body forever. Nothing lasts forever in the material world. This is a universal law. Every form that is created, including our bodies, also must die. This includes our thoughts, ideas, situations like jobs and relationships, and the things we build such as cars, airports, and houses. We confuse this knowledge of change and try to make things last forever. We believe in once and for all. And we confuse the process of dying. We think that once something dies, that is forever, too.

Oh, Great Mother of us all, without whom nothing is born or joyful, we pray that all beings awaken to the knowledge of interconnectedness and love. We pray that all beings experience peace and happiness.

DEEP SEEING

MAY 29

We are nature. We are nature seeing nature. The red-winged black-bird flies in us.

SUSAN GRIFFIN

Early morning walking meditations at Dhamma Dena Desert Vipassana Center are often held outdoors. The air would be cool and fresh before the heat of the day brought the temperatures above ninety. Ruth had several of her students create a circular path that wound around the creosote bushes. We would meet here in the beautiful, open space of the desert. Ruth would invite us to practice with these words, "Let us, through our movements, open in our bodies to the freshness of the air and the life above us, around us, and below us. Let us open and accept it." Ruth invited us to allow seeing, to see what the eyes actually see.

We don't often do this. We're so busy thinking about what we see. We may see a flash of color but it doesn't register deeply. The mind becomes busy with comparisons, evaluations, and memories. In the cool, desert air we trained to become present to our immediate experience. We learned to see and to notice that we were seeing. When we brought our attention to the world in this way, the seeing was direct. It wasn't clouded by either emotion or intellect. The barriers dropped and the students walking became the freshness of the morning air, became the butterflies alighting on the bushes, became the sand of the desert floor. Vibrant and alive, the perfumed desert air breathed us.

War will stop when we no longer praise it, or give it any attention at all. Peace will come whenever it is sincerely invited. Love will overflow every sanctuary given it. Truth will grow where the fertilizer that nourishes it is also truth. Faith will be its own reward.

ALICE WALKER

When my sons were younger and visited their grandparents I asked their grandparents not to take them to military parades. I did not want them to see war glorified. I wanted to teach my sons camaraderie with other people, with other men, not through the thrill and terror of war, but through shared excitement and curiosity about life. The children are our future. We need to love them, speak honestly to them, and teach them peace.

Once, young Mike was engaged with a friend in a verbal struggle that had the potential to become physical. I called both boys into the house, seated them at the kitchen table, and gave them a twig from a fir tree. I told them to discuss their differences, but that only the one holding the twig could talk. Amazingly enough they did as they were told. Talking in turn, passing the twig back and forth, they soon burst into giggles and were back to playing, their disagreement forgotten.

COMPASSION

What should you do?
Do good by doing compassion
to everyone
you know needs it.
Expect adversity.
Bear adversity with love.

MECHTILD OF MAGDEBURG

Here is some plain and simple advice. It is easy to be good to those who are good to us. It is easy to be compassionate and giving when things are going our way. We can be sweet when life feels sweet to us. It is not so easy when circumstances are hard. This is the true test of our openheartedness. And yes, the universe does test us! So expect adversity. This isn't negative. This is a realistic appraisal of life. It has ups and downs. If we can bring a sense of equanimity, a sense of balance, to life's trials, the trials will be less burdensome. Adverse conditions, like all conditions, can and do change. And we will come out lighter, without bitterness, if we bring a calm acceptance to these unavoidable times.

SISTERHOOD

Give birth to me, sisters, in struggle we transform
ourselves, but how often, how often
we need help to cut loose, to cry out, to breathe! . . .
This morning we must make each other strong.
Change is qualitative: we are
each other's miracle.

MARGE PIERCY

This is the power and the blessing of sisterhood: none of us is free until we are all free. Each time one of us makes the smallest act of courage, the energy of that act resonates throughout the atmosphere. We all benefit from this act because of the interrelationship of all life. Young women today have many opportunities that are easily taken for granted. Fifteen or twenty years ago these opportunities would not have been available. The opportunities are possible now because of the struggles of the sisters who went before us. We have not yet fully manifested the conditions of equality that are necessary to live in a caring, sharing world. While we have much to be thankful for there is still work to be done.

A sisterhood is created in the Women's Sacred Mystery School. We are not leaning on each other, we are walking together on the path. When one woman is tired or feeling her energy blocked, she can depend on the others to hold the integrity of the circle. At another time her strength will be called upon. We know that our strength is not for ourselves alone. We become stronger as we extend our strength to the circle of women and reach beyond our circle, to the circle of humanity and to the whole circle of life.

CONDITIONED BEHAVIOR

JUNE 2

The first crescent of the moon
Shows its form like a beauty's brow:
Paired with the light of the sun,
Its clear purity abounds.

CUI SHAOXUAN

Cui Shaoxuan was an accomplished Taoist. We know nothing of her personal life except that she was the youngest daughter of a Northern Chinese governmental officer. Through her poetry we have inherited the distilled essence of her wisdom. The translator of Cui Shaoxuan's poetry explains some of her symbolism. The first crescent of the moon signifies the initial awakening experience, that first insight which brings us out of the shadow of conditioned experience. The image of the moon and the sun as a pair symbolizes complete balance or full enlightenment.

Much of our lives are spent in the shadows. We think we are able to see and to understand, yet what we know is shadowed by our past experiences, our learned—or conditioned—behavior. Each time we see through that conditioning, each time we move through a fear or expectation, there is insight. The ability to reflect on our life's experiences, and to allow the insights to illuminate our actions brings about balance and integration. Intellectual understanding isn't enough. We must surrender to the knowing, allowing it to shine through all our actions.

To me the concept of the "Beloved" conveys not just a nice, cozy, warm relationship with God but one that is joyous, uplifting, and exhilarating because it is a recognition of who I am.

NANA VEARY

God as an entity separate from ourselves is simply another idea that we can either accept or dismiss. This mistaken idea leads us to another misunderstanding, that God is for or against us. Many religious wars have been fought with the belief that "God is on our side." Many small-scale wars are fought each day by people insisting that their way is the right way and the only way.

When we leave behind the world of concepts and go deeply into a direct experience of the body and mind, we uncover a cascade of changing sensations. There is nothing solid or separate or unchanging that we can grasp. Having the courage to confront the instability of this experience we open into a space that has been called the divine, the beloved, or the ultimate reality. It is through this direct experience that we realize we have no solid, separate, unchanging qualities. This realization brings joy.

LIFE SOURCE

JUNE 4

I ride the water's song
sleek as a dolphin.
Daughter, its constant pulse
belongs as much to you
as your own heart's ebb and flow.
This sea that carries me
is velvet with depth.
And wild with wave!
Come claim your place.

SUE SILVERMARIE

This excerpt from Sue Silvermarie's poem "Child to Your Greater Sea" reminds us that we all come from the same source, the vast ocean. The knowledge of our source, the ebb and flow of the sea, is within our hearts. It is within each heartbeat. It is within the rising and falling of each breath.

We can practice by going to the ocean or visualizing the ocean and watching the waves touch the shore and recede. Watch your breath filling and emptying, filling and emptying. Be still and become one with the ocean; breathe with the ocean until there is no difference between your breath and the ocean's breath.

A life of no-self is centered on no particular thing, but on all things—that is, it is nonattached—so the characteristics of a self cannot appear. We are not anxious . . . worried . . . don't bristle easily, . . . not easily upset, and most of all, our lives do not have a basic tenor of confusion. To be no-self is to be joy. Because it opposes nothing, no-self is beneficial to everything.

CHARLOTTE JOKO BECK

The concept of no-self is at the heart of Buddhist teachings. It is easily misunderstood, especially in the West where we have a heightened sense of our individuality and are taught how to "look out for number one." We make a mistake in equating no-self with no self-esteem or a lack of personal integrity. We believe that if we have a highly developed sense of self it will bring us what we need: happiness, success, popularity. This way of thinking always creates tension, if not from another person with conflicting needs, then inner tension, from fear of not getting what is wanted or losing what one has.

When we aren't attached to any particular thing, idea, attitude, need, or person, there is a beautiful peace that comes from the resulting lack of tension. There is a wider range of behaviors and options available to us when there isn't attachment to personal preference. Our ability to center comes not from our ideas about ourselves but from knowing that wherever we are and whoever we are, we are on the Earth, the sky is above us and we are breathing. This reality is quite impersonal, that is, nothing that we say or do makes this happen. Whether we are rich or poor, successful or unsuccessful, these facts are true. Centered in this way we are glad to be alive. We bring a gentle, open energy to everything we do.

LIFE AS SPIRITUAL PRACTICE

JUNE 6

Life is our practice. If we listen deeply to what's going on—if we're involved down to the very bottom with our life situation—this is our true teacher, the most venerable teacher. Life-roshi!

MAURINE STUART

Meditation retreats, ritual gatherings, periods of silence, weaving spells, chants, prayers, and yoga often come to mind when we describe a spiritual practice. These are the means to spiritual awakening and not to be confused with awakening itself. To bring that spiritual energy deeply into our lives, it is life itself that must be our practice. It is not enough to hear spiritual truth or even to have our own spiritual insights. Every aspect of what happens to us must become part of a learning experience. We must realize or embody these truths. We must integrate the truths into our consciousness, character, and conduct.

May we all trace our roots to the great Tree of Peace. May we honor the wisdom of our grandparents and caretake that wisdom for our grandchildren, unto seven generations. Let us recognize the sacredness of this time of transformation and choice, that we may truly manifest the beauteous family of humanity.

DHYANI YWAHOO

The confusion and conflict in the world today can deplete our energy. We have become accustomed to living in conflict and don't realize there is another way to live. However, there is enormous energy in conflict and confusion, and it is energy that is available for transformation. Once we are willing to directly perceive and deeply explore this conflict, the conflicted energy dissolves, and natural peace emerges. Each time a person transforms conflict in her or his own mind, the energy projected will be peaceful. The more conflict and fear in people's minds, the more conflict and fear are projected out into the world. When people's minds are calm and peaceful, peaceful energy radiates out into the world.

Each time I travel and go through customs, I'm struck by this thought: There are no real borders on Earth. Borders were constructed by people. Earth is Earth. We all live on Her. We all breathe the same air. Can we see ourselves as a planetary family? Can we imagine that people from different races and cultures are long-distance cousins we have yet to meet? These people have something to teach us, something to share. Can we let go of the idea that we have all the right ideas and the right ways of living, so we can learn from one another?

SOUL

JUNE 8

We consider our very souls to be like a
castle made out of a diamond or
of very clear cut crystal
in which there are many dwelling places.
The door of entry to this castle is
prayer and reflection.

SAINT TERESA OF AVILA

Saint Teresa of Avila, a sixteenth-century Spanish mystic, is considered one of the most profound spiritual teachers in the history of Christianity. She began to have visions, or trances, around the age of forty. One of the images that Saint Teresa saw during her visions was the soul as a diamond. Diamonds and crystals reflect light and have incredible strength and beauty. They are formed in the heart of the Earth through enormous heat and pressure. Likewise, we are shaped by the pressures of our lives. And we can become polished through the friction of living. We can open to this through prayer, an opening of the heart through gratitude. When we align ourselves with the beauty and power of the universe, we have access to its power and beauty. We need to reflect on our lives, to become conscious of the motivation, the volition, behind our actions. We are polished through this clarification. Then we are open to the full expression of the soul, and that is love.

She who loves roses must be patient and
not cry out when she is pierced by thorns.

OLGA BROUMAS

These are simple words of wisdom, yet ones we need to hear again and again. We work very diligently to attain the things we think will improve our lives. It is easy to delude ourselves by thinking that we can make things totally convenient and comfortable and eliminate all pain. This unrealistic thinking is disconnected from the truth of physical life. How do we learn to take the bitter with the sweet? We have so many cultural messages that deny this reality. "Don't take that lying down." "Get out there and fight." "Look out for number one." "You can have it all." The idea that we have ultimate control and can force the circumstances of our lives to be just to our liking dies hard. Even new age teaching with its holistic perspective falls into confusion with its dualistic thinking. The right affirmations, the right diet, the right thoughts, will bring you only pleasurable life experiences. This thinking is another way of disguising the ego's need for control with positive, upbeat language.

DIVERSITY

From all over the planet, the peoples of many nations come to bring wisdom and to learn wisdom. Let us be quiet enough to hear these first things of the earth wherever we are. The ground of our planet is continuous. Let us feel the whole earth Being in every part. Centering.

M. C. RICHARDS

Diversity is one of life's greatest gifts. Just as we can find joy in the infinite variety of flowers, we can learn to appreciate the varieties of human experience. Differences need not be a cause for fear. We can learn to recognize fear as it arises, and soften and open around it. In this open space there is room to wonder. There is room to greet one another with respect and a genuine curiosity that allows us to learn.

Inability to acknowledge differences is one face of fear. Openly acknowledging differences enables us to learn about one another's cultures and it transforms fear. A friend who works for a large organization told me a story that illustrates this. Although the staff includes people of many nationalities, these differences are not acknowledged. At a planning meeting one staff member, a Chinese woman, told the group that she worked well with their Chinese customers. She knew, for example, not to give them accounts with the number four. The non-Chinese staff had no idea why this was so. The woman explained that in the Chinese language the word for four is similar to the word for death; only the intonation makes it different, so the number four is considered bad luck. When we are willing to look at differences we open the way to more harmonious communication.

I am willing to abide by the mystery and to celebrate it. This I shall do as I die into each night's sleep that is rehearsal for the final one, just as each dawn's awakening is rehearsal for—what?

ELSA GIDLOW

Elsa Gidlow, honored lesbian feminist poet and philosophical anarchist, completed her autobiography with the above words. Elsa lived with Alan Watts and his wife, Jano, in an "unintentional community" that they named Druid Heights. Together they founded the Society for Comparative Philosophy, which has introduced Asian teachings to westerners. Over the years many artists joined their community, in which Elsa lived until her death at the age of eighty-seven.

Elsa's life is an inspiration for us, for until we have a direct perception of life's mystery, it is faith that enables us to believe there is a truth beyond what the senses can perceive. It is the celebration of this faith, sensing the awesome mystery of life, that lets us go to sleep each night filled with gratitude for all life's experiences. Can you let each day be complete as it was and go to sleep knowing that you may not wake up? This is not a morbid thought. It is embracing the reality that everything that is born must die. When night comes, the day has died. Can you awaken in the morning as a child, ready to explore the new day with excitement and curiosity: interested, open, and willing to take risks?

FORGIVENESS

JUNE 12

Mama Du said to take care of my children—to educate them. And do you know how? By teaching them to be soldiers or politicians or farmers? No. 'Teach them how to forgive, Bay Ly.'

LE LY HAYSLIP

We must begin to teach our children how to forgive. We have taught them how to hate, how to fear, how to create violence. This has not made life healthier or happier. In the United States alone we have created enough weapons to kill every person on the planet twenty times over.

Today there is much unnecessary pain and violence. Every one of us has experienced some emotional, mental, or physical pain. Refusing to forgive doesn't make the pain go away. In fact, it keeps the pain alive in us and we continue to hurt ourselves. Forgiveness does not mean we condone the harmful behavior. Forgiveness takes courage. We are giving away, releasing, our pain, anger, and fear. Forgiveness creates space inside us—space to heal, to love, to reconnect, to renew. We must soften and open our hearts to forgive. It is an act of power.

Spirit and energy should be clear as night air;
In the soundless is the ultimate pleasure all along.
Where there's reality in illusion
Is illusion in reality,
For the while playing with magical birth
In the silver bowl.

SUN BU-ER

Have you ever been in the country at night when the air is fresh and sweet? It is this delightful quality that we can express when the life force energy is flowing harmoniously through our bodies. Our modern lifestyle, with its excess work and worry and the lack of consideration for the environment, has weakened us. A friend who lives in the city related an experience she had while camping in the country. The night air was full, the energy was clear and high-spirited. She felt dizzy because her body had been weakened in the city and she couldn't take in the energy that was available to her

What will bring clarity to our spirit and energy? It involves surrender, a deep opening and letting go. Dominant Western culture puts much emphasis on appearances and discounts the inner reality that underlies all surface appearances. We might spend our whole lives attempting to gain sensory pleasures, yet pleasures are transitory. The belief that the physical world is solid and unchanging and can bring true happiness is an illusion created by the mind. The deepest peace and greatest joy are beyond material and sensory pleasure. It is through energetic practice that we see through these illusions and become adept. Then the mind is pure and we can create at will, without any confusion about cause and effect.

TRUE NATURE

What I have realized through practicing is that practice isn't about being the best horse or the good horse or the poor horse or the worst horse. It's about finding our own true nature and speaking from that, acting from that.

PEMA CHÖDRÖN

Competition is often assumed to be the natural way of life. A competitive attitude creates continual conflict: striving, doubt, or ambivalence in the mind. The training to compete begins in the home and is accelerated in the schools and workplaces. The competitive work ethic is found in all our relationships—in love, play, and work. This ideal creates the philosophy for our economy. These ideals are reflected in patriotism, racism, sexism. We work hard, struggling to beat our competitors; we play hard, competing to beat the other team.

We are ignorant of our true nature, which is peaceful. When my children were babies they were peaceful unless they were hungry, tired, wet, or hurt. They were born peaceful. They didn't read about peace, they didn't practice affirmations, they didn't attend a meditation retreat. As life goes on, conditioning to competition and its attendant conflict is strengthened and we don't believe we can live any other way.

We don't need to train ourselves to be peaceful and compassionate. We need to notice our competitive behaviors and thoughts that create conflict in the mind. With continued practice we can notice these thoughts arising and passing. Gradually the need to act out competition and conflict will lessen.

Like billowing clouds,
like the incessant gurgle of the brook,
the longing of the soul can never be stilled.

HILDEGARD OF BINGEN

Hildegard of Bingen began having divinely inspired visions at the age of six. These visions continued throughout her life. While we may not have had this experience, we all have an inner longing. It is this longing that is at the heart of the spiritual quest. It is our reason for being. The longing is for union, communion with the universal or divine. From the appearance of many people's behavior it may be difficult to believe this longing exists in everyone. We may make the mistake of separating ourselves and thinking we are better than those people whose interests are not in cultivating compassionate understanding. Yet even the person who is in pain and acts in the most despicable way has this longing. The longing may not be conscious, or it may be twisted into brutal control over others, or manifested in searching for fame or fortune. That person is searching in all the wrong places.

Those of us who do spiritual practice are indeed fortunate; our longing is conscious and we are looking in the appropriate places. We are practicing the discipline and activities that will bring us in communion with all of life. This communion is love.

STILLING THE MIND

To nurture essence,
First quiet the mind.
Why bother seeking skill
With thread and needle anymore?

FAN YUNQIAO

Fan Yunqiao's translator tells us that the thread and the needle refer to the daily tasks of life. This poem is telling us that the everyday world we know is impermanent. For us to live a life at the heart center, gaining fame or fortune in the material world is not important. What we must do is quiet our minds. Our usual method for seeking happiness is to become more and more active by gathering information, things, people, experiences. We create expectations and are concerned with our personal likes and dislikes. This doesn't bring us ultimate happiness. It takes us further away from who we are.

One way to quiet the mind is by using mantras, sacred sound syllables. Every religion has mantras, powerful spiritual formulas that transform consciousness when repeated aloud or silently. A few examples are "Hail Mary" for Catholics, "Baruch attah Adonai" (Holy One of Blessing) for Jews, or "Om Mani Padme Hum" (the jewel in the lotus of the heart) for Tibetan Buddhists. Choose a mantra that deeply appeals to you. Many women love to chant the name of a Goddess such as Tara or Kuan Yin. Repeat the mantra whenever you can, especially while doing mechanical tasks, falling asleep, or when frightened. The repetition of the holy name will steady the mind, keeping you relaxed and alert.

The one close to me now,
even my own body—
these too
will soon become clouds,
floating in different directions.

IZUMI SHIKIBU

For westerners, one of the most difficult truths to accept is our mortality. People want to feel invincible and refuse to look at the actuality of death. In the spiritual traditions of Eastern cultures in particular, great attention is paid to accepting the inevitability of death and working with the fear of dying. Everyone will die. The time of death is not certain. This knowledge need not make us angry or fearful. We can learn to die well. This means that we live well.

Living well means doing whatever we are doing in a whole-hearted way and without attachment, knowing that it won't last forever. We won't last forever. To be ready for death we make certain that what we do is complete. We don't put things off until tomorrow or wait for someone else to do our work. We don't hang on to pain and doubt. The person who accepts death doesn't rush to live as frantically as possible. She demonstrates a calm acceptance of herself. "These are my strengths and abilities. This is what I can do now." She undertakes her task to the best of her ability, without being attached to the outcome.

LOVE

Love transforms.
  Love makes empty hearts overflow.
  This happens even more
  when we have to struggle through
   without assurance,
  all unready
      for the play
        of Love.

MECHTILD OF MAGDEBURG

During my life I have met some of the kindest people who don't consider themselves spiritual at all. Yet their approach to life comes from a deep caring and concern for all human beings. It comes from a basic kindness. This is what spirituality is about. It is about our deep connections. It isn't about what gender we think God is, or whether we even think God exists or what rituals we perform or the creeds we profess. It is experiencing and acting from our deep connections. It is often done quietly, with no fanfare. People who are deeply spiritual don't call attention to themselves, but quietly go about expressing what comes naturally to them, loving-kindness. It is a friendliness to all life. This is the best care we can give ourselves, to give love. The more love we give, the more we are open to receiving, and the more we receive the more we have to give.

If you want peace, then do not look into anybody's faults. Learn to make the world your own. No one is a stranger; the whole world is your own.

HOLY MOTHER

It takes a pretty big heart to make the world our own, to extend a sense of friendliness to all life. We tend to reserve our friendliness for those people with whom we feel most compatible. We are friends with those with whom the communication is the easiest, people who have the capability to excite, inspire, or calm us. We're friends with those who satisfy our needs in some way. To see the whole world as our own is to bring a quality of gentleness and kindness to all life. We may not know a particular individual or culture or group but a friendly attitude toward life brings a warm, flexible gentleness to all. There is an open curiosity, wanting to know, to learn, to discover. The ability to meet another without barriers, without defenses, will bring peace. When we are concerned only with getting what pleases us we will try to manipulate situations to our benefit. We will try to limit, deny, or change people. Irritation, tension, and conflict will develop. When we act from our basic goodness and look to another's basic goodness with a light-hearted attitude, there will still be challenges, there will still be edges. The edges will soften more easily without an attitude of criticism and faultfinding.

COMMITMENT VOWS

I vow to hold you gently in my heart all my life.
I vow to be a clear mirror always reflecting your beauty.
I vow to keep my heart open through all doubt, fear, anger, and
*   pain.*
I vow to open to the truth of each moment.
I vow to cherish and honor your trust for the precious gift that it is.
I vow to be as spacious as the sky, and give each of us the space to
*   grow.*
I vow to love, honor, and cherish you always.
With all my heart, with a clear mind, and with each breath,
*   I commit to you.*

DIANE MARIECHILD

The vows my partner and I took at our commitment ceremony originally came into my mind quite unexpectedly during
a winter meditation retreat. They continue to serve us as a
daily reminder to abide in a state of loving-kindness. Sometimes we choose one vow, repeat it to each other while at our
altar, and then each use it as our mantra during the week. We
were happy to hear from several friends that they have in-
cluded the taking of these vows as part of their daily meditation practice.

SUMMER SOLSTICE

Love for the Unlimited is also unlimited; that's why our hearts have to be broken and become nothing to be able to accommodate the Unlimited.

IRINA TWEEDIE

The Summer Solstice is a time of magic. It is a marvelous time to explore and expand the openness of our hearts. Too often we limit ourselves, thinking that we can only love one person, or one family, or a small number of friends. Sadder still is the knowledge that many of us don't even love ourselves. Pray to the cosmic mother, make offerings of fire and fruit to the love goddesses. Remember that you are a blessed child of the mother of love. Whatever pain has prevented your heart from opening, imagine casting that pain into the fire of love. Let the fire transform it. Let no thing separate you from the ultimate truth. The fire of the goddess is within you. Let her fire bring warmth and light to your life.

INTERCONNECTEDNESS

Her words having nothing to do with this bird, except . . . as she breathes in the air this bird flies through . . . as the grass needs the body of the bird to pass its seeds, as the earth needs the grass, as we are made from this earth . . . and the sunlight in the grass enters the body of the bird, enters us.

SUSAN GRIFFIN

We could not live without the air we breathe, the air that all creatures breathe, the air through which the bird flies. We are not separate from the soil in which our food grows, nor from the farmer who plants and harvests the food. The farmer could not be here without parents to give her birth. No one could survive without the air and the water and the sun. If the sun didn't shine and the rain didn't fall the trees couldn't grow. The lumber from the trees made the paper on which these words are printed. Had I not been born I could not have written them and had you not been born, you could not be reading them. Is any one of us truly separate? Does any one of us exist alone?

The next time you feel separate from or unable to connect with others, look at a bird, look at the grass, look at the sun, and allow yourself to experience the connections that Susan Griffin has so clearly described. Take a deep breath, and know that the air you are breathing is being breathed by every person and every breathing creature on this planet. It is easy to get caught in thoughts of separation, thinking we don't need one another to exist. Take a minute to feel or remember the sun. No matter who we are or where we live or what we think, we could not exist on this planet without the sun.

*In everyday life, there is always an edge. Students do not cooperate,
bosses reject good ideas, children become ill before a vacation, traffic
snarls, the phone rings, a loved one dies. . . . Rather than ignore,
deny or fight them, we are called upon to actually dwell within them
calmly and to observe what use we can make of the tension there.*

CATHERINE PECK

Lessons don't always come from the large events in our
lives. We don't need to travel great distances to uncover our
wisdom. There are plenty of opportunities in life's small, daily
events. Everything that happens can be an opportunity for
growth. There are innumerable situations that cause us discomfort. Catherine Peck has named a few.

We can use the tension of everyday circumstances as a
means to soften and open. We can't force this receptivity. We
allow that it is OK to feel distressed or fearful. We meet the
tension with courage and look deeply into it. In that deep
looking, there is a softening. Within that softening is the wisdom to know which situations we can change and which we
cannot.

This is surrender. It is not a hopeless or helpless bowing
down. It is the receptivity that enables us to stretch and extend
beyond the tension to the calm space that is beneath.

MANY PATHS, ONE GOAL

Events themselves are not important, only the experiences and the lessons that you get from them. . . . On your way you will learn the same lessons as I on mine. There are innumerable pathways, but they all lead to the same goal.

ELISABETH HAICH

Life events don't belong to us personally. They are simply part of our path. What is important is how we relate to or respond to what is happening. We don't have to compete for experiences. It's not the outer event, but the inner response, that teaches us. We can choose to integrate or to resist. We don't need to imitate those we revere as leaders. We can draw from them the faith that it can be done. Each individual has her own ways of learning life's lessons.

SELF-RESPONSIBILITY

I am not blaming woman. I say that if we take the responsibility for our situation we can feel less helpless than when we put the blame on society or man. . . . Awareness can give us a sense of captainship over our fate, and to take destiny into our own hands is more inspiring than expecting others to direct our destiny for us.

ANAÏS NIN

When we take responsibility for something, it is not about assigning blame. It is about claiming our power so we can respond appropriately to something. This is a crucial distinction. If we blame ourselves or others, we can never totally effect a transformation. Blame puts the power outside ourselves. We can only change ourselves. We can practice empowering ourselves. Rather than allowing ourselves to become overwhelmed we can look at difficult situations with a kind and gentle eye. We can give ourselves the power to investigate deeply. Freely explore a situation by asking: If I try this, what might result? If I try that, what might result? In this way we have more options to test. Without blame, we are free to see our involvement, accept mistakes, and make changes.

INTERCONNECTEDNESS

Spirituality is not a very difficult thing—it is just an understanding of how we are interconnected. If we are interconnected, then we cannot damage the earth, and we can't damage or kill each other. We have to take care of each other because that is just taking care of ourselves.

MAYUMI ODA

True spirituality is not to be confused with religious dogma. It is not limited to one particular prayer, creed, or ritual. A woman I know once went to an acupuncturist for relief from pain in her shoulders. She was quite surprised when the acupuncturist put needles in her feet. "Why are the needles in my feet if the pain is in my shoulders?" she asked. "The body is all connected," the acupuncturist replied. "Take a look." It's time we took a look at the deep connections that are shared by all of life.

Begin with something simple. Wiggle your toes. Look and see how they are connected to your feet. See how your feet are connected to your legs. Follow these connections upward through your whole body. Easy, isn't it? Now look at someone else. Find one way in which you are connected. Look at all the drivers on the freeway and see that you are connected because you are all in cars, trying to quickly get from one place to another. Take a few minutes each day to play this game. Stretch the muscles of your mind by moving toward things or people whose connections aren't so apparent. After a few weeks check and see how you are feeling about connections. Is there a difference between how you perceive the world now and when you first began the game?

I tremble with bliss, remembering the words of the Divine Mother. Oh, my darling, come to Me. You have always been Mine.

HINDU DEVOTIONAL SONG

Devotion without knowledge can make us co-dependent. We can develop an unhealthy lack of concern for ourselves. This doesn't free us. It creates more attachment. We project our feelings onto the object of devotion, making ourselves less worthy. Yet the mental power of understanding without the sweetness of devotion can also be an entrapment. The understanding can separate us rather than awaken us to the connection. We can see ourselves as separate from the object that is to be understood. Understanding and devotion together bring mindfulness to all our actions. With this pure attention all acts become sacred. With this attitude the heart opens and there is great joy.

WOMEN LOVING WOMEN

Women loving women, and expressing it "publicly," if they choose, is part and parcel of what freedom for women means, just as this is what it means for anyone else. If you are not free to express your love, you are a slave; and anyone who would demand that you en-slave yourself by not freely expressing your love is a person with a slave holder's mentality.

ALICE WALKER

We deny freedom to others because of fear. Fear closes the heart and we project the fear onto others, trying to limit their behavior because it is different from ours or unacceptable to us. We split off into good, that's "us" and whatever we believe, and bad, that's "them" and their different beliefs. Why is lesbianism feared? I think most of us have loved a woman and can understand what it means to have a woman be the primary focus of our love and attention. We first knew gentleness and caring from a woman, usually our mother, and as infants we perceived our mothers as all-powerful. Men have had this experience too and in an unconscious way may fear this power and feel unneeded. I think this fear is the basis of woman-hating, and lesbian-hating is an extension of that. There is a fear that if we don't limit lesbian behavior then more women will become lesbians. I don't think this is true. There will always be women who are lesbians, just as there will always be women who are bisexual and women who are heterosexual.

The present is a freely given canvas. That it is being constantly ripped apart and washed downstream goes without saying; it is a canvas, nevertheless.

ANNIE DILLARD

We have a responsibility to life. We have the potential, the divine, within us. It is up to us to unveil this divinity. Everything that exists in the world exists within a framework of change. Nothing is permanent. There are both painful and joyful circumstances in life. True co-creation is not attempting to force only pleasant circumstances. It is seeing the larger picture. Freedom comes from acceptance of all life experiences. With mindfulness, every circumstance can teach us; every situation has the potential to take us beyond the ego concerns to the full expression of our divinity.

We can use Dillard's image as a visualization to create more spaciousness in our lives. Imagine you are an artist, and walk into your studio. See before you a large, blank canvas. Pick up the brush and begin to paint your day. It isn't important whether you paint literally or symbolically. What is important is understanding you have a choice in how you respond to the circumstances of your life. Now put down the brush, leave the studio, close the door, and get on with your day. In the evening return to the studio and create the image again. This time, wash away the pictures you have created. Make peace with your day's thoughts and activities. Make amends if necessary. Now you can go to sleep leaving the canvas blank, ready for the next day.

SPIRITUAL CHALLENGE

On the one hand I felt the call of God; on the other, I continued to follow the world. All the things of God gave me great pleasure, but I was held captive by those of the world. I might have been said to be trying to reconcile these two extremes, to bring contraries together; the spiritual life on the one hand and worldly satisfactions, pleasures, and pastimes on the other.

SAINT TERESA OF AVILA

We tend to split our worlds. We label things as spiritual or as material. If we have chosen the spiritual life we try to renounce the material world but we are often unable to do so. The spiritual goals can appear unrealistic and far out of reach. We live in the world. Our spiritual practice is to remain in the world, not of the world. We can welcome all of life's situations as opportunities to practice being kind and loving. If we feel too deprived it is difficult to walk the spiritual path and if we have an overabundance of material goods, we become attached to comfort and convenience and aren't willing to change.

We in the United States have a great challenge. Many of us have much comfort and convenience while others are wandering homeless in the streets. Our task is to reconcile these extremes. To do so we need to renounce attachment. It is not pleasure we want to deny: it is the pursuit of pleasure that we need to transcend. When the goal of our life is no longer the pursuit of pleasure we are able to enjoy the pleasures we have without feeling guilty and denying the pain of those less fortunate. When attachment is lessened, there is greater energy to warmly embrace all of life. Compassion ripens and is extended to all.

Limitless love,
from the depths to the stars:
flooding all,
loving all.
It is the royal kiss of peace.

HILDEGARD OF BINGEN

The rigid protection of our national interests, property, and welfare through armies and weapons will not bring us lasting peace. The rigid protection of our own interests in personal, one-to-one relationships won't bring us peace either. It is only the openness of love, the warmth and caring for each individual—making no individual more important than another—that will bring peace. It's easy to see how to care for those we love. It isn't as easy to show care for those we don't love. What this says is that what we call love is often mixed with much self-interest. If other persons are doing what we want them to do, then we love them. When we are displeased or disappointed with others, then we withhold love.

This dynamic is operating whether we're talking about individuals, groups, or nations. Peace will come when we are willing to take risks and express loving-kindness regardless of our personal interests. Loving opens us to a wider range of creative options for reducing conflict and thereby achieving peace. The solutions we arrive at when we have the interests of peace and both parties at heart will look entirely different than when we are pursuing our own selfish interests. As long as we are focused on getting the best for ourselves, we will run into conflict. We'll meet someone else operating in that same mode, and eventually the self-interests will collide.

ANGER

The trouble with anger is that it makes us overstate our case and prevents us from reaching awareness. We often damage our case by anger. It is like resorting to war.

ANAÏS NIN

Anger, one manifestation of fire energy, creates some positive but temporary changes. It is strong energy that enables us to take action we hadn't thought possible. Change in itself can be threatening, and if we are filled with anger when making the change, it creates confusion. Anger scares people and makes them angry in return, and the heat of anger can repress any kindness or connection we may feel. Then no one is heard. No one is in control. The anger controls. When anger controls us, our behavior becomes extreme. We have no space to see alternatives or more skillful ways of relating to difficult situations.

Here are some alternatives. Work with the energy of anger and see its potential for transformation. Feel, acknowledge, and accept this energy. It is okay to feel angry. Continue to work with the energy by using physical movements to disperse it; by asking a friend to be a witness as you speak the anger; by sitting, breathing, watching, and feeling the anger. Use visualization as a tool. Watch the anger pouring into the Earth and being transformed into energy with which you can make skillful changes. Now breathe in that transformed energy and you are ready to act, if necessary, with clear, calm, and compassionate energy.

Who says it is easy? But we have the power.
I watch the faces deepen all around me.
It is the time of change, the saving hour.
The word is not fear, the word we live,
But an old word suddenly made new,
As we learn it again, as we bring it alive:
Love. Love. Love. Love.

MAY SARTON

These lines from a poem entitled "AIDS" written by May Sarton powerfully depict a remembering, a relearning, of the power of love. We did not need AIDS, or any other disease for that matter, to teach us this. We don't contract a disease because we are lacking certain qualities, such as the ability to forgive, even though while having the disease we may develop these qualities. What is important to note is that mindfulness of any situation or condition brings forth wisdom and compassion. When we become mindful, we pay attention to what is needed in the moment and allow this knowledge to become conscious. We open to a wider range of possibilities. In the opening there is a release of whatever has hidden this inner knowledge.

PEACE

We will have peace, we will because we must
We must because we cherish life
And believe it or not as daring as it may seem
It is not an empty dream.

HOLLY NEAR

These words taken from a song by Holly Near, a singer and dedicated peace worker, speak the truth. Peace is not a fantasy. It can be achieved and will be achieved when we cherish all life. Too often our lives are run by fears. We fear difference and deny our connections to all life because of this fear. When the connections are denied, then we find it acceptable to destroy what we perceive as different and therefore threatening. Once we awaken to the interconnectedness of all life, we will cherish life. Those who cherish life do not harm life. When we no longer harm life, we will not create wars. We will invest as much time, energy, and money into finding creative and peaceful solutions to our differences as we do now to building military defenses and using war as the solution to problems.

War and violence only beget more war and violence. To create peace we must make peace a priority. We must choose leaders who make peace a priority. It must be a personal decision for each of us—to choose peace rather than arguments in our personal relationships. We must look at all our actions and ask, Will this create peace and harmony or conflict?

Mother earth, sister sea,
giving birth, energy,
reaching out, touching me lovingly.

MIRIAM THERESE WINTER

Mothers and motherhood have received a lot of "bad press" in Western culture. For years modern Western psychology blamed the mother for whatever difficulties the child encountered. As mothers we can and do make many mistakes, some of them seriously harmful. There is no attempt here to deny this pain. But the criticism is not merely a call to correct our honest mistakes. It comes from a deep fear and hatred of woman. This fear is calling for transformation. Mother love, the passionate all-embracing love that supports and transforms life, is the power we need to bring to the world today. Miriam Therese Winter's song expresses a consciousness we need to awaken: the knowledge of the creative, spiritual power of woman, the power of the Earth, the clay that shapes our lives. Her words honor the feminine power of the sea, its deep mystery, its tides of change. It is this power we call out in song. Its touch is loving and gentle. It renews us.

TRUE HAPPINESS

Genuine happiness, security, and love aren't products of anything. And if they are dreams and ideas they are not genuine. They come uninvited when the mind is still and open, not engaged in the conflicting movements of self-centeredness. They arise unexpectedly when the mind is not in want or fear and therefore not in pursuit of anything.

TONI PACKER

Raised in America, a country that has more consumer products than anywhere in the world, it is radical to suggest that our dreams and happiness don't come from products. Happiness isn't about acquisition. Toni Packer's words fly in the face of everything we've been taught about success. Where does happiness come from? Happiness is a state of mind.

It is true we need social action programs. We need laws to ensure equality and civil rights. Yet programs and laws alone won't effect the radical transformation our society needs. What is needed is a change of heart. This means every individual exploring the conflicts in her or his own mind. When inner conflict ceases, natural kindness and compassion will spontaneously be expressed. This caring will ensure the civil rights of all. This kindness will see that everyone has enough to eat. This caretaking will be demonstrated by people choosing to live in an ecologically sound way.

Take the time to pray—
it is the sweet oil
that eases the hinge into the garden
so the doorway can swing open easily.
You can always go there.

LYNN PARK

Praying is a means to attuning or bringing oneself into alignment with the power of the universe. We have often used prayer to plead with someone or something we thought outside ourselves and/or larger than ourselves. We hoped our prayers would be answered. We hoped because we feared. Without fear there is no need for hope. As we continue to mature spiritually we begin to grow beyond hope and fear. It is prayer that eases the way. We open our hearts in gratitude for the power of the universe, for the largeness of life. Gratitude opens us. We open into the universe. We breathe the universe and the universe breathes us.

Play with gratitude. Begin each day with a prayer of thanks. Whisper a simple thanks to the Goddess, to the universe, or to the spirit of love. Counting your blessings is another way of understanding prayer. It is grateful recognition that opens us.

ATTENTION

*True attention is rare and totally sacrificial. It demands that we
throw away everything we have been or hope to be, to face each moment naked of identity, open to whatever comes and bereft of human
guidance. . . . Another name for such full attention is love.*

FLORA COURTOIS

When I was young I was an avid reader, as I am now. I
would become totally absorbed in a book and not hear the
noise around me. In those moments I gave away my personal
identity, and I became larger than myself. A child's play is
practice for becoming an adult. We try on different identities.
As we grow older our identity becomes more firmly established. If we identify with our wants, our needs, our likes and
dislikes, the identity remains small. We'll become easily distracted or conflicted when meeting with difference. If we are
willing to approach each situation in an open way, without
clinging to our personal opinions, thoughts, and beliefs, we
become as large as life. We become love.

In Women's Sacred Mystery School and on retreats, one of
the ways we practice full attention is in the council circle. In
council, a stone is passed around the circle and the woman
holding the stone has the opportunity to speak. The only verbal response she is given is the Native American prayer phrase
"Aho" after she speaks. It affirms it is so. In the beginning it is
challenging to be the silent witness. Gradually it becomes a
meditative act and the whole circle experiences the silent
attention as love.

If we appreciate and respect the children that we were, the spirit of the child within each of us can emerge.

FLORA COLAO

Thousands of people are working to heal their inner child. This work entails confronting the painful and abusive aspects of their childhood. Adults who were physically or sexually abused, or who suffered emotionally from neglect or verbal ill-treatment, as well as any person interested in reclaiming curiosity, creativity, and the ability to play, are being healed through this vital work. All of us carry some embarrassment or shame from the past, whether or not it is conscious—times when we felt small and powerless. Our work involves more than healing the past abuse. It also looks toward remembering or re-creating a space of spontaneous delight in the world.

The inner child is healed through the cultivation of an unselfconscious attitude so we are able to relate to the natural world with curiosity and wonder, are able to take risks, and are willing to learn and grow. As we become attuned to that child's spirit and forgive ourselves for feeling clumsy, powerless, or ashamed, the natural loving connection and curiosity for life can re-emerge. When we can respect the child within us then we can reach out to the children of the world, making the world a safer and more welcoming place for all.

TRANSFORMATION

This feeling of being loved and supported by the Universe in general and by certain recognizable spirits in particular is bliss. No other state is remotely like it. And perhaps that is what Jesus tried so hard to teach: that the transformation required of us is not simply to be "like" Christ, but to be Christ.

ALICE WALKER

What a privilege to attend a concert of Sweet Honey in the Rock. This African American women's ensemble sings unaccompanied except for body and hand percussion instruments. Seeing these women is a visual feast and when they open their mouths, there is sweet power. The women speak and sing of incredibly painful conditions on this Earth: the oppression peoples of color endure daily because of the racist mentality that dominates the world; the struggles that women continually face to feed their families, to achieve self-respect, to stop rape and battering. Yet, there is no despair here. There is enormous energy. We are inspired and invited to make the changes necessary to make this planet a safe and welcoming home for all peoples, all races, and all creatures.

Bernice Johnson Reagon, the founder of the group, is courageous and creative in her work to transform racist attitudes. She speaks of building bridges, telling us it isn't comfortable work, and if we are comfortable, we aren't building bridges. This is the radical transformation that Jesus called upon us to perform. We must be willing to confront our conditioning: the fears, hatred, and prejudice. It isn't comfortable.

Mind like still water,
I'm naturally at peace.
Always calm yet ever alert,
I make good progress.

CUI SHAOXUAN

The Tao, the way of universal harmony, teaches us about the process of becoming human. First there is openness, openness becoming spirit and spirit becoming energy and energy becoming blood and blood becoming form. First there is the infant, then the child, the youth, the elder, and death. When you practice the Tao and become aligned with universal harmony, this process is reversed and immortality is possible. This doesn't mean you live forever in the same physical body. It is a way of saying you have a great understanding of energy—its source and manifestation.

Cui Shaoxuan was a Taoist practitioner who shared with us the secret of peace. Random thoughts in the mind create heat and are disturbing. When the thoughts settle we are peaceful. Without thoughts we don't become passive or unable to act. We become open and clear. This gives us greater energy to act and respond in appropriate and harmonious ways.

BREAD AND ROSES

JULY 12

Motheroot

Creation often
needs two hearts
one to root
and one to flower   *against winds of pain*
One to sustain   *the fragile bloom*
in time of drouth   *that in the glory*
and hold fast   *of its hour*
                     affirms a heart
                     unsung, unseen.

MARILOU AWISKTA

    I love Marilou Awiskta's image of the two hearts. I believe that women have two hearts. One heart is our womb, made of the same type of smooth muscle that the heart in our chest is made of. When we are rooted to the Earth, when our belly is strong, it supports the opening of the heart in the chest. Our creative energy lies in the belly bowl, in the second chakra. When the belly chakra is opened the creative energy can rise through the spine, opening the heart, and flow upward into the creative center in the throat.

    In Cambridge, Massachusetts, where I lived during the seventies, Bread and Roses, one of the first women's restaurants, was opened. Its name was a reminder that women need both bread (the roots that sustain us and enable us to endure) and the fragile, short-lived beauty of the rose. Let us pray this day that all women everywhere have bread and roses, that the hearts and bellies of all people are filled.

TRANSFORMATION

This very point when "I want" has been frustrated is the 'gateless gate'—because the only way to transform "I want" into "I am" is to experience one's disappointment, one's frustration.

CHARLOTTE JOKO BECK

Most of us believe that happiness comes only from having our needs met. We may feel successful at meeting our needs or resentful that many are left unmet. Our life experience is usually a mixture of both. Whatever level of success we experience, we all live with a fluctuating level of frustration. It exists whether or not we are aware of it. Even those who are successful have this frustration because one's needs are continually changing. More needs keep arising. We may meet our needs now but fear for the future.

Intuitively we sense there is more to life than satisfying our personal needs. We've all experienced glimpses of the larger picture, have recognized something larger than ourselves. Although living this insight is a challenge, there is great joy and contentment in this realization. When we experience frustration, rather than running from it or denying it, we can begin to soften and open out into the larger picture. Let us cultivate contentment and be happy with what we are doing rather than only doing what makes us happy.

COMMITMENT

To understand is not as important as to be, because understanding in itself implies a separation, someone to understand and something to be understood. The knowing is within you, the flow of breath.

DHYANI YWAHOO

As Ellen Serber guides our yoga class into various asanas she reminds us, "The commitment is to the breath." Throughout the session we are reminded to focus on the breath, to be mindful of the bodily sensations, whether painful or pleasurable, and to keep coming back to the breathing. We notice where the breath is in the body. We don't force any change. We watch as the breath becomes labored or relaxed, we see when it is fuller or deeper. We see when the breath becomes more aerobic or when it is being held back.

Making a commitment to the breath is making a commitment to life. We notice the inner and outer landscape but we don't get caught up in either. With a strong focus, we remain clearheaded. Ellen would invite us to receive the next breath "with joy" and release the breath "with joy." Breathing in this way, living in this way, we are one with the fresh, abundant flow of life.

Make a commitment to the breath. If you wear a watch, set it to beep every hour. Use that beep as a reminder to come back to the breath. If you don't wear a watch use the ringing of the phone or some other sound in your environment to serve as a reminder.

Sacred Corn Mother come to me
Make my way sacred, fill me with beauty
That I may bring others beauty.

LISA THIEL

Lisa Thiel's chant reminds us of the truth that we are gifted with beauty, with energy, and with power. In the Native American tradition the direction of south is the place of the Corn Mothers. We pray to become like the Corn Mothers. We pray for abundance, knowing that the more we have, the more we have to give. Our gifts aren't for our personal use alone. The gifts we have, our abundance, are shared so that the hearts and bellies of all people are filled

TRUE SELF

What if we smashed the mirrors
And saw our true face?
What if we left the sacred books to the worms
And found our True Mind?
What if we burned the wooden Buddhas?
Gave the stone Buddhas back to the mountains?
Dispersed the gurus with a great laugh
And discovered the path we had always been on?

ELSA GIDLOW

The running, hiding, and denial that has become so much a part of life often stems from fear of our true self. Our culture's methods of childrearing and education have contributed to the problems of self-doubt and lack of self-esteem many of us face. We have donned masks to cope with the feelings that we're not good enough or have to be different from who we are. When we look into the mirror we see the mask. What is hidden behind the mask?

One way to discover what lies behind the mask is to notice when the behaviors or attitudes of other people upset us. Those traits that are most upsetting in others are often part of us. The courage to see ourselves for who we are will transform the behaviors, attitudes, and beliefs that hide our true faces. To find that beauty, we must take off the masks. Who is willing to smash the mirror and see the true face?

*To have courage for whatever comes
in life—everything lies in that.*

SAINT TERESA OF AVILA

Western culture is filled with messages concerning the attainment of the perfect life. It is a life of ease, filled with material abundance. Whether we follow the puritan ethic of hard work or the new age method of affirmative thought, we are told we have within our power the ability to bring ourselves material abundance, the best of health, the perfect partner. These two philosophies seem like opposite ends of the spectrum yet they often lead us to two common problems. First, hard work and affirmations don't always bring the same results for women, poor and working-class people, and people of color, that they sometimes do for white men. Second, both hard work and affirmations can lead us to become manipulative and greedy. Those who are different from us are viewed as competitors or enemies who might try to take what we have. We use precious life energy trying to control all of life's circumstances to our personal advantage.

The courageous heart is one that openly accepts and works with all of life's situations. Every situation, whether it brings us happiness or sadness, is a potential gift, because it brings us energy that we can use to transform our conditioned mind. It is this transformation that brings true freedom.

GOODNESS

*The self—at one and the same time the self of all living creatures, and
therefore my self knows no bounds; so the entire universe is within
me, and my self fills all the universe. Everything that is—I am! In
everything I love, I love my self, for the only things we think we don't
love are what we haven't yet come to recognize within ourselves!*

ELISABETH HAICH

There exists within every human being a core of goodness.
An image I sometimes use to express this goodness is that of a
golden ring. It is the potential within us that is seeking to creatively and lovingly express life. When we are in love with
someone and we see this core within them, it makes us feel
wonderful. We love our partner and we love ourselves more
because of this. This is the energy that makes lovers seem to
glow. We don't need to limit the recognition of this golden ring
to our lover alone. We can move toward the recognition and
amplification of this golden ring in all people. This core is
boundless. Whenever this golden core is released it generates
good deeds, acts of kindness, and compassion.

Relax and imagine traveling very deeply within yourself.
Dive deep into the ocean of life until you come to a cave at the
bottom of the sea. In that cave is a ring of gold. Once you
touch this gold you can never lose it. Reach out now and take
the ring into your hands. Hold it to your heart as you swim
back to the shore. When you return you realize that the gold is
no longer in your hand; it is embedded in your heart. Imagine
that you are now filled with golden light and as you go
through your day you breathe this light and it surrounds you
and all beings. Notice your feelings, thoughts, and actions as
you go through the day encircled by this golden glow.

Taking refuge in the buddha, the dharma, and the sangha does not mean finding consolation in them, as a child might . . . in Mommy and Daddy. Rather, it's a basic expression of your aspiration to leap out of the nest, whether you feel ready for it or not, . . . It expresses your realization that the only way to begin the real journey of life is to feel the ground of loving-kindness and respect for yourself and then to leap.

PEMA CHÖDRÖN

When I left the spiritual community I had been a part of for many years I felt like a fledgling bird being pushed out of the nest. I didn't know if I was ready. I did know that for the time being I could not continue the relationship with my teacher and the community in the same way I had in the past. What I carried with me was the realization that I would reap the effects of my actions. Everything else was temporary. There was nothing I could cling to, not even the teacher or the teachings themselves. I could play with the question "Should I have left the community or should I have stayed?" in a way that evoked regret, blame, uncertainty, or despair. I could be angry at the circumstances. I could praise myself for making the right decision or castigate myself for making the wrong decision. Or I could make another choice. I could live the question. I could allow the question of staying or leaving to rest in my mind whenever it arose. I could become the gentle witness and allow the question to ripen. Working in a mindful way, the question of staying or leaving no longer became important. What is important is how I relate to myself and my present situation. Am I relating with loving-kindness to this unfolding process of life?

LOVE

Even when a river of tears
courses through
this body,
the flame of love
cannot be quenched.

IZUMI SHIKIBU

When we are alight with the fire of love, times of great sadness, pain, or disappointment cannot diminish that love. The connection to the source of life is so strong that it infuses all our actions. This doesn't mean that people who live from their source don't have grief or sadness. We all do. We can call forth courage and kindness even in the roughest of times when we see beyond the pain of our small self.

We often mistake pleasure for love. We think we love someone when actually we mean that what they do pleases us. Discussing this distinction with my friend Jodi she explained, "I'm very pleased when someone does show sensitivity and other wonderful characteristics and I'm not surprised when I see someone exhibit what I call 'feet of clay,' which used to cause me great disappointment." Jodi is fortunate. She loves beyond disappointments. The loving spirit isn't dampened when we experience our human failings.

That law (the Dharma) is such that every act we make, every word we speak, every thought we think is not only affected by the other elements in the vast web of being in which all things take part, but also has results so far-reaching that we cannot see or imagine them. We simply proceed with the act for its own worth, our sense of responsibility arising from our co-participation in all existence.

JOANNA MACY

The other night I watched a rerun of *Cagney and Lacey,* a TV series about two women detectives in New York City. Cagney and Lacey run into a group of people making a porn film. Cagney doesn't want to arrest the filmmakers because in the past the arrests never held. She figures it would be a waste of time and it was a victimless crime. Lacey believes there are victims. Later in the show Lacey gives an eloquent talk to one of the female actors who had been beaten and raped during the filming. Lacey wants her to think about what she was doing because the porn film would be seen by men who would think this is what women want. One of these men could eventually rape her daughter. The woman angrily replies, "Don't involve my daughter." "She is involved," Lacey argues heatedly.

Believe that your actions count. Know that your actions have an effect on other people and on the environment. Think about the kind of effect you want to have now and unto seven generations.

SHAME AND PAIN

Shall we grow one day wise enough
to love the way we long to,
to bleed away the fears that keep us green,
to change the vapors of shame,
and burn finally
into something else altogether?

SUE SILVERMARIE

We have all felt shame and pain. It isn't necessary to remember each doubt, insult, pain, or humiliation that has
added to the wall around our hearts. It is enough to know that
the wall exists. These feelings and experiences don't need to
keep us trapped. We can move through this pain to the love in
our hearts that is waiting to be expressed. This visualization
exercise will help purify the fear that inhibits love. Practice it
without worrying about the results. Let the fire do its work.
Imagine the flame of love burning at the base of your spine.
Breathe in and allow the fire to begin to rise up through the
spine. The flame burns brightly, bringing warmth and light to
your whole being. Breathe out and the shame, pain, and blame
leave your body in the form of smoke. Breathe in, letting
warmth and light fill the belly. Breathe out the smoke of
blame. Breathe in and the warmth and light of the fire rise
higher into the heart. Breathe out smoky fear. Breathe in; the
fire of love burns brightly in the throat. Breathe out the smoke
of shame. Breathe in and the fire of love warms and lightens
your head. Breathe out all pain. Breathe in and out as the fire
of love infuses your being. Your eyes see clearly, reflecting
great light. The flame has burned away the fears that keep us
green, leaving only warmth and light.

Thank you Mother Earth
Thank you Sister Water
Thank you for my birth
Thank you from your daughter.
Thank you brother sun
Thank you air in motion
Thank you everyone
Earth, Fire, Air and Ocean.

WOMEN'S ORAL TRADITION

This delightful song was created on a food line at one of the West Coast women's music festivals. We often sing it as grace at the Women's Sacred Mystery School or before early morning meditation.

One of the sure signs of a person who lives a spiritual life is gratitude. Such a person is filled with gratitude and it is this gratitude that brings joy. Without gratitude we can't receive what we have been given. Gratitude is thankful recognition for the precious gift of life. With this attitude one is thankful for the smallest things, a tiny blue wildflower, the rain after a dry spell, the moonlight that shines through the cracks in the roof, a stranger's smile. We can practice gratitude. To do this we give thanks for living through the night. We give thanks for the food we eat, the water we drink, the wind in our face, the sun on our skin. Each time we are mindful of what we have been given, a space is created within our hearts. We are open to widening our perspective and seeing more clearly, thus experiencing an ever-deepening joy.

COMMONALITY

JULY 24

The idea of commonality means standing exactly where you and/or your group . . . are, and noticing what part of you overlaps with others who are standing exactly where they are. . . . Commonality says that each element in the field equally matters and is centered in itself and in addition is in continual overlapping relation to every other element. . . . "What do we have in common" means how are we related. . . .

JUDY GRAHN

Too often we have fears in our relationships because we doubt that we will be truly seen or heard. We think that to eliminate conflict we have to feel, think, or act just like the other person. This mistaken idea has caused confusion and pain for many people. America's idea of the "melting pot" came from this fear of difference. America tried to make everyone accept the same white, male, middle-class, Anglo-Saxon values. Understanding how we are related means we can see and appreciate our differences while acknowledging our connections. To transform the melting pot into a beautiful kaleidoscope of dancing colors we need to neither minimize our differences nor deny our true connections.

To journey into this interior world within
love must already be awakened.
For love to awaken in us:
Let Go, Let Be, Be Silent, Be Still in Gentle Peace, Be Aware of
Opposites,
Learn Mindfulness and Forgetfulness.

SAINT TERESA OF AVILA

Here we are given a method for awakening love. We can't let love in while holding on to hurts and pain. Even when we clutch at pleasant memories we block the space for the heart's knowing to blossom. Let be. Change may not happen in the manner we would choose. If we can accept what we can't change, we are a step further in the awakening of love. Be silent. Instead of hurrying from one event to the next or from one thought to the next, listen quietly to the whisper of the trees or the song of silence. To be still in gentle peace we need to become aware of the parade of thoughts, judgments, hopes and fears that come and go in our minds. Hope and fear are a set of opposites: We only hope because we're afraid that what we want won't happen. Slow down and pay attention to the present moment. I am looking out my window and see the sunlight on the ivy leaves. I see the smile of contentment on my statue of Tara. When I absorb this I can bring the tranquility into all my actions, and let go of any pain.

When we forget our fear of not being enough, getting enough, or doing enough, we remember the truth of who we are and we are open to love.

DEEP SEEING

*If you take a flower in your hand and really
look at it, it's your world for the moment.*

GEORGIA O'KEEFFE

We may not have Georgia O'Keeffe's genius for painting,
yet we all have the potential to develop deep seeing. We can
develop this, as she did, by taking a long, close look at the
beauty of a flower. Take time to breathe deeply and look.
Bring all your attention, all your energy, to this flower. Let the
world outside the flower fall away. It will be there waiting,
with all its worries and demands, when you return. There is
only now, this moment, this flower. In our haste, we don't really see or absorb the beauty that is around us. Look closely.
Forget any other flower you have ever seen. Let this be the first
flower.

The God of curved space, the dry
God, is not going to help us, but the son
whose blood spattered
the hem of his mother's robe.

JANE KENYON

In order for our religious truths to transform the world they cannot be abstractions that we put outside ourselves, a pie-in-the-sky attitude. The truth must reach the nitty-gritty reality of daily life. There is pain in life. We can't change that. This is the richness of our lives; all that we experience can teach us, can transform us. What we can do is allow pain to break through the heart's defenses. We must allow it to touch us, like the "son whose blood spattered the hem of his mother's robe."

TRUE HAPPINESS

Yesterday, today and tomorrow, the days vanish one after another.
Does a splashing sound leave an echo? Only today is important. Suf-
fering from desire and delusion, most living beings are not free.

HER HOLINESS DAE HAENG SE NIM

People everywhere want happiness. Most of us are taught to seek this happiness outside ourselves. In the United States we call it the "American Dream." If we have the right job, live in the best house, have the perfect partner, buy the right clothes, then we will be happy. All of these things are temporary. With the present state of the economy, no job is secure. Our dream home could be destroyed through earthquake or fire. The perfect partner may leave us or we may become disillusioned when faced with their imperfections. The right clothes eventually go out of style or wear out. So we become disappointed and must continue our search to find a different job, a better partner, a new house.

Lasting happiness will only come when we are able to embrace all the circumstances of our lives with equanimity. When we accept what we have, whether or not we like it, there is no longer disappointment or tension from not having what we want or not wanting what we have. In the absence of this tension, we have greater access to the creative energy of life. In the absence of this tension we experience peace. And from this peaceful space joy arises.

Service was as much a part of my upbringing as eating breakfast and going to school. It isn't something that you do in your spare time. It was clear that it was the very purpose of life. In that context, you're not obligated to win. You're obligated to keep trying, to keep doing the best you can every day.

MARIAN WRIGHT EDELMAN

The ideal of service was similarly expressed in my family. "Actions speak louder than words," both parents were fond of saying. My mother gave fully of her time, energy, and talents. She was never too busy to bake cookies for a class party, sew uniforms for the cheerleaders, listen to the sorrows of a young mother, visit the sick or elderly, plant flowers for a community garden project. Our friends were always welcome in our home. No matter how little money there was, food could always be stretched to put an extra plate on the table. My father's life was also one of service—to his family, his church, and his community. Whether my father served as an usher at Sunday service or on the school board, or stopped during his workday to find a lost child or a home for one of my kittens, his life was lived according to this ideal: Do unto others as you would have others do unto you.

HUMILITY

*Humility says there were people before me who found the path. I'm
a road builder. For those who are yet to come, I seem to be finding
the path and they will be road builders. That keeps one humble.
Love keeps one humble.*

MAYA ANGELOU

Arrogant thinking is a deterrent to our spiritual growth.
The arrogant, self-centered person lacks a meaningful sense of
history. We need to take time to remember the people who
went before us and prepared the way for us. Our lives are
made a little easier because of their struggles. In the same way,
the lives of those who come after us will be easier because of
our struggles.

Politically, women have yet to win the struggle for equality.
Yet today we have more choices than our foremothers did. Let
us take a moment to remember the motherline. Relax, breathe
deeply, and let your mind travel back through the motherline,
in gratitude for those women who have gone before you.
Renew your strength and courage in this way.

Black mother goddess, salt dragon of chaos, Seboulisa, Mawu.
Attend me, hold me in your muscular flowering arms, protect me
from throwing any part of myself away.

AUDRE LORDE

I love Audre Lorde's prayer to the Black Mother Goddess, especially her use of the word *muscular*. The word *muscular* evokes an image of strength and power. I envision Mawu, strong and powerful, holding me and letting me know I'm all right just as I am. There is no part of myself I need to deny or hide or get rid of. Black Mother is fierce; she challenges me to face myself and the power that lies in my darkness. At the same time she nurtures me and invites me to nourish myself by allowing all of me to be. This gracious acceptance of self is truly empowering.

For the next few days call upon the Seboulisa to protect you as you sleep through the night. When you rise in the morning, greet Her with gratitude and ask for Her protection as you go through the day. Honor Her with a gift of flowers or fruit. Remember Her by sharing your good fortune with others. Make this prayer a mantra or an affirmation, and let it silently sing through your heart.

FREEDOM

Being in complete touch with each other means the absence of all division between "me" and "you." It is the absence of hurt and defense. It is freedom.

TONI PACKER

Have you ever noticed the difference in your responses when there is no defensiveness? When I'm in a grounded, openhearted space and my partner comes home tired and speaks abruptly, there's no pained or angry reaction. It doesn't bounce off me, it doesn't cut through me, it just goes into the air. If I'm tired or upset myself I might react. I sense an inner discomfort that isn't present when I'm open. The discomfort comes from the "me" who is tired and wants some attention or wants something different than what is happening.

If you have tasted the freedom from "me" and "you" then you have glimpsed a larger reality. This doesn't mean that we aren't human and don't have human responses to stress, or needs and desires. It means that there is a different place from which we can live our lives. Our self-centered nature is quite a formidable enemy and will struggle fiercely. It knows our weak spots, it will confront us when we are least aware. It takes strength to work with the conflicts that arise in the mind. This work is not about repressing the little mind or denying our feelings. We can't force ourselves to be different from who we are. We can choose to bring our attention to the larger picture. We can be mindful of the times we are closed down and not act out. We can focus on breathing, we can say a mantra. The less attention we give to the "me" the more room there is for the true nature to express itself.

We can all trace our roots to the Great Tree of Peace. Many roots, many nations, many religions, all on one Earth. And the root of that sacred Tree of Peace is also within our brain; the Tree of Life and the spiral of the DNA are symbols to remind us of continuity.

DHYANI YWAHOO

The hottest controversy in paleoanthropology today is what has been labeled the "search for Eve." Some paleoanthropologists believe that all human beings are descendants of a single woman who lived 200,000 years ago on the savannas of South or East Africa. This discovery was made by studying placenta samples and comparing variations between peoples of Asian, European, African, Australian, and New Guinean descent. Our genetic inheritance is passed through mitochondrial DNA, which we only receive through the mother. It is passed through the motherline, regardless of race.

While this research is exciting, it isn't necessary to wait until science has proven this link to recognize that as human beings we are part of a planetary family. We cannot wait for scientific discoveries or for the leaders of our governments to act. One way people have chosen to act is by joining organizations such as The Friendship Force, which sponsors American citizens who travel to foreign countries and are hosted by citizens of participating countries. Peace ambassadors strongly believe that whatever our racial heritage, we are all human beings and that creating cross-cultural friendships is a means of manifesting peace.

In honor of our planetary family breathe in, May I be peaceful. Breathe out, May all beings be peaceful.

WHOLEHEARTEDNESS

AUGUST 3

Wholeheartedness is a precious gift, but no one can actually give it to you. You have to find the path that has heart and then walk it impeccably. In doing that, you again and again encounter your own uptightness, your own headaches, your own falling flat on your face.

PEMA CHÖDRÖN

We have to choose to be present where we are, right now, in this moment. Only we can bring ourselves to this moment. In order to come to this moment we must leave behind the fears and doubts that take us away from the moment. Memories, regrets, fears, daydreams, and desires all drain energy. With this constant seepage of energy we are unable to be fully present. It takes practice to bring our full attention to the present moment. Being fully present is risky business. It takes enormous courage. We must risk making fools of ourselves, falling down and getting up, over and over again. No one can do this for us. As we continue our practice of falling down and getting up, we are purifying our bodies. We are cultivating openness. We are rewarded in that the openness extends itself and our vision is enlarged. Through our efforts we are given the gift of wholeheartedness. It is a gift of grace.

NO PRAISE, NO BLAME

Favor and disgrace are meaningless—
What's the use of contending?
Drifting clouds do not obstruct the shining moonlight.

WU CAILUAN

The light shines ceaselessly within us, waiting to be un-veiled, just as the sun shines always but is sometimes hidden by clouds. To unveil the inner light we must learn to shine like the sun, impersonally. We must shine because that is our true nature. We have no preference about who we'll shine upon or when we'll shine. We simply shine. It is challenging to practice this way of being. With courage, compassion, patience, and perseverance we learn to not take life so personally. Just as we learn to let a hostile comment roll off our back and not disturb our equanimity, so must we also learn not to let praise inflate us and disturb our equanimity. Both are ultimately meaning-less. There will always be those who are for us and those who are against us. If we are swayed by praise and criticism, our lives are in a constant uproar, and it becomes easy for us to be manipulative or manipulated. Living without attachment to praise or blame is living from the center of the heart.

WISDOM

Knowledge is not reality.
Experience belongs to the past.
Let those who lack immediacy be silent.
Let observers be content to observe. . . .

YOSANO AKIKO

Knowledge is often confused with reality. Knowledge helps us function in the world. We know how to drive a car, program a computer, knit a sweater, cook a meal. This knowledge helps us function in a physical world; it doesn't tell us about the ultimate reality of life.

All the experience we have comes from how we have related to situations in our past. Past experience is helpful in driving a car. We don't have to relearn each time we get behind the wheel. There is also a way in which experience can hinder us. When we rely solely on our past experience it can inhibit an accurate and appropriate response to a present situation. For example, we might rigidly hold to one way of doing things because it worked in the past. This prevents us from finding new, creative solutions to the present challenge. When a present situation reminds us of the past, the mind prevents us from seeing what is truly happening because it is clouded with old ideas and memories. In intimate relationships we often reenact old family patterns we learned from our parents. With our friends we reenact old patterns we learned from relating to our siblings. So we are reacting in a conditioned way. Keeping silent, being the witness, is often difficult to do. We think we're being helpful by giving advice. How can we truly know how another person feels or what we would do if we were in that situation?

We are all born of woman, in the rose
of the womb we suckled our mother's blood
and every baby born has a right to love
like a seedling to sun.

MARGE PIERCY

Over the last few years, several friends have gone to South America to adopt children. While I was pleased and happy for them, it brought up many questions concerning the right to take children from other countries and bring them to the United States. Was this yet another invasion by a "first-world country"?

I spent a day with one of the most recent adoptees. Just being with the sweet toddler and her mothers for a few hours reminded me that it is love and caring that are most important. The other adopted children I know are also loved and well cared for. All the parents continue to make efforts to keep in the home music, photographs, and objects from the children's homeland, as well as seeing that the children have loving connections with adults of their own racial heritage.

It is necessary to respect and celebrate the diversity of all cultures and races. It is equally important to remember that we are all born of woman. Dhyani Ywahoo, one of my teachers, would say that racial separation is one of the greatest illusions. We are a planetary family.

DIVINE LONGING

AUGUST 7

The woman I cry for smiles
right inside my heart.
My eyes go soft with surprise.

SUE SILVERMARIE

We are born with a longing for union with the divine. It is this longing that becomes the spiritual quest. The rituals, prayers, and religious traditions of the world serve to awaken us to the knowledge of our divinity. We travel far outside ourselves only to find that what we sought existed inside us all along. The spiritual search takes us on a spiral path. We have to get lost before we find this inner truth. This is the surprise and the wonder.

*The very word erotic comes from the Greek word Eros, the personi-
fication of love in all its aspects—born of Chaos, and personifying
creative power and harmony. When I speak of the erotic . . . it is an
assertion of the life force of women; of that creative energy empow-
ered, the knowledge and use of which we are now reclaiming in our
language, our history, our dancing, our loving, our work, our lives.*

AUDRE LORDE

Western culture, and we are not alone in this, is highly sex-
ualized. It makes sexual objects out of material possessions as
well as objectifying and harming women and children. Yet, we
are not a sex-positive culture. We may use sex to sell everything from cars to toothpaste, but we are not affirming of the
loving energy of life.

Women today are leading us in exploring and celebrating
this loving energy of life. Women are the birthers, the creators
of life. When we honor ourselves, we honor life itself. Women
are coming to this wisdom in many different ways. One way is
through the creation of a new vocabulary; we name or rede-
fine life energy. We are willing to explore this energy, to explore all aspects of ourselves, and to explore the diversity of
the whole circle of creation. Erotic energy, sexual energy, is the
creative energy of life. There is only one life energy. It flows
through all beings. We can use and abuse this energy. We can
tap into it and we can block it, but it is always present. When
we affirm this energy, Eros, love, the power to connect, we are
saying yes to life. We embrace all that life is.

KINDNESS

How should one live?
Live
welcoming
to all.

MECHTILD OF MAGDEBURG

It is easy to love or like those with whom we share the same religious, political, or philosophical beliefs. It is easy to like or find favor with those of the same race, culture, sexual orientation, or class background as our own. Most of us live as isolationists, tightly protected by our opinions, ideals, and attitudes. To be open to others would challenge the protection we have built around ourselves. Living life in a way welcoming to all is simply extending a basic level of kindness to everyone. We do not need to condone unethical behavior. However, if someone treats us in an unethical way, that does not give us the excuse to be unkind. Fears, selfish desires, and angry impulses prevent us from living as a friend to all. To follow these impulses doesn't make us bad. It just won't bring us happiness. The spiritual path is a rigorous training of the mind that enables us to turn away from such impulses. In this turning, love emerges.

Where the source of essence is clear,
The foundation of life is firm;
Turn the waterwheel nine times,
And the nine cauldron's complete.

CUI SHAOXUAN

The number nine in the Taoist system is associated with full development of the creative principle. The waterwheel is a Taoist exercise to circulate energy. Psychic heat is generated in the body through the psychic channels and is then visualized as traveling up the back of the spine and down the front of the torso so that it makes a complete circle, a wheel.

In the Cherokee tradition I studied in Sunray Meditation Society the number nine also signifies the realization of universal consciousness. An important part of the training in the Sunray Meditation Society is the Dance of the Four Directions. Each morning before sitting meditation we would do nine cycles of the dance.

Here is a Mindful Movement exercise: Bow to each of the four directions and move slowly from left to right around a circle. At each direction, step to the side with your left foot so that your feet are about three feet apart. Bring your palms together in front of your chest. Then stretch your arms above your head and slowly open them out to the sides. As you lower your arms, bend your knees in a deep knee bend. Then slowly straighten your legs and bring your arms back up, hands in prayer position at chest. Bring your right foot next to your left. Bow to the direction and turn by stepping with your left foot to the left. Bring your right foot to your left and you are ready to begin the movement again.

ATTENTION

To be absorbed in emptiness is not to know at all. In the radical unknowing of pure attention we sacrifice ourselves and discover our original wholeness.

FLORA COURTOIS

The sacrifice of the self that Flora Courtois speaks of is the sacrifice of the small self, the little mind. This is the ego that is attached to thinking that we know this or that or want this or that. It is the imposition of these ideas on our world that prevents us from seeing it as it truly is. We may see the beautiful spring flowers and for a moment be transfixed by their beauty. And in that moment we see. We see color and shape. Then we start thinking about the flowers: how the flowers are fuller this year because of the rain, or how much our friends would enjoy them, or remembering similar flowers from the past. Soon we are no longer present in the moment but off in fantasyland.

We can journey into the present by taking a deep breath and exhaling our memories. Just for a moment come to be where you are. Your feet on the Earth, the sky above your head, and the breath flowing. Who is breathing?

I do not like violence. So much has been done to me.
But having embraced my complete being
I find anger
and the capacity for violence
within me.
Control
rather than eradication
is about the best
I feel I can do.

ALICE WALKER

How many times do we point a finger at someone, saying that we would never act like that? As long as we see perpetrators of violence as totally different from ourselves we will continue to distance ourselves and deny our own violence. I don't believe we'll ever end violence until we come to the realization that violence is within each of us. When feelings are denied, they become out of control. The uncontrolled, untrained mind is dangerous. It is ruled by violence, greed, and hatred. When we are willing to see our own violence, our own hatred, our own fear, then we can learn not to act on it. Violence will never end violence. Only nonviolence will.

PRACTICE

Do not be dismayed, daughters, at the number of things which you have to consider before setting out on this Divine journey, which is the royal road to Heaven. By taking this road we gain such precious treasures that it is no wonder if the cost seems to us a high one. The time will come when we shall realize that all we have paid has been nothing at all by comparison with the greatness of our prize.

SAINT TERESA OF AVILA

Practice is tough. It can be discouraging. We fall down so often we wonder if we'll ever get up again. Some of us don't even start. It feels too scary to go for something we aren't sure is possible. We are pulled by life's pleasures, trying to obtain those that seem within reach. We are fortunate to have had great mystics such as Teresa of Avila who have followed the path to the end and discovered the prize. We can imagine Teresa and all those who have gone before us as cosmic cheerleaders, cheering us on through the pain and discouragement.

During a retreat at the High Desert Vipassana Retreat Center, one of the retreatants shared her experience after a movement meditation. She had played with the edge of her pain, choosing to work with her desire to run away by assigning herself five more minutes each time she wanted to leave. In that way she kept softening and opening to the pain. She said, "When I go home I won't be able to explain this to anyone. People would just ask me why I forced myself to do this when it was so hot and I was tired and in pain. They would think it was natural for me to want to leave and okay to do so." This is the discipline that we willingly undergo when we are working to transform the conditioned mind.

As writers we are always seeking support. First we should notice that we are already supported in every moment. There is the earth below our feet and there is the air, filling our lungs and emptying them.

NATALIE GOLDBERG

As women we receive conditioning that discourages our own strength. We are taught to look outside ourselves. In the struggle to name ourselves, to trust and empower ourselves, discouragement is a frequent companion. We've looked to other people, institutions, and governments, none of which has been effective. What if there isn't anything inside to support us? The inner journey asks that we see ourselves, not alone and isolated, but in the context of a full universe. This deep looking exposes the support that has been present from birth. We are held on this Earth by gravity, the force of the mother's love. The Earth is beneath our feet. The air supports us. We could only live minutes without it. To fill with air, to be inspired, filled with spirit, this breath is the gift of life. It is quite wondrous to experience the continuous support that is always available to us. In this way we are one with all creation.

JOY

The holy life cannot work without joy. It's as if it were yeast in bread. Without joy the holy life cannot rise to its full height. So enjoy every moment and especially the effort.

AYYA KHEMA

Polishing ourselves and bringing out the best in ourselves involves mistakes. The going will be rough at times. If the journey is joyless, it isn't a spiritual journey. It becomes a striving for something, a grasping in the way we grasp for material objects or people or situations. The holy life is concerned with the journey, not the goal. Those who share a puritanical heritage may think the spiritual life is hard and spare, that there is much effort and little joy. Reward will come in some distant future. In truth it is the spiritual life that brings great joy because it is a path of the heart. Discipline is needed; we need to put forth effort. The effort must be lighthearted. We can't be attached to our mistakes or any particular way of doing or being. We must be willing to fall down and get up, fall down and again get up, as though it is one movement. If we focus on the goal and think we can't be happy until it is reached then we'll never be happy. To make life whole, to make life holy, we bring a sense of equanimity to all life's challenges. We learn to laugh at ourselves, to not take ourselves so seriously, and to get back up when we stumble. This brings us joy. Joy makes life whole and holy.

Human beings are set apart from the animals. We have a spiritual
self, a physical self and a consciousness. Therefore we can make
choices and are responsible for the choices we make. We may choose
order and peace or confusion and chaos.

ROSA PARKS

One of my teachers, Lama Zopa, would often speak of the
pain of the animal realm. Animals don't have choices. Animals
spend most of their time trying to get food and protect themselves from other animals. They are used by humans as beasts
of burden or killed for food. Their lives are basically unsatisfactory because they can't choose to do other than what they
are doing. The Lama told us that human beings are most fortunate. Human life is a precious gift because we can make
choices and we have the opportunity to study the Dharma, the
law of interconnectedness, understanding, and love.

Rosa Parks, in her refusal to give up her bus seat to a white
man, made a choice that changed the course of human history.
Her action sparked a 381-day bus boycott, which ignited the
civil rights movement. She refused to deny her humanity and
her divinity, even if the dominant white culture refused to recognize it. Choice is a precious human opportunity. Will the
choices we make create peace or conflict? Will the choices we
make recognize the sacredness of all life?

GRATITUDE

AUGUST 17

Sometimes I'm overcome with gratitude . . . and feel that each of us has a responsibility for being alive: one, responsibility to creation, of which we are a part, another to the creator—a debt we repay by trying to extend our areas of comprehension.

MAYA ANGELOU

What a marvelous attitude! This is an antidote to the poisonous idea that the world owes us a living. Maya Angelou is speaking clearly, there is no guilt here. She recognizes the beauty and gift of life and does what she can to not only conserve and care for life, but to make it better. There is much laziness today. We see things that are beautiful and assume they are for our use. But we abuse them, instead of protecting and caring for them. I am impressed by her goal to comprehend better and more deeply. This is simple and it is enough.

The flowering of our practice is to see the whole range of experiences come and go. The potential for awakening is as existent and alive in any one of us as it was in the Buddha.

SHARON SALZBERG

There is plenty of love, goodness, and courage in the world today. These qualities are deep within the consciousness of every person. Our work is this: We must remove the impediments that have been built up by years of biological conditioning, shaking loose all the resentments, fears, and selfish desires. How do we remove the impediments? We can't force ourselves to be less fearful or selfish. As our practice deepens we become aware of our feelings and internal reactions. The next step in practice is to experience the bodily sensation that accompanies fearful, angry, and painful thoughts and feelings. There is always a contraction in the body. We learn to move from our thoughts to the experience. It may be a subtle tightening of the jaw or pressure in the chest or tingling of the skin. We don't try to remove or force anything. We keep coming back to our experience again and again. Simply experiencing, experiencing. In time (and it may take years) love will begin to flow from us, like water from a fountain, and all will be refreshed.

SANGHA

You need companions to travel
To the Isle of Immortals—
It is hard to climb
The azure cliffs alone.
If you take dead stillness for refinement,
The weak water brimming
Will lack a convenient boat.

SUN BU-ER

The Isle of Immortals is the legendary abode of the Taoist adepts. While we may never abide in this space, we do need to have the support of spiritual companions, whatever path we are following. As individuals we have an enormous capacity to fool ourselves. Our egos can function like tricksters and we can easily become lost in delusions. The *sangha,* or spiritual community, supports and challenges us.

One illusion is mistaking dead stillness, which is a stagnant state, for realization. We may appear peaceful and still but we are actually in denial. The stillness, the peace that we wish to open to, is a vibrant state, receptive and alive, able to respond appropriately in every situation. In Taoist philosophy weak water refers to not being able to hold any weight. So if we are weighed down by blocked energy, by attachments, by fear, then we aren't light enough to cross the water.

The next time your ego bumps into another ego take a deep breath. Before speaking or acting, reflect on what inside you is causing the conflict. Two prime times for bumping egos are when we are tired or hungry. If neither of these is the cause, then gently look deeper.

ENLIGHTENMENT

Though the mystic mechanism is right before us,
We need to look for it;
Only when you set eyes on it do you know
The depths of the ultimate design.

TAN GUANGZHEN

Tan Guangzhen was a realized Taoist practitioner from the twelfth century. Her poem reveals the paradox that enlightenment is within us yet lies there undiscovered. We need to look, that is, we need to put forth effort to bring it out. Dhyani Ywahoo, one of my teachers, uses the image of a treasure chest, filled with jewels. These treasures exist in our hearts. The first jewel is the diamond light of clear mind. Here we realize ourselves within the sacred flow of life. The second jewel is the ruby, the light of compassion. When this jewel is discovered so is the wisdom of forgiving and the wisdom of generosity. The third jewel, the yellow topaz, is the light of right action. When discovered, this jewel affirms our willingness to act in harmony with all creation. While this knowing is inside us we must practice diligently to bring it forth. We undertake training to accept responsibility for our lives. We can no longer blame others for our confusions and mistakes. We must learn to forgive, to release pain, shame, and blame. We practice generosity, sharing what we have. We must make peace a priority and work in harmony with all of life.

GODDESS

Lover-beloved, Woman
Small and strong in my arms
I know in you
The Goddess
Mystery
Fecund emptiness
From which all fullness comes
And universes flower.

ELSA GIDLOW

Let us make one day a week Goddess Day, a time to celebrate the Goddess in ourselves and in everyone we meet. Begin the day by greeting yourself in the mirror with a bow. Look into your eyes and reflect back as much love and caring and compassion as you can. Imagine love filling your whole being and that as you breathe out you are sending love out into the universe. Inhale again and fill with compassion, letting it move through your body, and as you exhale send it out. The energy is constantly moving through you. There is always enough.

Each person you meet today will receive your silent bow, your silent blessing. Mentally bow and silently say, I bow to the Goddess within you. Notice if this changes your interactions. The mental bow is a wonderful way to respond to someone who is challenging you by their angry, impatient, or uncaring behavior. It is a reminder that regardless of our behavior, we all have a divine nature. It gives us space to stop and respond mindfully, choosing words that are true, sensitive, and necessary.

Each woman has to know herself, her problems, her obstacles. I ask woman to take on intelligent responsibility for her development. I am not exonerating those who inhibited her evolution, but I want woman to realize she can be master of her own destiny. This is an inspiring thought.

ANAÏS NIN

Self-exploration is the way to self-knowledge, which opens into wisdom. In deep looking we penetrate the surface situation and see ourselves in a larger context. When I see myself in the broader context I know that I am part of a whole universe and that my needs are no longer more important or less important than anything else. The situation becomes impersonal, that is, it is not dictated by one's personal needs, likes, and dislikes. It is just a situation and we can respond creatively to it.

Here is an example of moving from a free or nonreactive state: One of my student's housemates was upset because she wasn't invited to a dinner the student was giving for some friends visiting from out of state. During the course of an extremely busy week, this dinner was the only event to which her housemate was not invited. The housemate blamed my student for making her feel uncomfortable and excluded in her own home. While my student could acknowledge her own frustration at being pulled into her housemate's scenario, she didn't have to act on it. She breathed through the tension in her own body and listened to her housemate's pain. She didn't need to feel guilty for not inviting her or justify her reasons. The housemate responded to my student's calm, realized her own reactions, and the problem was resolved.

JOYFUL ACCEPTANCE

A life of joy is not in seeking happiness, but in experiencing and simply being the circumstances of our life as they are.

CHARLOTTE JOKO BECK

A friend of mine had what she called the "red balloon theory." She used this theory to refer to people who weren't happy with what they had. They might have purple or green or blue balloons but it was never the color they wanted. They wanted a red balloon. We spend a good deal of time looking for that red balloon. The search always leads to disappointment.

Mindfulness of my back injury has given me a precious gift. It has taught me to find acceptance in my circumstances, whatever they are, especially on days when there are flare-ups. Rather than wishing I could be hiking a mountain trail, I have come to feel joy in listening to the sound of the wind chimes or watching the fading light of the setting sun. I have learned to become absorbed in the beauty of the sound or the light. The pain is still present but there is also a joy that comes from the gratitude of accepting what is here and possible for me now. Suffering comes from resistance, wanting to do something or be someone other than who I am.

Every moment lived in absorbed attention is simultaneously a begin-ning and an end, at once a birth and a death. In such attention we are radically open to the unexpected, to letting life live us. Any event, however small or seemingly trivial, properly attended, opens the door to infinity.

FLORA COURTOIS

Reading Flora's description of absorbed attention to some friends evoked shared laughter. We laughed because we were delighted with the truth Flora expressed. It is the small, seem-ingly trivial happenings each day that are so amazing. The problem is we don't stop to think about them. These moments tend to become one large blur because we are rushing forward to the next moment, the next activity. Paying attention stops the world. When we are awake, we notice the bright colors of the smallest wildflower or hear the sound of the crickets. Even the screech of the tire on the pavement can awaken us. This life is a feast for the senses if we are open to it. What makes it ironic is that in our quest for pleasure we miss the beauty that is right before our eyes.

ILLUSION

When, with breaking heart,
I realize
this world is only a dream,
the oak tree looks radiant.

ANRYU SUHARU

There are times I have felt the heaviness of depression that comes from grieving a loss or wanting things to be a certain way or wishing for something I didn't have. If I am open to experiencing the sensations of depression, such as its heaviness, and I can become a silent witness to it, I will receive a gift of grace. My heart breaks. I cry for myself, for all the losses, and for all those who are sad and despairing. As my heart breaks open and I feel the physicality of the pain I can see clearly the beauty that also exists in this ever-changing world. Then the oak tree is not clouded by any ideas, concepts, or judgments. It stands as it is. The oak tree is pristine in its beauty.

Holy Spirit, come into my heart,
by your power I journey to you, God,
and grant me charity with awe . . .

SAINT CATHERINE OF SIENA

Saint Catherine of Siena, a woman of humble birth, became an illumined teacher, a powerful writer, an incomparable orator, and a counselor of princes and pontiffs. The quote is part of a prayer she wrote after she miraculously learned to write. Her heart opened to a greater power and she acknowledged that it was through this greater power she was able to make this inner journey. She was praying for and acknowledging the gift of charity, which is love. She asked that this great love be filled with awe.

One of my favorite Lily Tomlin characters is Trudy, the bag lady. Trudy suggests that we practice "awe-robics," by taking time each day to appreciate something such as the beauty of the stars. Trudy says we're closest to understanding when we are in awe of what we don't understand. May our hearts open to a love that is awesome.

FREEDOM

Nothing
in the world
is usual today.
This is
the first morning.

IZUMI SHIKIBU

What freedom to be able to come to each day as if it were the first day of your life. One of the joys in my life was the opportunity to look and listen with my young children as they explored the world for the first time. Eager, curious, and with no preconceptions or expectations, they touched and tasted everything within their reach.

Put down this book and look at your hand. Look at it as though you have never seen it before. How does it move? Watch as it twists and turns. See the fingers one at a time. Play with each finger. Bend them this way and that. Feel the skin. What does it taste like? See this hand with awe and amazement and then deep gratitude.

in the northern mountains
Moon is a silver turtle
moving slowly through the stars

CHRYSTOS

Chrystos is a Native American woman who grew up in San Francisco, part of a group the government calls "Urban Indians." Her tireless work as an artist, writer, political activist, and speaker is directed toward better understanding how colonialism, genocide, class, and gender affect women and Native people. Through both her poetry and her activism Chrystos issues a thunder call to wake up. She shakes us out of our complacency.

When I read this poem, "Winter Evening," to a friend, her immediate response was, "I like the notion of the moon moving through the stars. My head knows the moon is close to the Earth and the stars are light years away. The image names a relationship between the moon and the stars that I don't usually think about." For me, the imagery turned the world upside down. Turtle Island is a Native name for the land Europeans call North America. We make our home on the turtle's back and in the sky above us another turtle crawls through the sky. The moon is a rock, spinning in space. She orbits the Earth and we who live below her can feel her magnetic pull. She causes the tides. The moon, with no light of her own, powerfully reflects the light of the sun. She plays with what is available to her. Does the silver turtle realize the deep and lasting satisfaction that can only come with the full acceptance of what is? Do you?

KINDNESS

What I want is so simple I almost can't say it: elementary kindness.
Enough to eat, enough to go around. The possibility that kids might
one day grow up to be neither the destroyers nor the destroyed.

HALLIE, a character in
BARBARA KINGSOLVER'S *Animal Dreams*

   On my walk today I saw a bumper sticker with Anne Herbert's words: PRACTICE RANDOM ACTS OF KINDNESS AND SENSELESS ACTS OF BEAUTY. Kindness isn't at the top of the list when we think of what is needed to alleviate many of the world's problems. We think of massive wealth, or large numbers of people actively organized, or government-funded programs. Yet it is simple kindness that can and does transform the world. There are countless ways to express elementary kindness: the smile, the touch of a hand, the phone call to say you care, the errand for a sick or elderly neighbor, the pot of soup for the new mother, or the planting of a community garden. Don't get lost in the global. Begin to change the world today with one simple act of kindness. Act as though this kindness were the most needed act in the world. It is.

All the deeds of life are creative, and bear within them the inner life-light, potentially. Artists need to see in this way. Lifting things and beings of the world into lifelight, or offering ourselves to them so that they may catch light from our inner flame, is artistic activity, is human activity.

M. C. RICHARDS

I was one of many proud moms and dads the day I attended my son's graduation from art school. Jake was the student speaker for his graduating class. He spoke of how his ideas had changed in the last four years. When Jake began his education he thought that his art would be a job that he held during the day. What he did at night would be his life, separate from his art. As Jake spoke he demonstrated his once polarized thoughts with two large flashcards labeled LIFE and ART. As he continued talking the life and art cards were separate, then interchangeable, until he reached his conclusion: Life and art are inseparable. Why is this so? Art, as Jake had come to understand, is not simply a medium such as painting or sculpture. "It is a mental state. An artist is someone who is continually learning. To question yourself is artistic. As artists we have a responsibility to bring the same process of exploration to all aspects of our lives. To be an artist is not to do art but to be art."

OPEN HEART

We need to retain an open heart so that whatever or whenever we do anything our action will be an act of love and compassion and nothing less.

DR. THYNN THYNN

The primary cause of friction in relationships is ourselves. We don't believe this, so we spend enormous amounts of time and energy trying to change the other person or trying to change our situation. If we truly understood how we act and react, then our relationships would undergo radical change. We can only experience a harmonious relationship with another person when we have a harmonious relationship with ourself. As long as we depend on another person for our well-being, our comfort, our emotional or intellectual support, that dependence will create fear and that fear will create sorrow.

When we are tranquil, people and situations can respond to us naturally. This kind of living and loving has tremendous power to create a harmonious and joy-filled life.

What I call innocence is the spirit's unselfconscious state at any moment of pure devotion to any object. It is at once a receptiveness and total concentration.

ANNIE DILLARD

One day a friend and I drove to Inverness and walked the Pierce Point trail. We spent several hours in the meadow watching the tule elk from a distance of about sixty feet. There was a herd of fifty females presided over by one huge bull with a great rack, who walked around and sniffed them and bellowed his mating call, which echoed over the ridge. The sound, which seemed to come from deep within his body, bore a faint resemblance to a horse's neigh but was deeper and felt more primal. The bull elk mounted several females, but each time he did, the female stood still for a moment and then walked away, appearing uninterested. The scene was peaceful. The herd appeared to be grazing as they might any day, yet the air was electric with promise. My friend and I became absorbed in watching this mating dance. We became so focused the world dropped away. It felt like we were in the center of the herd, part of the whole scene: the wind, the sun, the golden grass, the blue water of Tomales Bay below us. We lay among the thistles, breathing and watching, totally absorbed. In that moment we experienced our innocence, the original state of being one with creation

UNITY

*The dichotomy between the spiritual and the political is also false,
resulting from an incomplete attention to our erotic knowledge. For
the bridge which connects them is formed by the erotic—the sensual—those physical, emotional, and psychic expressions of what is
deepest and strongest and richest within each of us, being shared; the
passions of love, in its deepest meanings.*

AUDRE LORDE

In the 1970s this false dichotomy temporarily split the second wave of the women's movement. For a time, feminists
were labeled either political or cultural. The political feminists
were activists who took to the streets and demanded changes
for the enormous inequities in the dominant culture. The cultural feminists were concerned with self-healing and inner development, rituals and Goddess worship. During those years I
gave a public talk with a friend who was both a feminist and
an activist. It was a beginning attempt for us to dialogue and
develop bridges between the supposed polarities. We realized
that political action is inspired by a powerful concern, an
erotic connection with all life. Whether one person is harmed
or a group is harmed, we are all harmed.

One of the political slogans in the seventies was "We cannot be free until all women are free." Whether articulated or
not political work comes from this basis of concern for all life:
wanting equal care and equal rights for all Earth's children, regardless of gender, color, race, class, or sexual preference. The
urgency we feel for justice when seeing people denied freedom
for whatever reason, the longing for all people to share in the
bounty of the planet, comes from a kind, caring heart.

Although I try
to hold the single thought
of Buddha's teaching in my heart,
I cannot help but hear
the many crickets' voices calling me as well.

IZUMI SHIKIBU

Buddha means awake. It is waking up to the life that we are living and to the reality at the foundation of that life. It is to awaken from the illusion of a self that is separate from the rest of creation and know we belong to the power that creates and sustains the universe. The power of the crickets' call is not separate from the power of the Buddha's teaching. To be present for what is happening, even the sound of the crickets, is to know that the crickets' song is the Buddha's song, which is the song of the Goddess, which is the universal melody.

Here is an intensive listening practice that I have found helpful: Center yourself by bringing your attention to your breath. Now expand your attention to include sound. Listen to the smallest, quietest sound you can hear. Bring your full attention to that sound. When you return to your usual activities, take a few moments throughout the day to stop and listen for the smallest sound.

INNER BLISS

Machig appeared before me in the sky as a dancing red skeleton sur-
rounded by red gossamer scarves of energy. She said, "The experi-
ence of sexual union with an outer consort is something that can be
drawn forth from within yourself and need not depend on an exter-
nal partner. The potential for great bliss is always inside you."

TSULTRIM ALLIONE

While in meditation near Machig's cave in Tibet, Tsultrim Allione, practitioner and teacher of Tibetan Buddhist meditation, had a vision of Machig Lapdron. Machig was a beloved Tibetan woman mystic who originated the Chod practice, a practice that combines Buddhism and Shamanism, for the release of attachments and the cultivation of compassion.

In Tibetan practice the symbolism of sexual union is used as an analogy for spiritual bliss, since it is a more common experience. In her vision, Tsultrim was assured by Machig that we don't need an external partner; incredible reservoirs of bliss are to be found within. In our daily lives we tend to think that bliss or happiness lies outside ourselves, believing that it comes from union with another person. This bliss is only temporary and cannot compare with the greatest bliss that comes from within. Great bliss is experienced when we have actualized wisdom, insight, and compassion.

Perhaps the one certainty in life that I always come back to and that I find most reassuring is the knowledge of constant change; the certainty that spring will return. . . .

SONJA BULLATY

My son Mike and I once talked about similar feelings we had at the end of each summer. He went to school in Bar Harbor, Maine, and worked in a restaurant there during the summer. I grew up in a small New Jersey town on the Atlantic Ocean, and also did restaurant work during the summer season. We both experienced a sadness that seemed to hover in the air as the days grew shorter and the air became cooler. The fullness of summer was retreating and it was too soon to get into the faster moving energy of the fall. Each year, although we knew summer would return, we felt a transitory loneliness and loss at the change of season.

I remember saying goodbye to the beach each Labor Day. I would look back and reflect on the season's experiences. I did this summer's end inventory each year quite spontaneously. I appreciated the fun and acknowledged mixed feelings about the work. I felt a mixture of sadness at the end of another season as well as excitement and fear about the uncertainty of the future.

Now I see how fortunate I was to have been able to accept and explore my feelings. I was opening to a deeper understanding of impermanence.

BREATH

My roots are inside her
My roots extend to her center,
I draw her power up
Each long breath pulls up her power
sap through my trunk, my spine,
her life arising, arising in me.
Power bursts from the crown of my head
I feel it sweeping through my branches
in a gusty dance, up
and then down to touch the earth once more.

SUE SILVERMARIE

Hindus tell us that in the act of breathing, more important than the oxygen we inhale is the *prana,* the life force. It is this life force that keeps us alive. Yogis practice special breathing exercises to increase prana, which can be stored in the body for later use.

Try alternate nostril breathing to increase prana. Sit comfortably with the spine correctly aligned. Press the right thumb on the right nostril. Inhale deeply and smoothly through the left nostril to the count of five seconds. Close the left nostril with the fourth finger. Release thumb and slowly exhale through the right nostril to the count of ten seconds. Without releasing finger from the left nostril, inhale through the right nostril to the count of five seconds. Close the right nostril with the thumb and at the same time release the left nostril, exhaling to the count of ten seconds. This is one round of alternate nostril breathing. Practice a few rounds a day, gradually increasing the number of rounds as well as the length of the inhalations and exhalations.

We never lose an attachment by saying it has to go. Only as we gain awareness of its true nature does it quietly and imperceptibly wither away; like a sandcastle with waves rolling over, it just smoothes out and finally—where is it? What was it?

CHARLOTTE JOKO BECK

We live in a masculinist world where the active quality of mind has been overdeveloped to the extreme of aggression. Even those who are attempting to bring balance into their lives often continue to unconsciously operate in the forceful, masculine mode. The development of willpower enables us to have power over our attachments. We aggressively attempt to root out our attachments, to quickly change our limiting behaviors. Force begets force. The more aggressively we attack our weaknesses the more harm we do. The habit, even if changed, is soon replaced by another more strongly embedded. Our attachments lessen as we become aware of how attached we are. When we see the attachment, we don't resist it, force it, or deny it. Can we allow ourselves to be who we are— with all the attachments, limitations, and weaknesses? Softening and opening to who we are is love. As love grows, attachment lessens. It happens as part of the natural process of opening.

SHECHINAH

This generation is serving as the midwife for the rebirth of the Shechinah. . . . This Goddess who shines on us as we study sacred texts is found in redwood groves and apple orchards. She is coming to us in the wind and the water, in the ocean and the mountains.

RABBI LEAH NOVICK

In the Jewish mystical tradition there is a teaching called the "Shattering of the Vessels," which says that during creation, the divine light burst through vessels that were meant to contain it. Fragments of the divine light were scattered throughout the universe. These fragments were known as Shechinah, the feminine presence of God. Shechinah is now in exile from home, from the wholeness of divinity. This split from the sacred feminine has occurred in most spiritual traditions, and until the split is healed we will not know the fullness of either our human or divine potential. It is the present generation of women who are remembering the Goddess and calling her many names. When the Goddess comes home, we will have reunited the divided mind and achieved a full integration of the creative and receptive aspects of our being.

In the Native worldview there is no in or out; everyone in the circle is necessary for the benefit of the whole family of human beings and those that walk, crawl, swim, and fly. We are all relatives.

DHYANI YWAHOO

Can you imagine for a moment how the world would change if each of us believed, "I'm necessary for this planet. Who I am and how I think and feel are important. There's no one else who does it just like me. I'm truly needed." The key here is knowing that we are needed for the good of the whole planet. This is different from the self-inflated idea of thinking one is better than anyone else and working to get the best for oneself alone. In the Native view we realize our individual worth in relation to the whole community, the whole planet. We develop skills to share and to benefit the whole circle. Action manifested from an attitude of self-responsibility and a knowledge of co-creation will transform the world.

CREATIVE AND RECEPTIVE

The image of the creative is firmness,
The virtue of the receptive is flexibility.
Meditation is first sought in stabilization:
With a clear ladleful of the water of the jade pond,
Why should the bright moon
Need the adornments of seven jewels?

FAN YUNQIAO

In the *I Ching* the creative is activity, it is making. The receptive is openness, it is sensing. In Taoism, the creative and receptive represent energy and spirit. Meditation is the means for bringing spirit and energy or mind and breathing into harmony. Fan Yunqiao uses the image of the jade pond, which refers to the dwelling place of the Queen Mother of the West, the leading feminine immortal. The bright moon symbolizes pure awareness, and the "seven jewels" is a Buddhist expression referring to external adornments. This poem is yet another expression of the depth and beauty of pure awareness, which is far brighter than any jewels we could wear.

Imagine yourself climbing a mountain high into the clouds. At the top of the mountain, in a beautiful crystal palace, lives the Queen Mother. On the palace grounds is a sparkling jade pond. Drink a ladleful of water from the pond and then sit in stillness beside the clear water. Breathe deeply, allowing the fresh water to be a tonic for your mind, washing it clear of confusion and doubt. Breathe and enjoy the stillness. When the sitting is complete, rise, bow to the pond, and return down the mountain carrying the stillness within you.

SYMPATHETIC JOY

It's so clear that you have to cherish everyone. I think that's what I get from these older black women, that sense that every soul is to be cherished, that every flower is to bloom. That is a very different world view from what we've been languishing under, where the thought is that the only way I can bloom is if I step on your flower. . . .

ALICE WALKER

Matriarchal, or mother-wise, consciousness embraces all of life. This embrace is an acknowledgment of and respect for all life. From this respect comes a care that encourages the growth of every individual. We are raised now to believe that we must compete for life. For us to win, others must lose. Share has become a charged word. We are afraid that sharing means loss; in sharing we must give something away from ourselves. When we embrace all life, we are happy for the success of others.

We can learn to feel joy for another's success. It is the antidote to our competitive behavior. A first step is to become mindful of feelings of fear and scarcity. Whenever you have feelings of scarcity, notice how this manifests in the body. There may be numbing or sensations of tightness in the body. Notice your breathing. Is it shallow or rapid? Be kind toward your fear. Take a few deep breaths. It isn't necessary to try to make these fears go away. Bringing an interested and kind attention to the fear will gradually lessen it. A next step is to mentally repeat this phrase when you hear of the happiness and success of a dear friend: Your joy is my joy. Repeating this phrase even when your pleasure for your friend is mixed with your own needs will eventually soften and open your heart.

LAUGHTER

I weep a lot. I thank God I laugh a lot, too. The main thing in one's own private world is to try to laugh as much as you cry.

MAYA ANGELOU

The pursuit of success, whether it is material or spiritual, can turn life into a serious and grim adventure. In working for material success there is tremendous pressure to be faster and better than our competitors. So people tend to overwork and become burned out. And on the spiritual path we can get quite caught up with suffering, forgetting that joy is a necessity as well. A deep belly laugh has the power to shake loose troubles and pain. People that laugh easily don't necessarily have less troubles. What they do have is a lighthearted attitude that enables them to laugh at their own mistakes and at the trials and tribulations of life. Their laughter isn't a denial of pain. The same people probably have an easier time crying and expressing feelings of grief. Laughter is a healing balm. The open heart denies neither grief nor joy and accepts both as part of life.

Genuine, heartfelt ritual helps us reconnect with power and vision as well as with the sadness and pain of the human condition. When the power and vision come together, there's some sense of doing things properly for their own sake.

PEMA CHÖDRÖN

Pati Stillwater, a bodyworker who views her work as a ritual, described it to me: "There is the welcoming, the approach, the permission, the granting permission, the joining, the moving in deeper, the gradual return, and the farewell. Throughout the ritual there is consistent grounding. Every act, every part of the ritual, is a simple deed, and is powerful. I see both the sadness and the pain. The transformation can't happen unless there is a heartfelt intention, a willingness to realign. While I'm working, I see a vision of how the body is moving or I hear something from the client that lets me know why an energy might cause a distortion in a particular direction. I tap the place in them that wants the energy to move, and with skill, I can help the energy move and the distortion becomes a realignment. That is when the power and the vision come together. Like Pema says, 'things are properly done.' I see this as doing something for its own sake. When it is done, things fall into harmonious alignment."

Pati is describing balanced action. There is nothing superfluous, there is no reaction. The action is performed because it needs to be done. Balanced action restores harmony.

EXPERIENCE TRUTH

SEPTEMBER 14

Go your own way, on the path you select for yourself, corresponding to your own innermost inclination. Don't accept any statement because I made it. Even if it is true a hundred times over, it still is not your truth, it still is not your experience, and it will not belong to you. Bring truth into being, and then it will belong to you. Regard the lives of those who have achieved truth only as proof that the goal can be reached.

ELISABETH HAICH

We take so many things for granted. Much of what we accept as truth is actually hearsay. We haven't experimented and demonstrated the truth for ourselves. We confuse inner knowing with the knowledge we learn in school, a series of memorized facts. People often find a spiritual teacher and are so eager for guidance and feel so lost that they accept without questioning whatever the teacher says. We don't work with the teachings, test them, and see if they work for us.

In my own Buddhist practice I find in the teachings a map I can follow. I can investigate the process of my own mind and discover truth for myself. For example, I know in my own body the sensations I experience when I am clinging to or pushing away. There is a contraction or tension that is a very different bodily experience from when I am open and accepting without clinging or pushing. I know by experience the confusion and pain that comes from clinging and the freedom I experience when this tension is not present.

INFINITE LOVE

*The infinite is in the form of pure love. Meditate to reach it and you
will find infinite love, peace, and happiness.*

ANANDI MA

Anandi Ma, whose name means "One who is in Bliss and
keeps others in Bliss," is a Hindu woman and spiritual heir to
a realized master of Kundalini Maha Yoga. She was a very
quiet and devoted child who would sit for hours in temples
with her arms around the statues of deities and saints. Anandi Ma would spontaneously enter deep states of meditation,
often for long periods of time. At fourteen, she went into a
state of meditation so deep that neither her family nor her
friends could awaken her. Her concerned parents went to a
yoga master for help. The master, recognizing Anandi Ma as a
very advanced soul, gave her several years of spiritual training
to fully channel her energies for the benefit of others. Today
Anandi Ma travels widely, conducting meditation programs
and yoga retreats.

When I met her, I was moved by the peace and joy she radiated and I decided to study with her. As a child, I was very devotional and, although my family was actively involved in the
Lutheran Church, I spent time searching for something I could
not then articulate. I have since realized that I was trying to
find an embodiment of infinite love. The energy and guidance
of inspiring teachers can help us on our spiritual paths. Each
of us, however, must be committed to doing the work of meditation that will transform fears and doubts and release the
vast reservoir of love within our hearts.

JOY

If you feel the real joy and the real spirit within you, they come out naturally. If you really go deep inside, everything is there. You feel and, if you want it to come out, it will come out.

MAYUMI ODA

Mayumi Oda is describing the potential for joy within each of us. This joy is not based upon our external circumstances. The joy we experience when things in the external world are going our way is a temporary joy. When things change, and they are guaranteed to change, the joy changes also.

There is a deeper and more lasting joy that comes from within, and we can touch this joy if we are willing to do the necessary work to uncover it. We must have the courage to face whatever is hiding the joy. It is often hidden by the pain, anger, and fear our minds have generated in reaction to our life experiences. We can learn to stop running from these feelings and see them as energy seeking transformation. When we face our feelings without suppressing or expressing them, the energy is transformed and we experience that joy within.

This affirmation has been helpful for me: I have feelings, I am not my feelings. I have thoughts, I am not my thoughts. I have a body, I am not my body. I am love. I am joy. I am peace.

Live as if you liked yourself, and it may happen:
reach out, keep reaching out, keep bringing in.
This is how we are going to live for a long time: not always,
for every gardener knows that after the digging, after the planting,
after the long season of tending and growth, the harvest comes.

MARGE PIERCY

In the early seventies I belonged to a woman's moon circle and we celebrated the full moons and the changing seasons. These were special times of celebration and through our acknowledgment of the change of seasons we awoke to the sacredness of change. We were renewing an ancient ritual that has been performed throughout the world. The journey to unveil the power of love, the power of beauty within, is a process of accepting change. Each season has its time, and if the season is well lived and its lessons learned, we won't cling to the past. We will continue the journey of awakening, opening into the truth of each moment.

Honoring the turning of the seasons is a wonderful way to reconnect with the Earth. The ritual can be as simple as noting in your journal the qualities of the new season or the solitary lighting of a single candle to mark the season's change. You may want to gather with friends to sing, dance, and celebrate. What were the gifts of the past season? What is the new season bringing forth?

SELF-EXPLORATION

SEPTEMBER 18

A reformation of woman's emotional attitudes and beliefs will enable her to act more effectively. I am not speaking of the practical, economic, sociological problems as I believe many of them are solvable according to the attitudes women achieve which create clear thinking and intelligent solutions. I am . . . placing the emphasis on a confrontation of ourselves because it is a source of strength.

ANAÏS NIN

At the beginning of self-exploration we tend to want to control a situation; we want to protect our needs. However, wanting to maintain control and keep ourselves separate from the situation or the other person will continue to create tension. Once the tension is recognized it can be worked with, and the reaction stops.

This is easy to see with young children. When my children were young there were times when they would cry and demand something and I would have to say no. When I was tired or rushed it was a challenge not to react. When I could stop, breathe, and see my frustration in not being able to reason with the children the reaction stopped. I didn't need to get caught in my children's frustration. I could respond calmly, and the children, sensing that calm, would also begin to calm down.

Hold me, hold me
Never let me go.
Hold me like a leaf
At the end of the branches.
And when I die
Let me fly
Let me fly
Through the air like a leaf that is falling.

IZETTA SMITH

A friend sang this song to me when I was mourning the death of my father. It comforted me and has become one of the favorite songs we sing in the Women's Sacred Mystery School and at retreats and workshops. Izetta Smith works with grieving children who have experienced the death of a parent or sibling. The words beautifully express a gentle way of being, of living.

Can we hold one another as lightly and as firmly as a leaf holds to a branch? The leaf is whole unto itself, yet it is a part of the branch, which is an extension of the tree. The leaf remains part of the tree until the cycle changes and it is time for the tree to shed its leaves. The leaves fall, with utter simplicity and grace. They float away. The tree doesn't try to hold the leaves because she might never get another one. There is no pushing away or holding back. There is no thought process involved. There is no clinging. The leaves are part of the tree and part of the falling, a whole cycle that includes dying.

AGITATION

Everybody today seems to be in such a terrible rush, anxious for greater developments and greater riches and so on, so that children have very little time for their parents. Parents have very little time for each other, and in the home begins the disruption of the peace of the world.

MOTHER TERESA OF CALCUTTA

When we become emotionally upset the mind states change so rapidly that we are only aware of the stronger ones such as intense anger or hatred or deep sorrow. We do not see the quick and subtle changes that precede the intense anger state. It can begin with feeling pleasure; and then desire arises and can move to frustration until it builds to anger. When we take the time to explore our mind process, and become intimate with the workings of the mind, we can see the many changes, both subtle and gross. With practice we can notice the sensation of pleasure and recognize the desire that follows and not identify with, or become attached to, the desire so it does not escalate into frustration and anger. We become the gentle witness, observing the process. We are not bad because we have desires. We learn to notice and accept the desire. Desires arise endlessly. The stronger the mindfulness, the weaker the conditioned response, the attachment.

We are relinked, re-ligioned (that's what the word religion *means, to be relinked, bound together again, not with epoxy but with human concern)—relinked, re-ligioned, through our devotion to all the everyday acts, the humble humanity of each person, the mugs and saucers and napkin rings,* the power of the small *as the Chinese Book of Changes, the* I Ching, *calls it.*

M. C. RICHARDS

Devotion to everyday acts is mindfulness. It is bringing our full attention to whatever we are doing. Hexagram 9 in the *Chinese Book of Changes* describes those times when it is impossible to make a large change in our environment or situation. Success will eventually be possible if we take the opportunity to refine our nature in small ways. This calls for firm determination within and gentleness and flexibility in our relationships. It is well to heed such advice. Too often we feel discouraged when a situation seems impossible. We forget that change is both possible and inevitable. It takes both humility and high self-esteem to make those subtle refinements in character. And with mindfulness we are able to recognize the humanity of all people. When we are able to recognize our universal concerns, we recognize ourselves as part of the family of humanity. And it is this recognition, this compassion, that relinks us.

FREEDOM

The beginning of the sustenance of life
Is all in yin and yang.
The limitless can open up   *Diligently polished, the mirror of mind*
The light of the great limit.   *Is bright as the moon;*
                                    The universe in a grain
                                    May rise, or it may hide.

SUN BU-ER

The *I Ching* refers to the absolute infinite as the limitless. It is the foundation of the universe. *Wu chi* is the great limit, the primordial unity. From the wu chi comes the yin and yang. Sun Bu-er uses the phrase "the universe in a grain" to express the enormous potential of mind. Through spiritual practice the mind is mastered and one can act or refrain from acting by the power of will. One is no longer pushed and pulled by desire, controlled by feelings or life situations.

The following movement exercise keeps us grounded: Stand with your feet hip-width apart. Take a step forward with your right foot so that your feet are now about one foot apart. Keep your pelvis forward and begin shifting your weight from one foot to the other using a gentle rocking motion. As your weight shifts forward your right knee bends, as your weight shifts backward the toes and ball of the right foot lift and the left knee bends. Raise your hands in front of you, elbows bent and kept at your sides with your palms facing forward. As you exhale push your arms forward. As you inhale turn your palms over (facing the sky) and pull your arms back as you shift your weight to the left foot. With practice the movement becomes fluid. Remember to relax your jaw and shoulders, allowing the movement to come from your belly.

WITHHOLDING LOVE

Only fools hoard their heart.
You are no fool.
This grief and this longing agree on that.

Your love yearns to cry "yes."

LYNN PARK

In intimate relationships, no matter how loving the relationship is, there is often a part of us that holds back. The withholding may not be conscious and there are many reasons for such behavior. We withhold out of fear, in order to protect ourselves. We withhold because we fear we won't get what we want. We don't want to give unless we are sure we are going to get something equal or better in return. We withhold because we are afraid of being abandoned. Yet the withholding doesn't truly protect us, it inhibits us. The withholding mechanism works in such a way that we cannot withhold only the feelings or behaviors we want to withhold. The withholding gradually affects all our feelings and actions. Loving is risky business. And the person we love may not be able to love us back in return.

The love that Lynn Park speaks of goes beyond the loving exchange in relationships. Yet it is through our relationships we learn this greater love. And this ability to love is magical. If we love a little, we get a little love in return. If we love a lot, we get a lot of love in return. If we totally surrender, that is, open our hearts completely, we become love. If we truly knew the joy that is possible once we give all our love, we would never hoard our hearts.

HARVEST

We taste
Harvest: this instant
At the edge of green, on
The threshold of yellow,
Apple's perfection:

Taste frost, rain, sun,
White blaze of blossom
And celebration of the bees,
Taste labor of lady beetles
Keeping the tree clean.

ELSA GIDLOW

Select a beautiful, fresh apple or any favorite fruit. Make a silent ceremony. Carefully wash the fruit. Cut it into slices and lovingly place it on a beautiful plate. Place the plate on a tray and carry it to the place you have prepared for the ceremony. Walk slowly and mindfully to your place. You may sit at your table, at your altar, in your garden, or wherever you feel most comfortable.

Close your eyes and take three deep breaths. Slowly open your eyes and read this portion of Elsa Gidlow's poem. Read it slowly and reflect on the words. Think of the orchards and the abundance of the Earth. Think of the interconnectedness of life, all that was needed to support the growth of this apple. Now take one slice of the apple or fruit you have chosen, bring it to your lips, take a small bite, and place the rest of the slice back on the plate. Now begin chewing the bite. Chew in thankfulness for this life. With each bite make a prayer of thankfulness. Reflect on those people who do not have enough to eat. Hold gently, in your awareness, the whole Earth. When you have finished the fruit sit for a minute and look at the empty plate. Be aware of how you feel now that you have eaten. Then slowly rise and carry the tray with the empty plate back to the kitchen and mindfully wash them and put them away.

Goddess is Magic, the subtle forces of planets, moons and stars, and the Powers of our own Deep Minds. And She is our Ability to Call forth that which we have need of, and to Banish that which we no longer need. And therefore let us gather together in our communities, and join with the forces within and without, that we may together keep the Life and Death of our Selves and our World.

SHEKHINAH

Shekhinah, a present-day priestess of the Goddess tradition, has created this litany, a wonderful reminder to keep alive both the bitter and the sweet. Too often, the bitter or whatever we consider negative is denied. We only want the sweetness. A full experience of life challenges us to embrace it all, the day and the night, the dark and the light.

Goddess is the full circle. She is birth, life, death, and rebirth. Women need the Goddess. The planet needs the Goddess. We need to celebrate and embrace the full circle of life; to know that all of life is contained within this circle. There is nothing that is outside the circle. At times we may feel lost or doubt the vital energy of the Goddess, because the ever-present connection has been obscured by fear or pain. Goddess is energy, a way of balanced relationship, an openness of the heart that allows us to have a full experience of life, with all its pain and all its joy.

Find a quiet time during the day or the night when you can be alone and feel the energy of the world around you. Tune into the natural world—the water, the air, the light of the sun or the moon, the trees, the Earth. Can you sense this energy? No need to call it by any name. Sense. Breathe. Allow.

REST/RENEWAL

Now the wild garden and the ragged wood,
And the uncharted winter's fallow time
Become the source and the true reservoir:
Look for my love in the autumnal flower.

MAY SARTON

It is no accident that human beings spend one-third of their lives sleeping. We need this daily period of rest and renewal. This is a time to withdraw from our activities and replenish ourselves. Too often we do not allow ourselves enough sleep, or the sleep that we have is disturbed because of an inability to discharge the tension in our body and mind. We need to value times of solitude, contemplation, and rest as much as we value the active times. In order to grow and to blossom we need both times.

Give your body and your mind a rest with this relaxing pose: Lay down with your buttocks close to a wall and your legs extended up and resting on the wall. You may want to place a thin pillow or folded towel under your head for support. Let your arms relax at your sides. This position should be comfortable so that you can relax completely. Do not entertain any thoughts. Let your mind relax by focusing on your breathing. Keep your attention focused on the breath. Remain relaxed in this position for ten or fifteen minutes.

That prayer has great power which a person makes with all his might. It makes a sour heart sweet, a sad heart merry, a poor heart rich, a foolish heart wise, a timid heart brave, a sick heart well, a blind heart full of sight, a cold heart ardent. It draws down the great God into the little heart, it drives the hungry soul up into the fullness of God, it brings together two lovers, God and the soul in a wondrous place where they speak much of love.

MECHTILD OF MAGDEBURG

Goddesses, gods, demons, and devils are all powers within us. They are forces that either compel us to realize our own divinity—love, joy, and meaningful purpose—or obscure that impetus. Everyone has the potential to realize the indivisible unity from which we come. Whether or not we take the journey and how long it takes is up to us. We can stop and investigate the many distractions along the road of life or we can bring our energy into focus and take a more direct route.

Meditation and mindfulness provide a strong foundation for the spiritual life. It takes a great deal of inner strength to remain calm and compassionate in the face of opposition. When the mind calms, self-will fades and detachment emerges. We do not become detached from people. We become detached from activity that is motivated by self-interest. When the mind is calm, wisdom and compassion emerge. Yes, spiritual life is difficult. It tests our resources to the limit, but every human being can eventually come to the realization of her or his essential unity.

DEVOTION

Devotion without knowledge cannot free us. But knowledge without devotion is like eating stones. On the path of devotion we can enjoy the fruit from the very beginning, experiencing bliss in every action.

AMRITANANDAMAY MA

My teacher Ruth Denison told us a story about her training many years ago in India. While her teacher was giving his discourse Indian students would come, kneel at his feet, and place flowers on and in front of them. They would then touch their forehead to his feet in deepest reverence. The teacher would continue teaching as though this was not happening. One Western woman was upset by this. She thought the teacher was egotistical. Why didn't he notice and thank these students?

It wasn't until later in her training that Ruth more clearly understood this devotional practice. Ruth, eager to learn whatever she could, sat in the front row, day after day. One day the teacher beckoned to her, pointing to his feet. At first she felt awkward and embarrassed. But as she knelt and placed the flowers on his feet, she realized that she was bowing to the divine. It had nothing to do with the teacher personally. It was not about bowing to his particular personality. It was a surrender, an opening to the divine. The ritual was a means for the students to awaken to the divine source of life.

*Doorways are sacred to women for we
are the doorways of life and we must choose
what comes in and what goes out. Freedom
is our real abundance.*

MARGE PIERCY

Women's bodies are designed to create, to give birth, to nourish, and whether or not we give birth to children, we are the mother and creator of our own lives. Our freedom and our abundance lie not only in our opportunity to choose and to make creative changes. Life will offer us both pain and pleasure. Our most fundamental freedom lies in responding to rather than reacting to life's situations. In reaction there is a tensing and contraction; the reactive mind is burdened with self-interest. A woman who can respond has freed her energy, so she is not clinging to how things ought to be. She is open to a wider range of possibilities without attachment to the outcome. She sees a need and she addresses it.

There is much suffering in the world today. Women have been battered, raped, and incested. It is imperative we continue our political and social work to make the world safer and more equitable for women. We have a great inner power, even when we are not able to prevent such horrendous pain, and this power lies in how we relate to these life experiences. We can carry the pain, the rage, and the bitterness with us throughout our lives or we can move through it to a place of inner peace. We can heal this pain by our mindfulness. Freedom is our ability to transform the energy of even the most heinous circumstances.

ENJOYMENT

As I dig for wild orchids
in the autumn fields,
it is the deeply-bedded root
that I desire,
not the flower.

IZUMI SHIKIBU

Flowers have incredible power. Their fragile beauty and brief life can teach us to enjoy without attachment, to experience deeply while knowing full well the experience is temporary. It is the same with all of life. We will have pleasures and they too will be transitory. We are free when we are able to enjoy our pleasures without trying to hold on to them, when we are present without emotion-charged memories or looking forward to the next time. On the spiritual path it is not the pleasure we want to renounce, it is the attachment to the pleasure. Life will have its joys and its sorrows; to live fully we must live from the source, without attachment to either the pleasure or the pain.

It's the blood of the ancients that runs
though our veins. And the forms pass,
but the circle of life remains.

ELLEN KLAVER

Sing this chant. Let it spin around and around in your heart and mind. It is a reminder that we are always connected to the past. We can draw upon the wisdom of the ancestors. A simple observation of nature shows us this. The physical body arises from four elements: earth, air, fire, and water, which dissolve with death only to endlessly recombine again.

Look at a tree, watch it bud and leaf. Eventually the leaves wither and die. And in season the buds burst forth again. The sun continues to shine, the leaves become green, the circle of life remains. This deep and unending connection is what supports us. We can tap into it. In truth we are always within this circle, we have just forgotten. Our little minds tell us we are alone. We believe only what we see with our physical eyes. Let this chant widen your vision.

RESTRAINT

OCTOBER 2

Hesitation and restraint make altruism and kindness possible.

JUNE JORDAN

In a "me first" society we learn to actively assert our needs, to make clear our wants, and to obtain the objects of our desires. We learn to feel outrage when we can't achieve the object of our desires or when the pleasure doesn't last. Everyone has experienced some personal trauma, grief, or pain that can lead to feelings of outrage. Feelings of alienation and acts of violence are increasing daily. However, the expression of outrage will not heal the pain or stop the violence. It is restraint that makes the kindness possible. There is enormous suffering in the world: the numbers of homeless people, battered women, children who have been incested and physically abused, and the thousands who starve to death daily can evoke feelings of rage and despair. To refuse to act on these feelings may seem counterproductive. How can we make the necessary changes? How can we heal the inequalities? We need to balance our times of social action with times for solitude, meditation, and contemplation. During such times, if we are willing to sit with the outrage and notice the bodily sensations, we might find the outrage gradually dissolves. Instead of outrage we feel calm and joyful. It is from this space that altruism is possible.

When this black woman cook was asked for her recipes, she said, "I'll give you the recipes, but cooking is just like religion. Rules don't no more make a cook than sermons make a saint." I always remember that.

LEAH CHASE

The old cook's words are applicable to living a full, natural life. In Western culture we're educated with definite expectations of how things are supposed to be. We have limited and rigid definitions, as though by following a recipe, we'll become great cooks. We get fooled often. We live in the land of slick packaging, of supersell. Lost in the packages and the credentials we don't get to the heart of what is.

This quote humbles us. It asks us to open our eyes to the beauty and simplicity of life. Instead of going for the glamour, we are brought back to a centered place within ourselves.

EFFORT

OCTOBER 4

Effort has its own reward. . . . If the effort is just a little bit more than before, one stretches the mind, and if one keeps stretching it, the mind stays expanded. If one continues making the effort, then it will eventually stretch to the point where it cannot snap back, where the mind becomes pliable, malleable, extended, where it can see the whole rather than these tiny little specks of the universe that each of us occupies, like a pinhead.

AYYA KHEMA

When my children were babies I was told that given a choice of foods, babies will choose a balanced diet. We can't evaluate their nutritional intake on just one meal. We need to make this evaluation after several meals or over a few days. I like to look at effort in meditation in this way. If I evaluate each sitting I might not see much concentration or mindfulness. I might be very restless or tired or filled with thoughts. Yet if I continue to meditate each day and then look back over a period of time I begin to see the change. What once was a fleeting insight during a meditation period is now my daily consciousness. The mind is expanding, and as we go on, the changes become more subtle.

My friend and dharma sister Arachne once commented that the wonder of meditation was the fact you did not have to do anything, just show up for it. Just by practicing, day after day, a transformation takes place. It is not about doing anything. It is about being here, with all the resistance and watching, breathing and opening—watching, breathing, and opening.

To understand Mystery,
observe mind.
Stilling fear, mind moves clear.
Sing a song of equanimity
awake within serenity.
Affirm your voice
and choice.
Magnetize a potent dream:
World alight,
illumined peace.

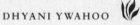

DHYANI YWAHOO

What was most memorable for me when I met Dhyani Ywahoo was the peace, joy, and equanimity she radiated. I felt great happiness. I felt all my sorrows and worries disappear. There was nothing else I wanted or needed on this Earth. It felt like everything in the universe was good and beneficial and no one needed to despair anymore. That feeling, like all feelings, didn't remain permanently with me. But I had a taste of freedom and I had found a way to practice it.

The peace Dhyani radiated is available to each of us. It comes from a mind that is trained, a mind without conflict. Classical Indian mysticism describes the mind as a lake. For most people, whose minds are untrained, the water is in a constant state of agitation. Anger, greed, fear, and selfish interest keep the waters churning. Even in those whose surface looks still, it is murky underneath. When the mind is trained, the lake becomes still and clear. We are all born with the potential to make this lake of mind still and clear. Training the mind is the surest road to peace.

AWARENESS

OCTOBER 6

I, we, Mothers, Sisters, Lovers,
Infinitely small out of her vastness,
Yet our roots too may split rock,
Rock of the rigid, the oppressive
In human affairs.

ELSA GIDLOW

Lily Tomlin's character Trudy, the bag lady, says that we are all specks in the universe. Trudy is an endearing character because of her humility. She sees herself as a tiny part of an awesome universe. She speaks the truth. She isn't attached to her personality or what others think of her.

We cling to our personality because we think that is all there is. If we didn't have a personality, who would we be? The more we risk letting go of the small self, the more we open to the larger self. As attachment to the personality is lessened, we stretch and grow deeper roots, deep into the Earth, into the vastness of our being.

Try playing with this image to cut through the place where you are rigidly attached to an attitude, belief, or behavior: Imagine swimming in a great ocean. Imagine expanding and opening, letting the awareness open out into the vastness of the sea. Imagine the waves gently rolling against the shore as the tide moves in and out. What was once a great rock becomes smaller and smaller, a tiny pebble, and finally a grain of sand. Allow the mind to become spacious and light. Give up expectations. Let be. Be at once the ocean and the wave.

Then the well spoke to me.
It said: abundance is scooped from abundance
yet abundance remains.

ANNE SEXTON

No one can give us enlightenment, joy, or peace. These qualities are latent within us, no matter how stained our personalities may be. If we dig deeply enough into the present moment, these qualities will pour forth. We will never use up all the joy, peace, and light. These qualities are abundant—the more we express them, the larger our capacity for such expression becomes.

This creative visualization practice can help restore energy and reconnect you with the universe. Sit quietly and imagine yourself in a calm, restful place beside a deep well. There is a bucket and a ladle beside the well. Lower the bucket and let it fill with clear, cool water. Take the ladle and drink as much water as you need. This well will never run dry. Let this pure water quench your thirst for freedom, for justice, for peace. Refreshed and renewed you will be able to meet the challenges of daily living.

INTERSTAND

OCTOBER 8

The question of how to "understand" her now clarifies itself, as the wrong question. . . . Perhaps interstand *is what we do, to engage with the work, to mix with it in an active engagement, rather than "figuring it out." Figure it in.*

JUDY GRAHN

Judy Grahn is talking about Gertude Stein but she could be talking about anything. When we understand something, we're separating from it. We have put it outside ourselves. Here is the person who needs to understand. There is the thing that needs to be understood. To *interstand,* we must be in relationship with what is happening. Related to it, not separate from it. We can respond to the information in the way that is most skillful. We open to it, or "figure it in." Learning to "figure it in" is crucial because many times throughout our lives we are so sure of our own ideas that we refuse to open to another perspective. Take time today to consider this. Is our knowledge preventing us from uncovering a deeper wisdom?

I made soup tonight
and all my ancestors danced
in the pot, with the barley,
the beans, the knuckle and neck bones,
enriching this brew;
Here women joined
love and ancient wisdom, the knowledge
salt and pepper bring; secrets
that are ritual and legacy.

ELSA GARCIA

Every act becomes a ritual when we bring mindfulness and simplicity to our daily lives. There is a fullness and precision to each act, making it complete in itself. The slow and simple days on meditation retreats, with alternate periods of walking and sitting meditations, support the development of mindfulness. There is nothing extraneous. As we grow in mindfulness, what used to distract us is no longer so urgent. When the mind is restful and no longer caught in conflicting thoughts, the energy is strong. We bring a simplicity with us, no matter how busy we may become. With awareness, each moment is experienced fresh and new. When the mind is calm and open, we realize the world is sacred.

FORGIVENESS

But remember to bury
all old quarrels
behind the garbage for compost.
Forgive who insulted you.
Forgive yourself for being wrong.
You will do it again
for nothing living
resembles a straight line,
certainly not this journey
to and fro, zigzagging
you there and me here
making our own road onward
as the snail does.

MARGE PIERCY

Dhyani Ywahoo writes of a Native American ceremony called the Friends Making Ceremony. It is a ritual of forgiveness in which the whole community participates by going down to the river's edge and throwing water over their backs seven times. In so doing they wash away any habits or thoughts no longer beneficial for growth. People forgive those who have harmed them and ask forgiveness of those they have harmed. Now they are ready to start the year anew.

In matriarchal times, water blessed and renewed was essential to fertility and creativity. It is time for us to remember the healing waters of forgiveness and allow ourselves to be blessed with the wisdom and peace that come through forgiving ourselves and others. Make a simple water ritual and perform it whenever necessary.

love is concerned
that the beating of your heart
should kill no one.

ALICE WALKER

True love never harms. When we are love, there is no room for harm because there is no fear. Without fear there is no need to hurt. Too much of what passes for love is attachment, grasping, trying to please someone to get something. We have so many hidden agendas. And some that aren't so hidden! The next time you feel you want to hurt someone, whether it's by making a critical or hostile remark or wishing someone ill, stop. Take a few deep breaths and begin to invoke the energy of love. You may need to imagine a person or a time when you felt loving. Let those feelings fill you. Imagine breathing in love with every breath you take. As you exhale imagine sending out love.

It may be difficult to immediately stop projecting angry feelings, especially if you've been working hard to know it is okay to feel them. It is not bad to feel angry. You notice and feel the anger and then make a choice to transform the anger. This is another way of working with the energy that neither represses nor expresses it. You can practice this at times when you are not feeling angry. Sit quietly and take a few deep breaths. Now feel warm, loving energy. Surround yourself with it. Feel it entering, filling, and leaving your body in a continuous flow. Practice this as often as you can.

FEAR

OCTOBER 12

*With the power of our collective imagination we can create a future that con-
tains us all, where those old divisions do not reappear to perpetuate inequality
among us. And because our (lesbian and gay) community crosses all boundaries if we can imagine ourselves into the future all together, true to our selves,
true to our love for each other, we will offer to the world the practical details
and the vision of a community creating change that is rooted in the liberation
of all people.*

MINNIE BRUCE PRATT

One of the many gifts that the lesbian and gay communities
bring to the larger community is the courage to look at difference. Everyone has some fear of difference, whether it is different color, different race, different sexual orientation, different
class, or different religion. In order for us to effect change at
the deepest level, our hearts must open and fear and prejudice
must be released. Acceptance of difference does not mean we
need to like everyone or condone behaviors that seem offen-
sive to us. It means that we refuse to react to our own or another's prejudices. Without reaction, our actions become clear
and compassionate. They do not harm.

Today spend ten minutes visualizing someone that you
think is very different from yourself. Imagine yourself standing face-to-face with this person. Imagine inhaling universal
love through your nose and exhaling that love through your
heart. Keep looking into the eyes of the person in front of you.
Without forcing, allow your heart to gently open. Even if you
think you have no loving feelings to give this person, remember that you are inhaling universal love and by exhaling that
love through your heart it reaches this person.

Blessed is the match consumed in kindling flame.
Blessed is the flame that burns in the secret fastness of the heart.
Blessed is the heart with strength to stop its beating for honor's sake.
Blessed is the match consumed in kindling flame.

HANNAH SENESH

Hannah Senesh is Israel's national heroine, a poet and a martyr. Hannah was safe in Palestine during World War II and she volunteered for a mission to help rescue Jews in her native Hungary. She was captured by the Nazis, stood up to imprisonment and torture, and was executed at the age of twenty-three. These words were taken from her journal. When I read them I am reminded of the power and the circular motion of love. The match is the catalyst to set the heart's love aflame. The one who inspires is like the match. She lights the kindling that is already present in our hearts. The match is absorbed, like the inspiration, and the heart's fire keeps burning. When the physical heart stops beating the energy of love continues and gives birth to a new flame. Hannah Senesh was killed by people consumed with hatred and violence, yet the love in her heart continues, its power igniting the fires of compassion in the world today.

PEACE

The ripening field, motionless in sunlight, seems the very symbol of peace. If the field is then gently brushed by wind peace becomes underlined by a reverence in which the whole conviction of creation for a purpose is indelibly coded.

RACHAEL PEDEN

Mystics from every spiritual tradition speak from their direct experience when they say we are one with the power that creates and sustains the universe. The Upanishads tell us that the power of nature is an expression of the more awe-inspiring powers of human consciousness. The delight we experience in nature is but a taste of the bliss we can experience when the heart is fully open. The peace that we can experience within our own minds and hearts is far greater than the peace that is evoked when we see fields ripening in sunlight. It is possible for each of us to directly experience this oneness. This is the purpose for which we are born and toward which we move.

Truth does not live at the surface, not yet. We are not transparent yet. Truth is occult. It lives in the depths, and materializes in a double realm, visible and invisible, like the seed. That's why we need an education that will help us to develop our powers of knowledge of the double realm. And that's why our great teachers ask us to experience paradox, to experience the opposites, to awaken in ourselves a soul-filled awareness, and an imagination, inspiration, intuition which are paths of knowledge between (human) and universe.

M. C. RICHARDS

In the Women's Sacred Mystery School we often do a drawing exercise. It is one I adapted from my years of teaching preschool and kindergarten. Using rolls of newsprint, the children would trace one another so that each child would have a life-size picture of themselves. In the Mystery School, women would trace one another and once everyone had a life-size outline we would do a guided visualization exercise on the *chakras*, the energy centers along the spine. Looking at one chakra at a time we would allow colors, images, and symbols that represented each chakra to arise. When the visualization was completed, each woman would take her outline and color it in with the symbols and images she discovered.

This is a practice in inner seeing. Working with the exercise once gives us a new tool for exploring ourselves. Continuing to work with the exercise develops the awareness that we are students of life, in a continual process of growth and change.

PRACTICE

My writing is a practice. It requires that sort of daily repetition and solitude—being with oneself—awareness—awareness of one's body, awareness of one's thoughts, awareness of one's own process. And meditation makes me more aware of everything I do, so it makes the movements within my writing process clearer to me.

SUSAN GRIFFIN

Practice and repetition are key words here. When we practice we repeat an activity again and again. One of the dangers we face in a culture with so many activities and experiences available is becoming quickly bored and jumping from one activity to the next. We never get to go beneath the surface. We lack the discipline necessary to move through the boredom to the passionate connection to all life. Boredom is the repression of passionate connection. We need to become disciplined. Discipline is not punishment: it is the courage to practice, to repeat an activity again and again until it is mastered.

I once studied tai chi with an elder, a Chinese master. He used to say, "Practice, practice, practice. I can't make you perfect. Practice makes you perfect." It is only through continued, disciplined practice that we can touch the wholeness, the perfection, that is within us.

Love has nothing to do with what you are expecting to get—only with what you are expecting to give—which is everything. What you receive in turn varies. But it really has no connection with what you give. You give because you love and cannot help giving. If you are very lucky, you may be loved back. That is delicious but it does not necessarily happen.

KATHERINE HEPBURN

We begin our search for love with a lot of selfish attachment. We are trying to get what we want, so we give with the hope that we will achieve the desired end. Love doesn't operate like a bank. We don't put energy into something with the expectation of getting interest. Katherine Hepburn is sharing with us the secret of nonattached loving. When we truly love and give from the heart, we have no expectations and we are not attached to any particular outcome. We can grow to our full potential to love. It is a skill that takes practice. Practice true loving by going against your own selfish desires. It is difficult, but it can be done. Practice by asking not what can I get, but what can I give? Gradually our capacity for love develops until we are giving love because it is our true nature, just as the rose emits its perfume.

COURAGE

*Dependency is like protection, and not being
dependent is like bravery, courage.*

PEMA CHÖDRÖN

Many people living in Western culture pride themselves on being independent. We find it easy to travel, to live alone, to work, and to be active in the world. If we stop and consider our independence we might be surprised. What if we didn't have access to a car or credit card or all the conveniences and comforts we take for granted? Whenever we are dependent on something that is outside ourselves, whether it be a relationship or some material object, a work situation or some attitude or way of living we take for granted, we have unknowingly created a trap. If circumstances change, how independent are we?

When my son Mike was in high school he received a scholarship to the Outward Bound program. He spent several weeks mountain climbing in Colorado. During that time the only people he saw were the others in his group. They carried all their food, clothing, and supplies on their backs. When he returned home he was exhilarated. Living so simply he realized that he could exist on much less food and with less of the material comforts he had come to take for granted. During rock climbing he had begun to face his fear of death. With solitude and the splendor of the mountains surrounding him, Mike called upon his inner strength and courage.

Are you black like night or red like clay
Are you gold like the sun or brown like the earth
Grey like mist or white like moon
My love for you is the reason for birth.

HOLLY NEAR

We are many peoples of many colors and many nations. What unites us is sharing life on Earth and having been born with a spark of love in our hearts. When we open to this love we open to the beauty of the world, the beauty of the many colors, the many traditions. It is this love that seeks expression. The fear of difference and the greed and hatred that control our lives can be transformed. We can let the fire of love burn away this fear. The policies of our governments can be based on love and the celebration of difference. We can begin to honor all peoples and look to learning from different cultures rather than automatically assuming our way is best. We all have something to share and something to learn. We have in common our home, the planet Earth. We have in common our humanity. We have in common our desire to be happy and free from suffering. We cannot sustain our lives on this planet without this recognition and working together—to bring peace to the Earth and to protect her precious resources.

HARMONY

When you have neither anger nor joy,
Your energy is harmonious;
Responding to events, according to situations,
Wind follows the clouds.

TAN GUANGZHEN

A life lived in response to our true nature is light as wind, able to move in all directions. Until then, we are controlled by our emotions. Tan Guangzhen isn't saying that feeling anger and joy are negative. What she is saying is that if we are controlled by our emotions then we're subject to upheavals. Our energy will go up and down depending on our emotions. Any strong emotion, whether anger or joy, disturbs the equilibrium. It throws us off-center. We may have an easier time understanding how anger throws us off-balance, yet excessive joy can also throw us off-balance. If our experience of joy is solely related to outside circumstances then we will try to hold on to those circumstances. In so doing we will have strengthened our compulsive behavior and when circumstances change, as they always do, the joy will leave also. We need to learn to enjoy ourselves calmly so that when something unpleasant happens, we also remain calm. When we are living in a state of harmony, there is joy. It is the joy that comes from within; it arises naturally, when there is no conflict in the mind. Then, whether the circumstances of our lives are going well or poorly, we are calm and happy. In Buddhism this state is referred to as "calm abiding joy."

From every branch
flowers drift and mingle down.
Saying, "Now!"
the spring departs until the paths
she takes in leaving cannot be seen.

IZUMI SHIKIBU

My home is a beautiful house on a small, shaded lot but there aren't any flowers. Not having a flower garden for the first time in many years has taught me a deeper appreciation of their incredible variety, beauty, and delicacy. I now take a daily flower walk. Winding down the hill, I drink in the beauty of my neighbors' gardens. The flowers aren't for me to own. Their beauty is for all and it lasts for such a short time.

This is true for any beautiful moment. It lasts for a short time. If we are willing to stop and experience it, drink it in with gratitude, then we'll be open for the next time it happens. We know all experience is temporary and nothing lasts forever. Holding back and not looking because of potential disappointment over its impermanence prevents us from seeing and causes us pain. Grasping and trying to make the experience last also causes pain.

Take some time to be with a flower, whether it is in your garden, your neighbor's garden, a field, growing by the side of the road, in a flower box, a park, or a florist's shop. Look at the flower and see its color and shape. Just see the color and shape. Breathe. Drink in the beauty. Give thanks.

DEEP SEEING

OCTOBER 22

For the ultimate revolutionary act is not giving up our lives literally but direct, immediate seeing which is our own true nature.

FLORA COURTOIS

People have had ideas about changing the world for hundreds of years, but fundamental change cannot happen because there can never be a radical transformation that is based on ideas. Replacing one idea with another is simply a reaction, one idea reacting to another, and that is conflict. We can only act in a harmonious way when our minds are free from ideologies, religious beliefs, dogmas, patterns, conditioned behaviors. Ideas and beliefs divide people and lead them to war. When our minds are free from such ideas we can act. If we are patriotic, we can never be sisterly. All our actions are conducive to war. Minds can be freed from ideas through self-knowledge. It is only through vigilant practice that we can see the hindrances, the impediments, that block us and prevent harmonious action.

Living is moving; time is a live creek bearing changing lights. As I
move, or as the world moves around me, the fullness of what I see
shatters.

ANNIE DILLARD

"What a vivid, descriptive, and poetic description of impermanence," my friend Arachne, a practitioner of Buddhist
vipassana meditation, exclaimed. "It is remarkable in that it is
the quintessential anicca (impermanence, flux, change) insight—'the fullness of what I see shatters.' As you look at
something in a concentrated way, it does shatter. You see that
it isn't as you thought when you were looking at it superfi-
cially. Annie Dillard experienced this while looking at a creek.
You could experience it while looking at your breath or body
or speech."

On a long retreat we have the opportunity to look deeply
into our body and mind. With concentration we look carefully, and what first appears to be one sensation is actually
many tiny sensations rapidly arising and falling, arising and
falling, until the whole thing breaks apart and there is no solidity. Sitting and breathing, the simple sound of a sneeze shattered me. I no longer felt the boundaries of my body. It became
sparkling light. Sounds were no longer outside or within me.
Everything arose and fell, again and again, in the vast space.

RELATIONSHIPS

The point of a relationship has nothing to do with the relationship itself. The point of the relationship is the added power that life gets in working with it as a channel. A good relationship gives life more power. If two people are strong together, then life has a more powerful channel than it has with two single people.

CHARLOTTE JOKO BECK

Joko Beck's reason for being in a relationship is probably radically different from the reasons most of us are in relationships. We strive to find relationships that are mutually satisfying. We ask ourselves, "Am I getting enough of my needs met to stay involved in an intimate relationship?" We work to be able to voice our needs, to communicate clearly, to negotiate. We want pleasant and exciting companionship, trust, loyalty, and passion. Without negating these needs can we open out into a wider perspective of relationship? Can we look in a practical way at our relationships and ask if the relationships serve life? Do we add to the clarity or the confusion? Do we hurt or do we heal? Do we build or do we destroy? Do we create conflict or peace?

Each time the heart opens, the power of love is strengthened. In this way, strong relationships are gifts to the world. A strong relationship is an interrelationship: one in which we do not depend on the other to express what we cannot, but in which each partner is committed to helping the other achieve the fullest expression. The more openness there is in love, the more energy there is to give to the world.

Imitate the trees. Learn to lose in order to recover, and remember that nothing stays the same for long, not even pain, psychic pain. Sit it out. Let it all pass. Let it go.

MAY SARTON

Growing up on the East Coast I witnessed the yearly explosion of fire on the hillside as the leaves turned brilliant shades of red, orange, and gold before they drifted to the ground. On the days when sadness creeps in because the painful arthritis in my spine has flared up, I recall the beauty of the trees in autumn. When I'm experiencing a lot of physical pain, I can't make it go away. I can't force myself to stop thinking about it. I can practice mindfulness. I can become acutely sensitive to what I am experiencing moment to moment. This kind of attention is loving-kindness. Befriending this pain, being present with the experience, may mean I embrace the sense of hopelessness I feel in dealing with a situation that has become chronic regardless of the care I take with exercise, diet, and various healing modalities. It may mean I have a good cry or call a friend who is experienced in relating to physical pain and in being mindful of it. In befriending the pain, there is a letting go. The ability to let go calls forth wisdom and sensitivity. It is not something that can be forced. The physical pain may or may not go away. Yet, my mind becomes more spacious and I feel lighter.

INNER PEACE

And when the soul reaches the stage
at which it pays little attention to praise,
it pays much less to disapproval;
on the contrary it rejoices in this
and finds it a very sweet truth.

SAINT TERESA OF AVILA

The truth that Saint Teresa of Avila is sharing with us is this: Inner harmony and peace come from within. This joy-filled state is not dependent on outer circumstances. We do not base our feelings about ourselves on the feedback of others. As long as we are attached to seeking praise, we cannot move from the deeper joy that is inside. Our actions will not be authentic. They will be coming from trying to please others and get their praise. When we are less motivated by praise, we find that we are less angered or saddened by disapproval. Life brings both praise and criticism. As long as we are swayed by either, our actions will not be balanced. Everlasting joy comes from the peaceful heart that has ceased all conflict.

Giving oneself completely is the most difficult thing to do for most people. One thinks one is losing oneself. Actually one gains everything. All religions agree on that.

AYYA KHEMA

Confusion reigns when we see life only as sensation, that is, when we are solely identified with the body and its desire for pleasant sensations. The selfish attachment that causes us to manipulate others to conform to our desires is the root of all problems. Egotism is a formidable enemy. The ego is fighting for survival. The Hindu scripture *Chandi* depicts the battle in gruesome detail. The Goddess Durga is fighting Red Drop and each time a drop of his blood is spilled in battle it becomes a new warrior. The Divine Mother transforms into Kali who swallows the blood before it can touch the ground. Seasoned meditators realize this battle is analogous to the struggle to control one's thoughts and desires, which seem to replicate magically. To stop the endless cycle we must catch them before they take root. With meditation and mindfulness we learn to detach from our ego's desires. What is gained when we lose the ego's desires is the full awareness of life's unity. We live, giving and enjoying, sharing in one another's joys and sorrows, always aware that the world comes from and returns to a divine source.

TRUE SELF

As a hungry cat stalks the fish for a chance to eat it, as a baby longs for its mother, so must one long for one's true Self, ju in gong. Unconditionally surrender all one's being to this Self, the actual owner of all actions. With this letting go, your totality will be organized by the very energy, the impulse which actually guides the whole universe. Then, your life becomes invincible.

HER HOLINESS DAE HAENG SE NIM

The understanding of *ju in gong* is central to Dae Haeng Se Nim's teaching. Different Koreans translate it with different English words. True self is what we in the West refer to as Buddha nature or Christ nature. It is the heart energy of the universe. It is the energy that connects us and the power that remains when there is nothing else. We are part of it and it is part of us.

Our concept of an individual self makes it difficult for us to understand how deeply we are all connected. Our concept of self creates complicated problems. We have problems with relationships, problems with self-esteem, problems with work, problems with lack of time. We often intuit the longing for the true self but not realizing this, we spend all our time, energy, and money developing the individual self. This creates enormous fear. There is so much to protect and control. Awakening to the deep interconnectedness of the universe lessens the individual self; therefore, it lessens the fear. We become invincible.

Love as a power can go anywhere. It isn't sentimental. It doesn't have to be pretty, yet it doesn't deny pain.

SHARON SALZBERG

Love is often confused with romance. In romance we have projected an idealized image onto the loved one. We do not really see the other person. Gradually the high intensity of the romance fades and we see the person with flaws. The love we expressed has been limited. Both partners have been projecting their illusions onto each other. We have been using the person as an object to meet our personal needs. Sometimes the illusions remain in place and we feel as though we have won. Other times the illusion slips away and we lose.

True love has no object. It is a warm, caring, kind attention that is given without expectation of any return. When we have expectations, we are bound to be disappointed. When we have expectations we are not able to receive what is there. We are too focused on what we want. To some it may seem unrealistic, being able to give without expecting anything in return. The miracle of love is that it moves in a circle, so when we give love in an openhearted way, it does come back to us.

MEETING THE SHADOW

OCTOBER 30

*Many traditions have incorporated the (evil) side in Goddesses like
Kali and Dakini and concepts like "hell realms" encountering your
shadow side. There's a tremendous richness in the idea that you can
see your hell realm . . . we can meet and embrace our evil.*

MAYUMI ODA

There are many special celebrations in the Women's Sacred
Mystery School. Two in particular encourage us to meet the
shadow. Hallowmas is an auspicious time to meet the darkness. Dances are created to encourage meeting the dark energy.
Dancing, we touch the Earth, we spiral around and down, we
dance into the dark. We meet this energy and move with it,
opening ourselves to its transformation. The night of the winter solstice we hold an all-night vigil without sleep. We chant,
we meditate, we dance, we sing, we cry, we pray, we laugh.
There is storytelling and there is silence. The lack of sleep invites us to drop our defenses and we avail ourselves of the precious opportunity to meet the shadow and dance with our
demons. Yes, there is fear and trepidation. The courage comes
from our willingness to meet together, to dance with and embrace the fears. Then there are no surprises. We know the evil
inside. This creates safety. There is less danger of entrapment
from the unconscious. There is power here. It is the power to
act in balance, the power to give and the power to be.

CHANGE OF THE GODDESS

Let my worship be in the heart that rejoices, for behold—all acts of love and pleasure are My rituals. Let there be beauty and strength, power and compassion, honor and humility, mirth and reverence within you. And you who seek to know Me, know that your seeking and yearning will avail you not, unless you know the Mystery: for if that which you seek, you find not within yourself, you will never find it without.

DOREEN VALIENTE

This quote is excerpted from Starhawk's adaptation of Doreen Valiente's *Change of the Goddess*. The moon circle group in which I was a participant for many years would recite "The Change of the Goddess" at our monthly full moon meetings. We welcomed the reminder that the rituals we performed were the means to awaken an inner spiritual power. The happy heart is one that is filled with gratitude. A simple ritual such as bowing and breathing deeply to greet each day awakens joy within us. Each day, each season, each cycle offers something of beauty. Let us notice and give thanks. The essence of all spiritual traditions is this: The divine that we seek, the beloved for which we yearn, lies within us. Each tradition has its rituals, prayers, and practices to unite with the divine. The qualities we need to cultivate and uncover this divinity are love and compassion. We need to find joy in the simple things in life. The heart that is joyful is the heart that is open. The heart that is open is the heart that is love.

Take time today to celebrate the love that created the beauty in the world. Now look in the mirror and see it in your own eyes and smile, reflecting back that beauty to all you meet.

WARRIOR/CHOD

Since you are wholeheartedly committed to the warrior's journey, it pricks you, it pokes you. It's like someone laughing in your ear, challenging you to figure out what to do when you don't know what to do. It humbles you. It opens your heart.

PEMA CHÖDRÖN

The path of the warrior is not a comfortable one. We're at war with the thieves who would rob our mind of its natural peace and clarity. They are quite formidable demons: greed, hatred, and delusion. It is all too easy to become entrapped. The trickster blows our cover. We are shaken from our core. In the shattering, we are humbled, and compassion emerges.

Machig Lapdron, one of the most renowned and beloved Tibetan women mystics, developed the *chod,* a meditation practice to cultivate compassion. Our natural feelings of compassion are inhibited by our fears and grasping. To remedy this, we visualize our dearest possession, our body, and give it as an offering. First the practitioner performs purification rites, then she visualizes cutting off her head, dismembering her body, and transforming it into nectar and making an offering of it to all beings in all dimensions.

At times during meditation practice a vision of Machig, with her dark, wrinkled skin and pendulous breasts, naked except for adornments of skulls and human skin, would appear. She would act crazy, dance wildly behind my back, encircle my body, and shout in my ear, "you think you know it all." She would taunt me and demand that I come to my edge and go beyond. At times the feeling became quite tangible as she made a slit down my back, reached through, and grabbed my heart.

God has not absconded but spread, to a fabric of spirit and sense so grand and subtle, so powerful in a new way, that we can only blindly feel its hem.

ANNIE DILLARD

The idea that God is dead was popular during the sixties. I think what died for many people during that time was a childish concept of God as a benevolent father who would grant our wishes, who would take care of us. We were growing beyond that idea. We were growing into a place of self-responsibility, a place of understanding God as part of our consciousness. God is that aspect of ourselves that senses the connection with the whole fabric of life. It is this connection that calls forth the responsibility of caretaking.

The concept of God as parental figure is limiting, as any concept of God is limiting. Concepts are abstractions. They are created by the mind. They are ideas about reality, not the reality. As Annie Dillard writes, the truth is so powerful and so subtle that our attempts at understanding can be like groping in the darkness. God isn't a concept. God must be directly experienced by each of us.

IMPERMANENCE

Come quickly—as soon as
these blossoms open,
they fall.
This world exists
as a sheen of dew on flowers.

IZUMI SHIKIBU

Izumi poetically describes the changing nature of a world we think of as solid and permanent. The seasons come and go, the moon waxes and wanes, day gives way to night. There are losses and gains. We cannot prevent the changes but we can allow our hearts to break open to the losses and hold the joys of life also. Attachment causes suffering. In my acupuncturist's office there is a sign that reads: PAIN IS INEVITABLE. SUFFERING IS OPTIONAL. There will always be pain in this world. It is the attachment to the pain or the joy that creates suffering. Here is where we have a choice. Clinging prevents us from experiencing and enjoying the delights of the world. We're either too busy to notice them or frantically chasing after them, as though this is what will bring happiness. Both attitudes cause pain. To walk unattached through this world means to walk with an open heart, present for all of life's pains and joys.

Take time today to appreciate something that you assume will last forever. Let its impermanence into your heart. A friend may die, a job may end. Notice how this awareness changes your experience of life.

ACCEPTANCE

When we understand how precious each moment is, we can treat each breath, each moment as a newborn baby. Awareness can become that tender.

MICHELE MCDONALD

When I started spiritual practice years ago I wanted a lot from it. I wanted to be happier and more peaceful. I didn't want to feel angry or upset. I wanted pleasant life conditions. While there is nothing wrong with wanting these things, it isn't what practice is about. And by fantasizing the achievement of such benefits, I was living in the future. And the future was all about me. As I continued to practice I began to see that I didn't need to force myself to be other than I am. I learned to watch my thoughts and feelings come and go. Each moment became precious. I didn't need to change it, only to experience it.

Mature practice is learning to serve life well. It is being able to create harmony and growth for everyone. I'm still in the picture but I'm not the center. Of course, I still have preferences, and haven't become completely selfless. My attitude is changing, and rather than thinking of practice as someplace to go, I know it is about being where I am now, doing the best I can, and learning from the results. This is tenderness.

DESIRE

Sleep, sweetly, dear sister
in the robe you have made.
Your desire is still,
like dried up vegetables
in a pot.

ANONYMOUS WIFE

The Therigatha is a collection of seventy-three poems in the canon of early Buddhist literature. *Gatha*s are poems, songs, or verses and *Theri* means women elders. Thus, the Therigatha are the poems of the wise women of early Buddhism. Susan Murcott, in her book *The First Buddhist Women,* tells us that although the Therigatha commentary speaks of this nun as a devoted wife, we can tell by the poem that she prefers the life of a renunciate to that of a wife. The legacy of the Therigatha is women's spiritual authority. We have the right to control our own bodies, minds, and spirits. We have the right to lead, teach, publish, and hold any position within an institution. We must be our own light. We must not imitate others but rather use their creative examples to question all of the illusions created by materialism, consumerism, and violent aggression.

This nun, through deep looking, explored desire. To explore desire is to explore our effort to control. We feel betrayed when we are separated from the objects of our desire. We try to achieve the objects of desire and then we must guard them so they won't be lost. These qualities of seeking and guarding cause suffering. The nun, cutting through attachment, gained peace.

Love knows no fear and no dependency. It has no possessions and no attachments. Love is without sorrow.

TONI PACKER

Love is the absence of fear. Without fear, there is no dependency. It is our ego that fears for survival. The ego attempts to create for itself a safe, convenient, pleasant situation. It then attempts to defend this situation, so nothing can be taken away. The ego is dependent on the situation and on whomever or whatever is involved in keeping it comfortable. When change inevitably happens, there is a feeling of loss and sorrow.

Raised with a romantic notion of love, we may find these words hard to believe. We believe that if this love does exist it isn't within our reach. It is the love of saints and mystics, not the love of lusty, flesh-and-blood people. Before you quickly agree or disagree with Toni Packer's words stop and take a deep breath. Make a choice to patiently explore this love. Play with the words "love is without sorrow" as an affirmation. Say it several times daily for a week. At the end of the week, what have you discovered about love? What have you discovered about yourself?

IMMORTALITY

You should know there is also
A heaven in the earth;
To seek it singlemindedly
Is to seek immortality.

CUI SHAOXUAN

Most of us see reality as something permanent and solid, that exists outside ourselves. The real world is the business world, the material world, and we are taught how to succeed in this world, how to get things that will make us happy. There are many who think the existence of a reality beyond what they know with their five senses is simply fantasy. Others believe there is something else, but that it is only after death and if we are blessed or saved that we will reach this other world.

It isn't known when Chi Shaoxuan practiced. What is known is that she achieved immortality, that is, she understood the true nature of reality. A name for this understanding is enlightenment. Enlightenment is the development of virtuous action and wisdom to the highest degree, and it is possible while living within the material world. The Tao is the natural law. The mind of the Tao is within the human mind. To study the Tao is to study the natural order of things, to work with this natural order rather than against it.

It is a long baptism into the seas of humankind, my daughter. Better immersion than to live untouched.

TILLIE OLSEN

Life with all its changes can sometimes cause us to become fearful and confused. Holding back from fully participating in life won't keep us safe. We need to immerse ourselves, open ourselves to all its joys and all its sorrows. Where can we find refuge in this changing world?

When we take refuge in the Buddha we are affirming belief in the possibility of becoming awake. We vow to spend our whole lives stripping away layer after layer of fear and doubt, so we can uncover the awakeness that has always been present. Each time we open and let go of a personal need—wanting to get this, fearing to get that—we become less dependent on other people, things, and situations to make us happy and secure. Our security comes from the breath. The breath moves and changes. Life moves and changes.

EARTH WISDOM

The earth is my sister; I love her daily grace, her silent daring, and how loved I am, how we admire this strength in each other, all that we have lost, all that we have suffered, all that we know: we are stunned by this beauty, *and I do not forget what she is to me, what I am to her.*

SUSAN GRIFFIN

To call the Earth sister is to acknowledge a most sacred relationship. We could not live without this Earth. Earth's atmosphere enables us to breathe. We could only live minutes without air. The Earth's waters quench our thirst. We could only live hours without water. We are fed by this Earth. We are fed by the bones of our ancestors, which have fertilized the soil in which we grow our wheat. We could live only for a few days without food.

Native Americans bring us the gift of Earth wisdom. They teach us how to respect the Earth and how to walk in balance. Indigenous peoples across the planet have Earth wisdom. It is time to listen and learn this wisdom. It is time to stop the destruction. The Earth will last. Will we?

Woman, so gentle in my arms
Loving, you have opened to me
Fierce, my own dark heart
And found therein and to me reflected
My source of light.

ELSA GIDLOW

One of the gifts an intimate relationship between two women offers is the safety and joy of similarity. Women know how a woman's body feels, how a woman's mind thinks, how a woman's emotions respond. In the arms of our beloved we can find a mirror, a reflection of ourselves. Mirroring can be incredibly powerful. We have an opportunity to see the shadow, the aspects of ourselves we keep hidden in the dark. This can be uncomfortable, but if we are willing to face the fear and work with the shadow, a great healing and transformation are possible. We have access to resources of power previously unavailable to us. We uncover our wholeness and holiness.

TRUE HAPPINESS

NOVEMBER 11

Poised
between death and conception
the moon rejoices
quietly
that emptying has ended.
Her invisibility
satisfies her.

She rests
from the gaze of her children.
Yet she teaches us:
Empty your heart.
Imagine no weight in your heart.
It will make you happy.
It will make you true.

SUE SILVERMARIE

We all want happiness and we often try to collect what we think will bring happiness, such as material objects, success, or praise. We may find possessions become a burden or we lose interest in what we have and need to seek more. The endless search for praise is like always being "on stage" and will prove to be exhausting. When we are no longer tied to or swayed by either praise or blame, we have found equanimity. We can find happiness in invisibility. This is not a state where people deny our existence or reject us, but the invisibility that comes through openness. We release our grasping and become transparent. When the mind isn't grasping it is at peace. This is true happiness.

Tonight, and every night for a month, spend some quiet moments watching the moon. Watch her move through her cycles from new moon to full moon, waxing and waning. What does grandmother moon teach us?

We came to the Earth as absolutely loving beings.
That is our basic nature. And all we want is to have a joyful life together—a peaceful, harmonious, laughter-filled, song-filled kind of life together.

BROOKE MEDICINE EAGLE

Several babies have come into my life recently. What joy to hold these tiny, sweet beings. I am reminded of how precious life is and how simple our true needs are. A baby's needs are simple. She wants to be fed, held, kept warm and dry. Everyone began life as a tiny baby. As we get older our needs seem to grow. Yet if the simple needs of a baby were met no matter what our age, there would be more peace and contentment in the air. That baby lives inside us. Take care of your baby today. When your inner baby is cared for you will see to it that other babies are cared for. It will no longer be acceptable to allow children to starve and homeless people to wander the streets. A great teacher once said that we have enough in this world for everyone's needs. We don't have enough for everyone's greed.

SILENCE

You are made whole again in silence.
Solitude shatters the illusion that you
and I are separate.

NANA VEARY

There is a great difference between loneliness and solitude. In loneliness we feel cut off from other people, from the whole of creation, and from our inner wisdom. With solitude we have the opportunity to reach beneath conventional reality to a deeper truth, that of the interconnectedness of all beings, of all life.

Our education has taught us to actively seek out information. We're taught that growing and learning is a process of acquisition and expansion. We have not been taught to simply be or to sit still and listen. Silence can feel so frightening we rush to fill it up rather than sitting and listening to it. We all need periods of reflection, time to integrate and absorb. Otherwise we become like a filled glass to which water is still being added. The glass overflows, unable to hold any more.

Let's begin now to stop and empty our mind of chatter. Sit quietly and observe the breath. Don't allow thoughts to disturb you. Just watch them come and go. With practice the thoughts will slow down, become further and further apart. Maybe then the still, small voice of the spirit will be heard. It is always present. We must learn to listen.

I say that if each person in this world will simply take a small piece of this huge thing, this tablecloth, bedspread, whatever and work it regardless of the color of the yarn, we will have harmony on this planet.

CICELY TYSON

Cicely Tyson's words encourage us to believe that every individual can make a difference. Rather than feeling despair and hopelessness we can act. Together we are weaving the tapestry of life. We can choose to ignore the tapestry, to tear a hole in the tapestry, or we can take up a piece and begin to work it. Working together cooperatively creates harmony. We have many excuses about why we cannot work with someone. Veils of fear, hatred, prejudice, and denial block our innate ability to cooperate. Cicely Tyson addresses this in a direct and simple way. Regardless of our color, we all have the same yearnings, fears, hopes, and desires. We're all connected. If we act upon our connections we can create harmony. It depends on each of us.

My mother embodies this harmonious way of thinking. Rather than become engulfed in despair she will see what is directly in front of her and work with that, however small the task is. With a good-natured attitude and a willingness to work she encourages us all to live in harmony.

RELEASE

What, after all, brings joyful release
After long illness, after near despair,
Better than four ducks and two geese?

MAY SARTON

One early fall weekend I was delighted to have the opportunity to visit Lake Tahoe. The visit came at the perfect time as I was just recovering from an injury. In front of the cabin was a lily pond where a gaggle of geese lived, thirty in all. I was reminded of May Sarton's poem "After Long Illness."

Sickness and pain can make everything look dark. We lose our perspective, unable to notice anything of joy or beauty around us. Pain tightens us. It drains our energy, leaving room for little else. There's an intensity in pain that makes it feel endless. There's a release when the pain stops—akin to a rebirth. I've felt a rush of relief when pain has subsided, tears of joy mixed with sadness wet my face. When my whole world was pain there wasn't room for the sadness. I felt a prisoner to my body. Once the pain-free space opens up I feel sadness for myself for having had to suffer and sadness for all people who suffer. The sadness is temporary. With deep acceptance, it thaws like ice and the crystal-clear water of wisdom flows. I can enjoy times when pain is absent or lessened, knowing that when pain returns, I can open to space—the whole body of the universe.

If we try to dance the spirit without knowing the shadow side that we all have, we can't really dance with our full grace and divine spirit. Once you have started to see the shadow side . . . nothing is hidden. If you can fully see, you don't feel fearful.

MAYUMI ODA

When I think about the shadow side, I'm reminded of an article in which Alice Walker responded to criticisms of her fictional character Mister in *The Color Purple*. In it she speaks of the maiming that takes place when we try to deny a part of ourselves. The slave and the slaveholder, the oppressor and the oppressed are within each of us. Wholeness will not emerge until this is acknowledged. Mayumi's message is the same.

It takes great courage to face fear. Only weak people are harsh and vengeful. Often the most aggressive people are the weakest and most fearful. Women, by grace or design, are often willing to face that shadow. Maybe it is in part because conditioning allows us to show fear. Courage, however, isn't the absence of fear, it is the willingness to face the fear, to dance with it. And in fear's embrace courage is born.

SELF-RESPONSIBILITY

When we fail to love our neighbor we are lost. . . .
When you see yourself lacking in this love,
even though you have devotion and gratifying experiences that make
you think you have reached (union)
and you experience some suspension in the prayer of quiet,
believe me, you have not reached union.

SAINT TERESA OF AVILA

Everything that happens to a woman is a private matter. She is dying of cancer. That's a private matter. Her husband is beating her. That's a private matter. If she is divorced and her husband won't pay child support, that's a private matter. This is the kind of patriarchal thinking that seeks transformation. We need to care for women, to be responsible to situations that our culture considers private matters. If we aren't caring for our neighbors, no matter how deep our meditative concentration is, we have not achieved wholeness.

UNDERSTANDING EMOTIONS

When you look at things emotionally you will not see them clearly.
When you see things spiritually you will understand.

PEACE PILGRIM

It is important to be in touch with our emotions because they can guide us to a deeper truth that is more inclusive than our own personal feelings. When we can feel or understand ourselves more deeply, we can also feel or understand others more deeply. We begin to realize that even our enemies are people who want to be happy and don't want to suffer. It is the attachment to the emotion that limits our perceptions, not the emotion itself.

Moving beyond emotions is not saying that emotions are bad. It is not repressing emotions. It is directly perceiving the pure emotion, not confusing it with our personal story. Take sadness as an example. I can look deeply into sadness by noticing and feeling the sensations of sadness within my body. I may experience it as a heaviness in my chest or a tiredness in my body, a lack of energy. When these sensations are recognized and deeply experienced I can see that they are changing. They don't remain constant. In the beginning I am not able to fully integrate the flow of change. So the sadness quickly returns. When I hold onto the sadness I get lost in all the memories and experiences that saddened me. The sadness infuses my thoughts and actions. Then I am not in control of my life. The sadness is in control of me. As I continue the deep exploration, my concentration becomes more stable and I am able to bring a sense of equanimity to times of both sadness and joy.

FRIENDSHIP

*Each friend represents a world in us, a world possibly not born until
they arrive and it is only by this meeting a new world is born.*

ANAÏS NIN

It was a beautiful sunny day. Several dear friends from the
East Coast were visiting and four of us gathered on a deck
overlooking Tomales Bay. We talked of the importance of
friendship and how we are mirrors for one another in our
growth. We agreed that friendship is sacred and were delighted to share such sacred space.

"I used to think that with a group of friends, there would
be one particular friend that would be like the hub of the
wheel. Now I realize that the sacred space in which the friendship moves is the hub that connects us all together," Pati
remarked, sparking an exploration of the similarities and differences between lovers and friends.

Linda considered the sexual sharing of the body the only
difference between a friendship and a marriage: "The space
between you and your lover or you and me is the same in that
it is sacred space. What you share with your lover will be different but it isn't a loss for your friends. They won't have less
because of it. I used to think there was more to a lover relationship than there was to a friendship. I was violating the
sacred space with that thought."

INTERCONNECTEDNESS

Weave real connections, create real nodes, build real houses.
Live a life you can endure: make love that is loving.
Keep tangling and interweaving and taking more in,
a thicket and bramble wilderness to the outside but to us
interconnected with rabbit runs and burrows and lairs.

MARGE PIERCY

We have been conditioned to fear, envy, and compete. These false ideas keep us isolated and unable to establish real connections, making truly intimate relationships difficult. Even if we act warm and friendly, we often keep relationships on a surface level. We fear letting people too close because our security will be compromised. The only true security is the direct experience of our divinity. The more we are able to open to and experience this divinity, the more we know there is nothing to hide, nothing to lose. Awakening to the divine nature enables us to live freely on Earth. And it is this firsthand knowledge of our divine nature that is the antidote for envy. The deeper we go in meditation the clearer our divinity becomes. The more we practice the more we see ourselves in everyone. There is nothing left to envy. Knowing this we can "weave real connections."

BALANCE

We choose as we go along, little by little, the way our ancestors did living in the fields since creation. We take some of this and leave a little of that. . . . We balance things out just the way nature tries to balance things around us. [We let go] of all the labels that got us into trouble in the first place.

LE LY HAYSLIP

Le Ly Hayslip is writing about her ancestors in Viet Nam. She is reminding us of living simply on the land and "walking in balance." When food or herbs were gathered the people were careful to take only what was needed, taking care that the balance of nature was maintained. We need to look to this balance today.

We need to become mindful of our thoughts. Are the thoughts we hold thoughts of harmony or conflict? We don't need to condemn or repress these thoughts, just see them for what they are: thoughts. This seeing will slow down the thinking process. All the labels, the ideas that we are better or worse than others, all the greed and the grasping, need to be seen clearly for what they are. The wanting, the disappointment—wanting what we don't have, not wanting what we do—it is this that causes the mischief in our minds.

Reading Le Ly Hayslip's book *When Heaven and Earth Changed Places* we see how the suffering in Viet Nam continues, long after the war is over. We need to bring this mindfulness to our actions and see what the effects will be, not only for us, but unto seven generations.

It is now time for all women of the colorful mind, who are aware of the cycles of night and day and the dance of the moon in her tides, to arise.

DHYANI YWAHOO

Dhyani Ywahoo teaches that race is one of the greatest illusions, or obstacles, that prevents us from knowing ultimate truth. We divide along lines of color and race, using the differences to oppress and create harm. The fear of difference has dulled our perceptions, limited our ability to be in the world, narrowed our range of behaviors. Dhyani teaches us that in the circle of life, each individual has particular gifts to share and each race has its particular wisdom, which is necessary for all.

If we look around this amazing planet, there is so much beauty, so many colors. Dhyani powerfully and poetically plays with words: to calm, to caress, to startle, to excite, to shatter our usual perceptions. I hear in these words a call to women to awaken to this beauty. Women are deeply connected to the seasons and cycles of the Earth through our own bodies, our menstrual cycles. The colorful mind is the mind that is infused with rainbow light. The colorful mind is vibrant, alive, beautiful, sensuous, passionate, connected to all of life.

LOVE

The soul is made of love and must ever strive
to return to love. Therefore it can never find rest
nor happiness in other things. It must lose itself
in love. By its very nature it must seek God, who is love.

MECHTILD OF MAGDEBURG

    Human behavior is motivated by the search for love. Each person intuits this. It is what separates us from the animals. The motivation is not always clear or conscious so we can be derailed on the search, willing to accept worldly pleasures as substitutes. The happiness we find is always temporary, however, and eventually we are left unsatisfied.

    Do not accept expensive substitutes. The journey to reveal the beloved is neither safe nor comfortable, yet the rewards are well worth the risks. Begin now to still the mind and listen to the Goddess. She is in our hearts.

No lesson is learned immediately. There is a phrase used in West Africa, deep talk, which means that anybody will understand it on a certain level. People who are interested in really understanding more take that lesson deeper. As far down as you take the advice you could still go deeper if you lived long enough.

MAYA ANGELOU

Learning a new skill can initially be awkward and burdensome. As experience develops, what was tiresome becomes effortless. It takes patience and courage to keep going deeper. Living in a quick-fix culture we don't often get support for the continuous, meticulous exploration that meditation requires. The spiritual path is like this. In the beginning it seems like we are depriving ourselves in seeking silence, solitude, and little sensory stimulation. With patience and balanced effort we can reach beneath the truth of ordinary life. We will still be able to function and carry out our responsibilities in the world. Yet we will no longer be confused by the world, mistaking a label for the truth.

WHOLENESS

It is important to keep the picture of wholeness alive in our under-standing of ourselves: the center we live within, *the life we live* within, *the love we live* within, *the connections we live* within. *All Beings of dark and light are the center we live within. To feel our-selves in touch with the wholeness of life is . . . to be on center, to be in* love.

M. C. RICHARDS

It is so easy to get lost in the details of everyday living and lose sight of the larger picture. The personal drama, the story of "my" life, what I do day to day, how I think, what I feel, be-comes what is most important. The dominant culture's mes-sage reinforces our conditioning to get for ourselves the best, the most pleasant, the most comfortable. In this quest to feed my sense pleasures I divide people, things, and experiences into good and bad. I work to obtain more of the good and eliminate the bad. Trying to get, trying to keep, and trying to push away create an ongoing level of stress and tension. To be on center, we must cut through the fantasy of total comfort. To be on center, we must embrace the whole of life. In love with life, and with a balanced state of mind, peace and joy come from accepting all of life's experiences.

With greater concentration and deeper penetration we will notice constant movement in ourselves. The mind realizes that if there's constant movement inside, it must be outside, too, so where can any solidity be found? The body is moving. There isn't anything I can hang on to. The thoughts are moving, so where am I? Impermanence has to be experienced.

AYYA KHEMA

Medical science teaches us that the body is in a continuous process of transformation: old cells die and new cells are born. The entire body is changed on a cellular level every seven years. So who we are today is not the same person that we were seven years ago. Our bodies are continuously undergoing change even though we may think they remain the same.

When we practice meditation, when we practice awareness of breathing, we notice how the breath does not stay still. It moves in and out of the body. The same is true with our thoughts and feelings. When we pay close attention we find that each thought is only held for seconds; the thoughts change so rapidly we experience them as one continuous thought. With closer attention we directly experience this movement. Change is no longer a scientific fact that we have read about but something that we experience firsthand.

ANIMAL PROTECTION

NOVEMBER 27

The task is to learn from the animals. And to learn from them is to provide for them, that is to preserve their territory, that is to withdraw, as the Ein Sof withdrew for the sake of creation.

DEENA METZGER

At Dhamma Dena Retreat Center all the water is brought in on trucks because the local people are concerned about the natural environment and wish to protect the turtles, which would be seriously disturbed by water that was piped in. Most of us grew up in homes where the water flowed quickly and easily from a tap and we didn't pay much attention to where the water came from or where it went after our use. Addicted as we are to convenience, it may feel like a hardship to limit our water usage. Yet, when we look at the whole picture of the planet and want to live in harmonious relationship to all life, it is a simple task. Retreatants learn to become aware of the source of the water, and it is an opportunity to use water mindfully. The gray water is collected and used to water the plants. We see how much water we use when we wash dishes or take showers or brush teeth. Far from being a hardship conserving water becomes a delightful meditation of thanksgiving for the blessing of water and a deep practice of mindfulness.

Social change must start in our hearts with the will to transform our own egotism, greed and lust into understanding, love and commitment, and sharing responsibility for the poverty and injustice in our country.

SISTER CHAN KHONG (TRUE EMPTINESS)

Gentleness can be difficult to maintain, especially in the face of our fears. Fears often cause us to react in a defensive manner. We become either physically or verbally aggressive. Fears can also cause us to react by withdrawing or running away. Gentleness evokes a quality of centeredness, a peace of mind, an ability to see beyond the pain that confronts us. It is a deeper wound that we need to address while we attend to the more obvious physical suffering. The horrors of war, for example, go deeper than the amputated leg. The horrors of war are the fear, hatred, and violence that make it possible for us to kill. Calmly bearing witness opens us to the realization of our own hatred and pain. The direct experience of this pain is transformative. A gentle heart is a compassionate heart. Most of all, a compassionate heart is kind.

Make gentleness your affirmation and activity this day. Keep the focus on your breath as you breathe in and out. Whisper gently, gently on the in breath and gently, gently on the out breath. Allow gentleness to manifest in all your actions.

EXPERIENCE TRUTH

The more one researches these small things, such as the purple-blue violet I picked this morning and brought in to examine under a microscope, the more clear it becomes that nothing on Earth exists totally separate and unrelated, and that everything is composed of even smaller parts.

RACHEL PEDEN

The Upanishads, the mystical Hindu texts, tell us it is not the world that is unreal—it is the belief that the world is separate from ourselves that is unreal. What is unreal is the idea that an individual exists separate and unconnected from the world around her. Truth is the interconnectedness of the world, and this truth will prevail. Unreality is negativity and separateness, and we must turn away from these ideas and beliefs to realize truth. These writings are not dogma. There is nothing that we are asked to believe. The writings come from the direct experience of the mystics.

These truths are available to each of us. Many of us, like Rachael Peden, begin to understand this unity through our experience with nature. We must come to "see" the truth through a direct experience. We cannot know the spiritual truth unless we deeply explore the mind. This exploration is possible through the practice of meditation—training the mind to become focused on an inner object such as the breath so that the energy becomes concentrated, and deep exploration and insight are possible.

The woman's place of power within each of us is neither white nor surface; it is dark, it is ancient, and it is deep.

AUDRE LORDE

This deep, dark womanpower is clearly portrayed in the ancient Hindu scripture known as *The Glory of the Goddess,* or *Chandi.* Like the better known Bhagavad Gita, the *Chandi* revolves around the battle for inner peace. The story in brief is this: Self-Discipline, Universal Love, Selfless Service, and other divine beings have been thrown out of heaven. They must fight the fiercest warrior of all: Egotism. Ego is aided by his demons Greed, Lust, and Anger. These demons come upon a beautiful woman (the Goddess) seated on a mountaintop. They ask her to become slave to the Ego and promise her all the wealth of the world. The Goddess shyly states that she has taken a vow that she can only marry the man who conquers her in battle. What follows is a fierce and grisly battle between the ego and Shakti, the purifying power of Supreme Consciousness.

Western culture's reluctance to accept the Goddess tradition may be the reason why this text is not well known. The Chandi, or Kali, scripture offers us the fundamental tantric realization that the world is pervaded by a Divine Unity or Goddess. Awakening to this reality overcomes our dualistic, self-centered way of being.

JOY

Joy, love and compassion are essential ingredients in spiritual growth. We are enriched by their nurturing, and our world is enriched by their actualization. Profound joy is a celebration of our vision of connectedness, a vision that dissolves division and the myth of separation. We must let our hearts dance and rejoice with love and compassion and yearn wholeheartedly for oneness and for wholeness.

CHRISTINA FELDMAN

Transcending our individuality will not make us inactive. It will transform selfish activity. What is destructive within us will become creative. Our sensitivity will grow so that we become incapable of thinking of our own needs in isolation from the rest of life. As our joy expands, the perceived need to exploit others will shrink. The rites, rituals, and mantras of all religious traditions serve to help us establish the conditions of freedom, love, and wisdom within us. We cannot cling to any of them. They are only a means to making our own lives part of the selfless work of divine energy. Firmly established in this, there is no greater joy.

Ordinary women of grace are, in a sense, my real role models. What always struck me is how unbitter they were. They had the capacity to keep struggling.

MARIAN WRIGHT EDELMAN

The ability to work hard without bitterness is of utmost importance. When we are bitter and resentful, that bitterness clouds all our thinking and activities. It is how we perceive life, how we respond to life, that makes us graceful or not. "Women of grace don't view life as a struggle, " my friend Pati told me. "There is an acceptance and therefore an ease. When I see women like this, I know that they work hard but inside they are peaceful. I watch them and learn from them because to me, that is true meditation. I've seen this in my grandmother. She lived a private life. She kept things in her heart. I could see she took pleasure in little things. Flowers, butterflies, and dragonflies had the capacity to fill her. My grandmother walked in a centered way through life. She never moved faster than her feet could take her. 'You just don't go faster than your feet can take you or do more than what your hands can do,' she was fond of saying. Now, that's grace."

MEDITATION

The state that one arrives at in meditation is very much like that ex-pansive state of creativity, which is, on the one hand, very calm and very quiet, but on the other hand, abundant—a sort of fountain of everything.

SUSAN GRIFFIN

The Upanishads teach us that the essence, self, or ground of being is the same in everyone. As long as our sense of identity is solely within the body, others are viewed as separate and different. The Reality underlying life, which is the essence of every created thing, is what is real. The illusion is that we ap-pear separate. We are one with the power that creates and sus-tains the universe, and the direct and deep perception of this unity is the purpose for which we were born. The ego cannot perceive this unity. We can train our minds to dwell on an inner focus until it becomes absorbed in the object of concen-tration (such as the breath) and the outer world falls away. We are aware of, but no longer distracted by, the sights, sounds, and sensations of the world. Becoming awake to this divine nature is a peaceful, joy-filled, and creative state of being.

We need to approach our state of mind with curiosity and open wonder. That open curious listening to life is joy—no matter what the mood of our life is.

CHARLOTTE JOKO BECK

In my work as a counselor I hear many stories of self-hatred. We are often hard and unforgiving of ourselves for being fearful. The attitude is one of shame and embarrassment or anger for having felt something that the ego considers unacceptable. The process of living, of coming alive, is a process of befriending the self. We need to love our inner child—all those hurt, scared, sad, and angry places. When we bring love and forgiveness to that child we transform childish attitudes and become more childlike. To be like a child is to be delighted with the world, curious and unafraid to take risks, eager to grow and learn. It is a most creative space.

The next time you feel fear or shame or numbness, stop and take a deep breath. Now picture yourself as a young child and take that child into your arms. Love and appreciate her. Breathe deeply again and let the feelings of love and appreciation fill your whole being. Now imagine the child dissolving into light and becoming a tiny spark who lives safely sheltered within your heart.

GRATITUDE

I remember when I used to dismiss the bumper sticker "pray for peace." I realize now that I did not understand it, since I also did not understand prayer; which I know now to be the active affirmation in the physical world of our inseparableness from the divine; and everything, especially the physical world, is divine.

ALICE WALKER

Human life is precious. We could not live without the sun shining down upon us. We could not live without air to breathe or water to drink. We cannot receive the joys that life has to offer if we are not grateful. It is gratitude that opens the heart. Prayer is a means for opening the heart. We do not pray to appease a wrathful god. We do not pray to seek favors, as a child might from a parent. Prayer is the courageous opening of the heart that will bring us into clear alignment with this divine source of life.

Will you take the time today to be grateful? Will you take the time to pray? Do you have the courage to open your heart to this world, to open to both the happiness and hardships?

God loves me. Each time I allow myself to say the words I am suffused with tears of gratitude and wonder. And I am re-established as a giving, living, full human being with every right to everything right on this earth.

MAYA ANGELOU

God loves me. Goddess loves me. Goddess is love. I am love. Awareness of ourselves as Goddess is a gift of grace. I have been graced during walks in nature, chanting, meditation, rituals, and dance. Knowing I am Goddess continues to give me the strength and courage to investigate the truths beyond conventional reality. Knowing I am Goddess, I am loved, enhances my self-esteem; it allows me to know that I am worthy. This knowing, in turns, empowers me to give. I can't give from a place of scarcity. I can't give away what I don't have. When doubts overtake me and I forget I have the right to be, I must heal that pain. The healing comes through caring for myself, even the doubting self. Those old doubts will recycle through my mind. I can watch them come and go. I don't need to be held hostage to my thoughts. Breathing out, I release them. Breathing in, "I re-establish myself as a giving, living full human being, with every right to everything right on this earth."

RESPECT/LOVE

A crust of bread in a simple hut where you are honored and loved is worth more than living in a palace with no love and respect.

MARIA LORUSSO

These are the words of my grandmother. Orphaned in her teens, she was sent from the farm in Italy that had been her home since birth to live with relatives who had immigrated to the United States. She never learned to read or write but she gave much wise counsel to her daughter, Marie, and my mother passed these words to me.

The words "I love you" come easily to many. But much of our loving is mixed with self-interest. Respect means treating another with esteem. To respect someone is to refrain from intruding upon them. The greater our self-interest, the less respectful we become. It is a challenge to get our egos out of the way so that we can draw upon a deeper will and a higher wisdom. Our personal relationships provide us with the greatest opportunity to practice patience, forgiveness, and respect. Relationship is an art. There will always be differences and times we will provoke one another. It takes enormous endurance to have respect for and to be kind and patient to those we don't like, or that which threatens or disgusts us. It isn't necessary to like everyone and everything. But we can love them in the sense of not doing anything to harm them, not being vindictive or dwelling in hostility toward them. Let us always remember that love is complete and sincere respect for another being.

I don't think I can learn from a wild animal how to live in particular—shall I suck warm blood, hold my tail high . . . but I might learn something of mindlessness, something of the purity of living in the physical senses and the dignity of living without bias or motive.

ANNIE DILLARD

Vipassana teacher Ruth Denison is a master in working with body movement as a means for awakening compassion and experiencing insight. Ruth uses slow, gentle stretching, with attention to the breath and sensations in various parts of the body, to bring students into a deep awareness and experience of life. Without losing the focus on the breath or the strength of the stretch, Ruth guides students in simple circle dances. The movements are precise. Students are guided to remain present and not fall into thinking, dramatization of the movement, or excessive emotional expression.

Sometimes Ruth will have students raise their arms above the head or extend them to the sides long enough to feel the tension that comes when the body tires of its weight. Students are encouraged to see how the mind wants to change, run away, or stop when experiencing something unpleasant. What is discovered during body movement sessions is integrated into the sitting periods. When there is tension in sitting, Ruth encourages the students to make subtle changes in position, which she considers taking care of oneself. There is no sense in experiencing excess tension that distracts the mind from the experience of breathing.

SPIDER WOMAN

In the beginning was thought, and her name was woman. . . . She is the Old Woman who tends the fires of life. She is the Old Woman Spider who weaves us together. She is the Eldest God, the one who remembers and re-remembers.

PAULA GUNN ALLEN

Earth as mother, mother as creator, woman as nature, woman as teacher of the culture, emerges in the legends and images of many Native American peoples. The Pueblo of southwest North America know Spider Woman as creator. In one such legend Spider Woman spun a line from north to south and she spun a line from east to west. Spider Woman sang as she sat by these four lines that spanned the four corners of the universe and from this spinning two daughters were born. Spider Woman and her two daughters gave birth to the sun and the moon and the stars and to the Pueblo people and to all the other peoples of the world. Upon each person was placed a covering of creative wisdom and each was attached by a thin thread to Spider Woman's web. We have forgotten this link. Several times the world has been destroyed, and each time Spider Woman saved those who remembered. It is time for each of us to remember this link, to call upon the creative wisdom, and to become co-creators, creating together a world of peace and harmony.

We all share a deep vulnerability. Everything changes. Wisdom is the ultimate protection because it helps us face life as it really is. Concentration doesn't lead to wisdom, it makes exploration possible. Concentration builds the strength and courage needed for deep exploration.

MICHELE MCDONALD

Concentration practices, such as mantra recitation or visualization, seek to narrow the awareness by shutting out the senses. The mind is steadied, energy is collected, and states of bliss and tranquility can be experienced. I like to do concentration practice if I'm in a lot of pain. It gives me a temporary relief. Visualizations have a powerful transformative effect on one's energy. Some lamas say that visualizations are easier for women to practice. Mantra recitation can be done throughout the day, and you don't have to be formally sitting. However, the states attained in this way don't last forever and often emotions that have been silenced during practice become quite ferocious when the practice stops.

Awareness practice is open to any present experience. One teacher calls it "touch and go." One lightly touches the breath, the sound, or the bodily sensation with awareness and then goes to the next predominant experience. Awareness practice is a hard practice. We notice our thoughts and the contraction in the body and come back to the present moment, over and over again. This is a very grounded practice and through it I have learned to take life less personally. Life is rapid change and we can't know what will happen. We can learn to be fully alert in the present moment, the only moment there is.

EFFORT

DECEMBER 11

Our essential victories ultimately must be only our own; nevertheless the knowledge that someone else has preceded us and returned alive and well to tell the tale is a major consolation.

BARBARA MYERHOFF

Barbara Myerhoff is speaking of surviving cancer. Truly, our essential victories must be our own, and we need to put forth vigorous effort to transform ourselves. The great teachers and mystics can inspire us and point the way but we must do the necessary work of transformation. The spiritual journey is a long and arduous one. To attain purity of heart we must have mastery over the senses, freedom from self-will and likes and dislikes, and be without selfish bonds to people and things. The difficulty of the journey is demonstrated by how few people consciously step on the path. We are either totally caught up in the world and have no interest or we feel that such purity is unrealistic and therefore unattainable for us. Having the teachings of the mystics to tell us that it can be done is enormous support. For myself, knowing that it is hard does not deter me. It gives me comfort to know that it can be done and that it does take enormous effort. All I need is to show patience and kindness toward myself while I continue to put forth effort.

O my friends,
What can you tell me of Love,
Whose pathways are filled with strangeness?
When you offer the Great One your love,
At the first step your body is crushed.
Next be ready to offer your head as his seat.
Be ready to orbit his lamp like a moth giving in to the light,
To live in the deer as she runs toward the hunter's call,
In the partridge that swallows hot coals for love of the moon,
In the fish that, kept from the sea, happily dies.
Like a bee trapped for life in the closing of the sweet flower,
Mira has offered herself to her Lord.
She says, the single Lotus will swallow you whole.

MIRABAI

To open to love, the small mind (the intellect, the ego) must give way to a larger knowing. Some of us never experience this opening until near death, others not even then. For those who do, death is experienced as wholeness. When death is near there is often a luminous quality. The air surrounding the person is vibrant and alive even though there is almost no life left in the body. There aren't any barriers. Everything is open and fluid.

When I was young I would often accompany my mother on her visits to sick parishioners. She would bring them the flowers that had been on the church altar. I remember one woman in particular. She had cancer and only a few weeks left to live. There was such a light around her she appeared almost translucent. She manifested no fear. I have never forgotten my experience with that woman and the peaceful energy that surrounded her.

PEACE

It is not a matter of thinking much, but of loving much. So do whatever most kindles love in you.

SAINT TERESA OF AVILA

Saint Teresa of Avila reformed the Carmelite Order and founded seventeen convents throughout Spain. Although the nuns were strictly disciplined, they had time for recreation in which they often danced. Saint Teresa even played the drums and the tambourine.

Our culture places great emphasis on thinking and not as much emphasis on loving. A number of years ago I was teaching a week-long retreat on peace. The week was experimental, with times for silent sitting and walking meditations as well as interactive exercises, movement, and rituals. The first night we held a sacred circle that began with drumming. One of the participants was upset because he didn't understand what this had to do with peace. He stayed for the next day or so and then dropped out. He thought that a workshop on peace would have more of an intellectual "brainstorming" approach to finding peaceful solutions for the national and international problems we are facing. My intention, though, was to cultivate a space in which the experience of peace would be possible. This experience would come from exploring our inner landscapes and finding ways to create joy within our small community. Such experiencing would then inform our thoughts and actions when we returned home to our daily lives. People who love peace bring that love to every situation, and that love and deep interest will enable them to find ways to create harmony rather than conflict.

PRECIOUSNESS OF LIFE

Let us accept the nectar that is always being given to us. No matter how old, we are still children in the womb of our Mother Earth.

DHYANI YWAHOO

Each day is a precious gift of twenty-four hours in which we can choose to live in a way that will bring peace and happiness to ourselves and others. Peaceworker and Zen meditation master Thich Nhat Hanh travels throughout the world reminding us that we can find peace in every moment. We have a choice. We can smile, eat, walk, and breathe in a way that invites peace. There is no place we need to go and nothing we need to buy. We can begin each day in a peaceful way by smiling and remembering that we are all children of the Earth.

SELF-RESPONSIBILITY

DECEMBER 15

It is not enough merely to call for freedom, democracy and human rights. There has to be a united determination to persevere in the struggle, to make sacrifices in the name of enduring truths, to resist the corrupting influences of desire, ill will, ignorance, and fear.

AUNG SAN SUU KYI

Aung San Suu Kyi was awarded the Nobel Peace Prize in 1991 for her work in leading the movement for human rights and democracy in Burma. This quote is an excerpt from her essay "Freedom From Fear." While legislation can do much to give, preserve, and protect human rights, it will take more than enforcement of laws for democracy to last. Aung San Suu Kyi says we must resist the corrupting influences of desire, ill will, ignorance, and fear.

These influences are states of mind that we have all experienced. How do such mind states corrupt us? Anger and greed can cloud our vision so that it looks like what we want is right. When we are deluded we are not able to see any possibilities beyond our own needs or we do not believe that right action, harmonious action, is possible. When we truly live in freedom, that is, free from selfish desire, we ask what we can give and not what we can get. Through the practice of meditation and mindfulness we can lessen our attachment to selfish desire and transform those mind states that hinder our wisdom and compassionate action. Virtuous action and wisdom are the most precious things in life. These are qualities we all have and they can be developed to the highest degree. Through virtuous actions our wisdom shines forth. In turn, wisdom enables our actions to become more virtuous.

It is this natural freedom in us that is the only permanent thing, because it is innate and the essence of our being; it is life's natural gift. Everything else outside of ourselves is contrived, and, as such, is unsatisfactory.

DR. THYNN THYNN

One of the best-loved allegorical Hinda epics, little known to westerners, is the *Durga Sapta Shati,* or Seven Hundred Verses on the Mother of the Universe. One episode tells the story of a king and a merchant who become thrilled by the revelation that everything in the universe is the play of the Goddess: both the liberating power of Divine Consciousness and the stranglehold of the ego. This insight inspires the two to begin a deep spiritual practice. They develop great concentration by focusing their minds on the Great Mother. After three years the Goddess appears to them and because of their devotion offers to grant them a wish. The king asks to regain his lost kingdom and the Goddess makes him the most powerful ruler of his time. The merchant stops and thinks about this. He reasons that if his friend lost his kingdom once, even though he has regained it, he could lose it again. He decides to ask for something that he can never lose, something that no one can take away from him. He asks for spiritual freedom. In that moment he becomes enlightened.

BELONGING

You say you belong to me.
I become frightened.
Then I remember the stars
belonging to each other.
I think how the wind
belongs to the sky.
This is the way I belong to you.

SUE SILVERMARIE

Sue Silvermarie's poem spoke directly to my partner, who responded with delight, "This is the only way we can belong to each other. Anything else is possession or ownership. It doesn't work. It is frightening for me to hear that someone belongs to me because then I feel responsible for them in ways that I'm really not. It is a burden. It is also frightening to feel that you belong to someone in that way because you try to make them responsible for you in ways that they are not. The image of belonging like stars means that we are there in relationship to each other. That is how we belong. We belong in relationship to each other. We don't own each other. We don't owe each other."

Being responsible *for* someone brings with it ideas of ownership and expectations, guilt and blame. If we exist in open space together like stars in the sky then we are interrelated to each other. There is no entrapment. We can become responsible *to* each other. In this open space, free of attachment, we are able to respond to each other in an authentic way. Natural kindness and compassion can be expressed.

WHOLEHEARTEDNESS

Wisdom comes from applying yourself wholeheartedly to whatever you're doing. The lessons of life are in everything.

PEMA CHÖDRÖN

We can bring a sense of wholeheartedness to every task we do, beginning with something as simple as brushing teeth. Really brush, without thinking of what you're going to do next or looking back to what you have already done. Bring all your attention to this act. Do it with reverence. Now go through your day in this way. Bring all your energy to each task, however large or small. Wholehearted attention to every task, whether drinking a cup of tea, writing a letter, traveling to or from work, waiting in line, or listening to music, requires being where you are and nowhere else. Let go of thoughts of what needs to be done next or fears or expectations about what you are doing. Just do as though your life depended on it. It does!

LOVE

There is one goal: the experience of love. . . . This entire universe is the pulsation of God. In this pulsation, there is opening and closing, opening and closing. As you do your practices, you experience the opening. . . . The whole universe opens itself for you.

GURUMAYI

We can be careless with the words "I love you," using them as an excuse when we disrespect or harm another. The love of which Gurumayi speaks is a basic warmth and friendliness to all life. It is not determined by whether or not you are personally satisfied by another human being. It is without conditions. There is no love without respect.

When my partner and I had our commitment ceremony, my son Jake spoke of the clarity that is born of openness and respect. "Within a relationship there is a space between two people that is sacred, in which any emotion or thought can be explored without judgment. Then there is an understanding that comes. It is as simple as deciding that the two people wish to understand and be together. Next, it is going and doing it. This is what I hold most dear—being clear and directed in your actions."

It takes practice to love. Respect is an energy that grows. Begin today to investigate your own actions. Are they coming from a place of respect?

This dawn, facing the year's decline as we begin to move toward the Winter Solstice—feeling it more imminent since the recent blessing of early rain—there is the additional awareness of being between life and death. We rarely think of it, but is this not where we always are, whether at the high noon of our day or our year or of our individual life cycle?

ELSA GIDLOW

A person who is fully present and awake to life is a person who has befriended death. Death is part of life. People raised in Western culture often fear death and deny its inevitability. We are taught that to think about dying and death will make us morbid. To face the fear of death, to let it tear our hearts open and to go beyond the fear, is to live with the knowledge that life is precious. Life is sacred. Life matters.

What would you do differently if you accepted death? How would this acceptance inform your life? Play with this image: Imagine that death is sitting on your left shoulder. Go through the day with death. Notice what thoughts and feelings arise through this exercise. Does this change your priorities? Perform each act as though it will be your last.

GREATNESS

I long to accomplish a great and noble task, but it is my chief duty to accomplish small tasks as if they were great and noble.

HELEN KELLER

    In many spiritual traditions, the winter solstice, the longest night of the year, is a traditional time for an all-night vigil. It is the time when spiritual aspirants willingly face their fear of the dark, the unknown, the great mystery. By consciously going into the night they are able to bring to light what has been hidden within. The spiritual practitioner is not trying to get rid of anything. She is facing fear with courage. She is embracing all of life.

    As individuals we may not do all-night vigils, but we do have many opportunities in our daily lives to face fear, doubt, and confusion. Greatness in a human being is evoked when we are able to demonstrate kindness, compassion, clarity, and insight. It comes through living life with integrity and authenticity. How do we live in this way? By bringing mindfulness to each task, accomplishing "small tasks as if they were great and noble."

I was trained to be numb, I was born to be numbered and pegged,
I was bred and conditioned to passivity, like a milk cow.
Waking is the sharpest pain I have ever known.
Every barrier that goes down takes part of my flesh
leaving me bloody. How can I live wide open?

MARGE PIERCY

Freedom demands that we awaken to the truth. For too long we have closed our eyes and denied both senses and feelings. We have denied the existence of our own wisdom. These uncomfortable but familiar limitations provide us with a security that is deceptive. Whether we place these limitations on ourselves or they are forced upon us by others, illusions serve to stifle and imprison us. It is neither safe nor comfortable to wake up. We have to be willing to feel pain. We have to be willing to risk uncertainty, inconvenience. We have to face the fear of the unknown. Without the risks, without the tearing, we will never open.

CHILDREN

My mother always said that children were gifts from God who were loaned to us. We had to love them with open hearts and with open hands. We had to have the wisdom to know when to let them go.

MARIE SHERMAN

The birth of Aaron Michael, my first nephew and my mother's third grandson, brought much joy to our family. When Aaron was two months old, his mothers held a naming ceremony in their home. In this beautiful candle lighting ceremony, surrounded by family and friends, Aaron received his Hebrew name. The ceremony acknowledged that by gathering in community we make manifest the unity of the universe that gives us all birth. My sister and her partner promised to love and guide Aaron and prayed to know when that time was done. Together they pledged "with grace and respect, we must return to you what has been ours only in trust—that which has always been rightfully yours: yourself."

TRANSFORMATION

Taking in new information completely honestly means believing it and not believing it at the same time, taking it for accurate and not accurate at the same time. Information being something new . . . is a state of being "information," in the act of being, of admitting. This is a transformational state, a state of possibly changing one's mind.

JUDY GRAHN

What a marvelous description of how to hold one's mind open to new experiences. Too often we don't hear. Our minds are so busy judging whether we agree or disagree that we are unable to receive. Judy Grahn clarifies the difference between blindly accepting and totally rejecting new information. The next time someone speaks to you, even if they are telling you a story you have already heard, listen as closely as you can. Imagine that you are hearing for the first time and you are very curious and you want to discover what the speaker is saying. Do not compare it with a different time, a different person, a similar idea. Feel that you are wide open and have plenty of room to take it all in and let it float in your mind.

MOTHER OF US ALL

When God was knitted to our body
in the Virgin's womb,
God took our Sensuality
and oned it to our Substance.

Thus our Lady is our Mother
in whom we are all enclosed
and in Christ we are born of her.

JULIAN OF NORWICH

In the Christian tradition, when Jesus took physical form in the virgin's womb he embraced the physical senses. Christ was an embodied spirit, as we all are. Jesus demonstrated, by his example, the power of personal transformation. The body is what the genes make it but character and behavior are neither limited nor fixed by the genetic code. We can change from angry to compassionate, from greedy to generous, from fearful to courageous.

Through this precious body, through these five senses, we have an opportunity to recognize that we are not limited by the body or the senses. We are spirit. We can explore our aliveness and discover the source. We will find that the power that creates and sustains the universe is the true self and is within each individual. Another way of saying this is: The Mother of God is the Mother of us all. Not one of us would be alive were it not for the air we breathe or the water we drink or the sun that shines down upon us. In this way we are all relatives, we are all in relationship to the Earth. A Native American teacher expressed it this way: "We are all children in the womb of the Earth."

We are never separate from this divinity. We are never alone.

Growth is not to be understood in terms of infinite expansion. It is helpful to notice in life and work how the motions of widening and narrowing follow rhythmically, as in centering clay on the potter's wheel, to produce a quality of being. In order to make the form, the clay must be brought into the compass of the hands.

M. C. RICHARDS

The dominant Western culture sees growth in terms of acquisition: more is better. This greed is thinly disguised by such words as growth, progress, development, and evolution, all of which are considered essential. It is an attitude causing the destruction of the Earth. Now more than ever, we need the voice of woman, whose intimate connection with the natural, cyclical nature of life can guide us back to an ecologically sound and harmonious way of living. We will honor both the times of expansion and the times of contraction.

To bring this understanding to a personal level we can look at the times we feel stuck, and understand these times as part of a natural cycle. We need times of rest and absorption, just as the fields need to rest and the crops need rotation. When we honor these cycles in our personal lives we will insist this knowledge be reflected in our government's policies.

BEAUTY WAY

*The quality of our laughter and joy, the knowledge of our voices,
thoughts and actions are weaving beauty around the land.*

DHYANI YWAHOO

The Beauty Way in Native American teachings is the way of
balance, of living in harmonious relationship with all of life.
The harmony and balance we seek is within us. We are born
with this knowing. There are many reasons this harmony is
lost to us through our racial, cultural, and gender experiences.
The times we live in seem particularly difficult for re-establish-
ing this harmony. Yet we can take great comfort and joy in
Dhyani's words. Wherever our lives take us, harmony is there
inside us, waiting for our discovery. Expression of this inner
harmony creates balance and beauty in the world. Our knowledge, our thoughts, and our actions count. We can make a difference. Awakening and bringing forth this natural harmony
in the world is a responsibility that each of us shares. This
is not a burden. Creation and transformation are delightful
tasks in which we may all take part.

This simple music meditation is one I have often used: Sing
the "Ah" sound, the first sound a baby makes. Sing it in any
key; play with this sound. Explore it, singing "Ah" higher and
lower, louder and softer. Let the vibration of "Ah" fill your
body. Move and stretch while making the "Ah" sound. See
how the simple sound invites the body to open and extend.
Now come to stillness, keeping the "Ah" sound going. Let it
bring you to your inner harmony. Then sit in the silence.

Formerly I too used to notice others' faults. Then I prayed to the Master and through his grace got rid of this habit. It is the very nature of man to see defects. You should learn to appreciate virtues. People are liable to err, but you must not take notice. If you constantly find fault with others you will see faults alone.

HOLY MOTHER

Everyone makes mistakes. We can't take risks and grow without making mistakes. Our culture's educational methods have stressed constant feedback concerning our faults so we can "fix" them. The intention is good, but unclear, and it often leaves us feeling insecure and unloved. It also creates a negative habit—looking for faults. The more we look, the more we see. It is a misuse of energy.

We can transform the fault-finding habit into one of affirming the beauty in all. Begin to notice the tendency to criticize. Take an honest inventory of yourself. Is this fault you find in another also found in yourself? Each time you find fault, stop, breathe, and say, "I forgive you this fault. I forgive myself for finding fault." Imagine the waters of forgiveness showering down upon you and the other person. Now you are clear and can ask for information or express how you are feeling without pointing blame. When we focus our energy on the positive in ourselves and others, it is the positive that increases.

DEATH

DECEMBER 29

Why did you vanish
into the empty sky?
Even the fragile snow,
when it falls,
falls in this world.

IZUMI SHIKIBU

   Izumi's poem portrays the profound sorrow of a mother mourning the death of her daughter. The pain is palpable. There is no disguise. There is no attempt to cover the pain with intellectualization. We can watch to see where the snow lands as it falls. We can't see what happens after death. Any thoughts we have about what might happen are just that, thoughts. It is only our ability to directly experience this world, the sorrow and the joy, that brings us to a space beyond intellect and emotion, beyond hope and sorrow.

From diaper change to diaper change and wash day to wash day, there is more profound change happening—the diapers are softening, becoming more and more absorbent and forgiving, and finally wearing out to rags. And the baby grows . . . the tedious, smelly processing of diaper washing reveals what in our universe can be done—the world gives renewal to us as a gift.

SUSAN ACKLEY

Religious traditions throughout the world have often directed their spiritual teachings and practices to men. The monastic tradition of a man going off to a temple, cave, or monastery to deepen his practice is seen as the ideal. Women are not taken as seriously. Many teachers feel women cannot practice because they have children who get in the way of the practice.

In truth, children are the practice. Here we meet on a daily level the bodhisattva vow, to live in service to others, to be as concerned for another's life as our own. In the simple chore of diaper washing we see the truth of change. In caring for the child we learn to be present, without preference. The smiling baby comes with the smelly diaper. We learn to embrace both.

IMPERMANENCE

DECEMBER 31

In this world, where not even a drop of dew on a leaf of grass remains, what word or saying should I leave?

ASAN

Zen dialogues can appear to be strange because they are a shorthand language dealing with experiences that cannot be put into words. Asan was a greatly enlightened woman from Shinano, Japan, who studied with renowned Zen Masters. When Asan was old and dying her family gathered around her, asking for some last words of wisdom. She laughed and gave the response above.

So now we have come full circle. In this constantly changing flow of human experience is there anything that remains the same? Is there any thread of continuity?

Grateful acknowledgment is made to the following for permission to reprint material copyrighted or controlled by them:

Jean Boughton for "Longing," reprinted by permission of the author.
Tsultrim Allione, newsletter, 1991.

Reprinted by permission from "Nurturing Compassion" by Christina Feldman, in *The Path of Compassion: Writings on Socially Engaged Buddhism,* edited by Fred Eppsteiner, Parallax Press, Berkeley, CA, 1988.

Reprinted by permission from "Rape" by Judith Ragir, in *The Path of Compassion: Writings on Socially Engaged Buddhism,* edited by Fred Eppsteiner, Parallax Press, Berkeley, CA, 1988.

Reprinted by permission from "In Indra's Net: Sarvodaya & Our Mutual Efforts for Peace" by Joanna Macy, in *The Path of Compassion: Writings on Socially Engaged Buddhism,* edited by Fred Eppsteiner, Parallax Press, Berkeley, CA, 1988.

"Looking At Stars." © 1990 by Jane Kenyon. Reprinted from *Let Evening Come* with the permission of Graywolf Press, St. Paul, MN.

Dhyani Ywahoo from *Voices of Our Ancestors.* © 1987 Dhyani Ywahoo. Reprinted by arrangement with Shambhala Publications, Inc., 300 Massachusetts Ave., Boston, MA 02115.

Lynn Park, for excerpts from *Poems After Rumi.* Reprinted by permission of the author.

Le Ly Hayslip from *When Heaven and Earth Changed Places.* © 1989. Reprinted with permission of Doubleday Publishers.

Camilee Campbell from *Meditations with Teresa of Avila,* by Camilee Campbell. © 1983, Bear & Co., Inc., P.O. Box 2860, Santa Fe, NM 87504.

Gabriele Uhlein from *Meditations with Hildegard of Bingen,* by Gabriele Uhlein. © 1983, Bear & Co., Inc., P.O. Box 2860, Santa Fe, NM 87504.

Brendan Doyle from *Meditations with Julian of Norwich.* © 1983, Bear & Co., Inc., P.O. Box 2860, Santa Fe, NM 87504.

Sue Woodruff from *Meditations with Mechtild of Magdeburg.* © 1982, Bear & Co., Inc., P.O. Box 2860, Santa Fe, NM 87504.

M. C. Richards, excerpted from *The Crossing Point.* © 1973 by Mary Caroline Richards. Published by Wesleyan University by permission of University Press of New England.

INDEX

ABUNDANCE October 7
ACCEPTANCE April 10; August 28;
    November 4
AGITATION September 20
ALONE JOURNEY March 6
ANCIENT WARRIOR GODDESS
    November 30
ANGER January 18; May 26;
    July 2
ANIMAL PROTECTION November 27
ATTACHMENT January 26; February
    20; May 22; September 7
ATTENTION March 27; July 8;
    August 11; August 24
AWAKENING LOVE July 25; August 18
AWARENESS October 6; December 10
AWE August 26

BALANCE November 21
BEAUTY WAY December 27
BEING February 24
BELONGING December 17
BLACK MOTHER GODDESS July 31
BODY MINDFULNESS December 8
BREATH January 29
BEAUTY February 17; April 2; April 16
BITTER/SWEET March 22; June 9
BREAD AND ROSES July 12
BREATH September 6
BUFFALO WOMAN April 24

CHANGE January 7; January 12;
    September 5
CHANGE OF THE GODDESS October 31

CHILD OF GOD February 15
CHILDREN December 23
CHOICE August 16
CIRCLE OF LIFE October 1
CLEAR ENERGY June 13
CLEAR ESSENCE August 10
COMMITMENT March 18; July 14
COMMITMENT VOWS June 20
COMMONALITY May 8; July 24
COMPASSION January 14; January 28;
    April 12; May 31
COMPASSION/JUSTICE March 23
CONDITIONED BEHAVIOR June 2;
    December 22
CONFRONT DARKNESS May 19
CORN MOTHER July 15
COURAGE February 28; July 17;
    October 18
CREATIVE AND RECEPTIVE September
    10

DARKNESS/LIGHT April 21
DEATH January 10; June 17;
    September 19; December 20;
    December 29
DEEP SEEING March 16; May 29; July
    26; October 22
DESIRE November 5
DEVOTION June 27; September 28
DHARMA May 1
DISCIPLINE May 17
DIVERSITY January 15; June 10;
    October 19
DIVINE LONGING August 7

EARTH WISDOM January 9; January
    21; April 18; May 13; November 9
EFFORT October 4; December 11

ENLIGHTENMENT April 17; August 20
ENJOYMENT September 30
EQUALITY March 31; May 5
EQUANIMITY March 10
EROTIC POWER March 13; August 8
ETERNAL LIFE May 28
EXPERIENCE TRUTH September 14; November 29
FEAR October 12; November 16
FEMINISM/SPIRITUALITY March 8
FORGIVENESS June 12; October 10
FREEDOM February 5; March 24; August 1; August 27; September 22; December 16
FRIENDSHIP November 19

GENEROSITY February 25; May 12
GENIUS March 11
GENTLENESS November 28
GIVING October 27
GOD April 19; June 3; November 2
GODDESS August 21; September 25
GODDESS/DEVOTION February 19
GODDESS within April 9
GOD'S LOVE December 6
GOODNESS July 18
GRACE December 2
GRATITUDE July 23; August 17; December 5
GREATNESS December 21
GREED April 3
GROWTH December 26

HARMONY October 20; November 14
HARVEST September 24
HEALING, FORGIVENESS January 8
HEAVEN ON EARTH March 25

HUMILITY July 30; October 3

ILLUSION August 25
IMMORTALITY November 7
IMPERMANENCE May 24; June 29; October 23; November 3; November 26; December 31
INFINITE LOVE September 15
INNER BLISS September 4
INNER CHILD July 9; November 12; December 4
INNER HARMONY March 7
INNER PEACE February 4; October 26
INNER TRUTH October 15
INNOCENCE September 1
INTERCONNECTEDNESS January 1; February 29; June 22; June 26; November 20;
INTERSTAND October 8

JOY February 6; August 15; September 16; December 1
JOYFUL ACCEPTANCE August 23

KEEPERS OF THE FIRE January 31
KINDNESS May 3; May 15; August 9; August 29

LAUGHTER September 12
LETTING GO March 1; October 21; October 25
LIFE AS ART January 4; August 30
LIFE AS SPIRITUAL PRACTICE June 6
LIFE/ESSENCE February 26; May 9
LIFE'S OBSTACLES April 4
LIFE SOURCE June 4
LISTENING April 13; September 3

LOSS January 20; February 21
LOVE January 23; February 14;
    February 22; March 29; April 1;
    April 7; April 11; April 15; May
    14; June 18; July 3; July 20;
    October 11; October 13; October
    17; October 29; November 6;
    November 23; December 12;
    December 19
LOVING-KINDNESS March 14

MANY PATHS, ONE GOAL June 24
MEDITATION March 20; December 3
MEETING THE SHADOW October 30
MIRACLE OF BIRTH March 26
MOTHER/FATHER GOD February 1
MOTHER LOVE July 5
MOTHER OF US ALL May 18;
    December 25
MYSTERY January 3; June 11

NATURAL CURIOSITY February 27
NONVIOLENCE August 12
NO PRAISE, NO BLAME August 4
NO-SELF May 7; May 25; June 5
NOURISH SPIRIT April 29

OBSERVATION April 20
OPEN HEART August 31

PAIN, PLEASURE February 10
PEACE April 22; May 2; May 30; June
    19; July 1; July 4; October 5;
    October 14; December 13
PERSEVERANCE February 18
PLANETARY FAMILY June 7; August 2
PLAY January 22

PRACTICE August 13; October 16
PRAYER January 5; February 2; July 7;
    September 27
PRECIOUSNESS OF LIFE December 14
PRESENT April 23
PROGRESS ON THE PATH July 11
PURIFICATION March 2; April 27
PURPOSE April 28; May 11; May 23

RACISM/SEXISM May 21
REFUGE May 6; May 27; July 19;
    November 8
RELATIONSHIP AS MIRROR January 13
RELATIONSHIPS October 24
RELATIVES September 9
RELEASE November 15
RELIGIOUS TRUTH July 27
RESISTANCE January 17
RESONANCE April 14
RESPECT/LOVE December 7
REST/RENEWAL September 26;
    December 30
RESTRAINT October 2
RITUAL September 13; October 9

SACREDNESS OF LIFE February 7
SACREDNESS OF WOMAN September
    29
SACRIFICE January 27
SANGHA August 19
SEASONS September 17
SELF-CREATION/PELE March 28
SELF-ESTEEM February 16
SELF-EXPLORATION September 18
SELF-RESPONSIBILITY March 12; June
    25; August 22; November 17;
    December 15

SENSITIVITY May 4
SERVICE July 29
SEXUAL ABUSE March 19
SHAME AND PAIN July 22
SHECHINAH September 8
SILENCE February 11; November 13
SISTERHOOD June 1
SMALL CHANGES February 12
SOCIAL CHANGE February 13
SOUL June 8
SOUL LONGING June 15
SOURCE OF LIFE January 11
SPIDER WOMAN December 9
SPIRIT March 4; April 26
SPIRITUAL CHALLENGE June 30
SPIRITUAL GARDENING January 16
SPIRITUAL HUNGER April 6
SPIRITUAL LIFE March 21
SPIRITUAL PATH January 2; January 6;
    January 19; November 24
STILLING THE MIND June 16
STILLNESS April 8
SUMMER SOLSTICE June 21
SUPPORT August 14
SURRENDER June 23
SYMPATHETIC JOY September 11

TENDERNESS February 23
TIME/ILLUSION March 9
TRANSFORMATION July 10; July 13;
    December 24
TRUE SELF July 16; October 28
TRUE HAPPINESS July 6; July 28;
    November 11

TRUE NATURE January 24; March 1;
    May 10; June 14
TRUE SAFETY February 3

UNDERSTANDING EMOTIONS
    November 18
UNITY April 25; September 2
UNIVERSAL CONCERNS September 21
UNIVERSAL CONSCIOUSNESS February
    8
UNIVERSAL LANGUAGE January 30

VIRTUES December 28

WARRIOR/CHOD November 1
WEB OF LIFE July 21
WHOLE/HOLY May 20
WHOLEHEARTEDNESS August 3;
    December 18
WHOLENESS November 25
WISDOM August 5
WITHHOLDING LOVE September 23
WITNESS March 3
WOMAN January 25; March 17;
    March 30; April 30
WOMAN BORN August 6
WOMAN POWER May 16
WOMEN LOVING WOMEN June 28;
    November 10
WOMEN'S ABUNDANCE February 9
WOMEN'S TIME November 22
WOMEN'S WISDOM April 5